ENCOUNTERS
WITH STRAVINSKY

BY PAUL HORGAN

NOVELS

The Fault of Angels
No Quarter Given
Main Line West
A Lamp on the Plains
A Distant Trumpet
Far from Cibola
The Habit of Empire
The Common Heart
Give Me Possession
Memories of the Future
Everything to Live For
Whitewater

OTHER FICTION

The Return of the Weed
Figures in a Landscape
The Devil in the Desert
One Red Rose for Christmas
The Saintmaker's Christmas Eve
Humble Powers
Toby and the Nighttime (juvenile)
Things As They Are
The Peach Stone: Stories from Four Decades

HISTORY AND OTHER NON-FICTION

Men of Arms (juvenile)
From the Royal City
New Mexico's Own Chronicle (with Maurice Garland Fulton)
Great River: The Rio Grande in North American History
The Centuries of Santa Fe
Rome Eternal
Citizen of New Salem
Conquistadors in North American History
Peter Hurd: A Portrait Sketch from Life
Songs After Lincoln
The Heroic Triad: Essays in the Social Energies
of Three Southwestern Cultures
Maurice Baring Restored (editor)

ENCOUNTERS
WITH
STRAVINSKY

A Personal Record

Paul Horgan

THE BODLEY HEAD
LONDON   SYDNEY
TORONTO

Publisher's note:
This book is a shorter version
of the original American edition.
The abridgement was done by the author.

© Paul Horgan 1972
Quotations from
Poetics of Music in the Form of Six Lessons
by Igor Stravinsky,
© 1942, 1947, 1970 by the President and Fellows
of Harvard College, are reprinted by
permission of Harvard University Press.
ISBN 0 370 10299 1
Printed and bound in Great Britain for
The Bodley Head Ltd, 9 Bow Street, London WC2E 7AL
by C. Tinling & Co. Ltd, Prescot.
Set in 11 on 12 pt Imprint
First published 1972

For V. de B. S. and R. C.

CONTENTS

ILLUSTRATIONS

FOREWORD

As will be immediately clear to the reader, this book is neither a musical study nor a complete biography. Rather it is a sketchbook in which I attempt to bring to page by recollection and anecdote various details for a portrait of Igor Stravinsky in terms of his meaning to me, both before I came to know him personally, and after.

His presence was as uniquely expressive as his music. To capture something of his likeness I have tried to reflect the special character of his speech and gesture. To describe gesture is not difficult. It is another matter, however, to try in writing to capture a highly flavoursome accent of speech. To resort to continuous mimicry by spelling out approximations of Stravinsky's spoken accent in English would do the reader a disservice in two ways: first, this would, like unrelenting printed dialect, soon become wearisome to the eye; second, it would seem to narrow the range of Stravinsky's verbal expressivity. I have limited my use of such means.

Stravinsky's English was filtered through a rich Russian accent —but with what precision, originality, and amplitude of vocabulary! His extraordinary intellectual awareness and breadth of learning were commonly in evidence, but never with pedantry—he was saved from that by wit, ranging from pranks of thought to total demolitions of luckless targets. Now and then his effects were incidentally enhanced, for an American ear, anyhow, by the foreignness of his pronunciation; and therefore in a few episodes in my text where this was particularly telling, I have resorted to phonetic approximations of his accent, to suggest the vividness of his presence.

For the rest, when I quote Stravinsky from life, I do so without mimetic effect, and would only ask the reader to remember a rich, burry, virile, pan-European sound, in which Russian consonants stud his words with a result at times unconsciously comic, and at other times intentionally emphatic.

Finally, I mean this personal record as a modest act of homage to a transcendent artist who for almost four decades indirectly and

9

impersonally brought aesthetic fulfilment to my life and learning —an experience which then for another decade and a half was crowned by personal friendship with him and his wife. The value to me of this double friendship lives, I hope, as much between the lines of this book as in my efforts at reconstruction in words of the enriching relationships which I trace.

P.H.

We always feel the immediacy of Stravinsky's sense of
the inner coherence of his material, no matter
how long it takes him to establish succession.

—ROBERT CRAFT:
Commentary to the Sketches for 'The Rite of Spring', 1969

The art of the biographer—devilish art!—is
somehow practically *thinning*. It simplifies even while
seeking to enrich—even the immortals are so helpless
and passive in death.

—HENRY JAMES TO HENRY ADAMS,
quoted in Leon Edel's 'Henry James: The Master', 1972

Book 1

BEFORE

I HAVE often returned in thought to the moment early in my life when I first became aware of Stravinsky as the prime source of style in the arts of my century. For me, he was a remote personage —powerful, exemplary—while I was still a schoolboy. As the years passed I came to know him through works of criticism, and by his own writings, by recordings of his works, and finally by live performances of his music in concerts. I knew him as most of the world knew him—on our own worldly terms: by reputation and the lustre of his unique creativity; and like the rest of the world, I never expected to meet him. He grew in a one-sided intimacy by which I, with all the countless others, helped to make history's response to him. He was, then, woven through the fabric of even my earliest—most remote, youthfully imprecise—discoveries of the meaning of the word 'modern' in the style of my time.

In 1915, by which time I was twelve years old, there was already a new energy of general style in the visions of the Diaghilev Russians in Paris. In particular this was expressed through *L'Oiseau de feu*, *Petrushka*, and *Le Sacre du printemps*. If their initial impact was great, the diffusion of this has made them the most enduring works of the capture of the cultural West by the whole Russian enterprise. For more than six decades, these first statements of an astonishing temperament were sustained by an unbroken line of musical masterpieces. Many of these were composed to meet the needs of theatrical productions; many were not; but their effect was always prophetic in terms of artistic idiom— so much so that they were almost always denounced on first hearing by critics and accepted by them only years later. It was the artist and the gifted amateur who generally understood the works of Stravinsky as they first appeared. Further, his creations so acutely brought to fact in performance the essential spirit of the age in its successive airs that Stravinsky not only led the musical discoveries of his time, but also expressed an energy which touched and even influenced all the other arts. Fifty years ago he

was a model of prophetic style such as all precocious youths—in any provinces (even New Mexico, where I lived)—somehow discover for themselves; and such a prophet he remained, in each of his successive revelations, for succeeding generations.

By a fine absurdity, it was a military academy which in my second year of attendance—1920–21—brought me into the direction I sought with nothing but the temperament of a nascent artist to compel me; or rather, it was an exceptional officer of the school who served as my guide. Though I never had a class directly under his tutelage, he became aware of me, and presently allowed me to sharpen my claws upon him. This, finally, may be the only thing a teacher can do for a student whose die of vocation and character is already cast. In any case, in him I met a tangent of the great world of which I was already an imaginary inhabitant. Making points, just as I hoped he would, about the aridity of much of American provincial life, he was a poet, a recognised poet, who published his lines in *Poetry: A Magazine of Verse*, and in *The Dial*, and showed them to me. His name was Charles DeGuire Christoph, in itself sufficiently un-American as to be culturally subversive, and therefore satisfactory to me. With the gentle, intelligent local girl whom he was courting, he read what I wrote, listened to me read back to him the early poems of T. S. Eliot, and above all, he gave me the monthly issues of *The Dial* as they reached him.

The magazine entranced me. It was the period of H. L. Mencken and *The Smart Set*, and the volumes of his *Prejudices*, and the climate of roaring scepticism and iconoclasm which he let loose upon my generation. He was a sort of national 'village atheist' and cultural radical—though politically conservative. I read Mencken with the rest, and often laughed out loud at his inspired hyperboles, but even then, I felt the presence of a sort of showmanship which took the place of knowledgeable reflection in his work, and which in the end anchored him to a sophomoric though funny cleverness which would not long outlive the generation which acclaimed him.

No, it was *The Dial*, and its concerns, its visions of the outriders of the new culture, its fine format, its reproductions of art in the new spirit, and its chronicles of criticism, which became my Baedeker in my inner journey, and it was in its pages that I first encountered the name of Igor Stravinsky. Thereafter I looked first in every issue for news of him.

Christoph of course knew of him, and was able to repeat to me vagrant details of his already established legend. It was splendid to hear of the Russian Ballet in Paris, and especially of its most notorious event, the uproar of the première of *Le Sacre du printemps*, which Christoph always referred to by its French title. Repeating it in some dim sense of ownership, I would marvel how the worlds of my French class and the Théâtre des Champs-Elysées could be so far apart.

I asked Christoph what *Le Sacre du printemps* was like.

He did not know, he had not heard it, it had not been played in America.

Why had it made such a commotion?

Oh, so far as he could gather from what he'd read and heard about it, he thought that violent dissonances together with rhythms previously unheard in serious music, and described by everyone as primitive, even barbaric, were what had set off the work's career in a marvellous scandal.

What was it about?

Oh, some imagined recreation of a pagan ritual in ancient Russia during which a maiden was sacrificed in a spring ceremonial.

Even so sketchy a synopsis was enlivening. I was suddenly reminded of something I had witnessed the previous summer. Christoph agreed to hear about it.

With friends of my parents in Albuquerque, who unlike us were long-time residents of New Mexico, I had been taken by motor car to the pueblo of Santo Domingo to see the annual Corn Dance. The Indians allowed entrance to a certain number of white spectators depending upon proper behaviour. This meant decorum on the part of visitors, a sense of attending a religious ritual, abstinence from taking photographs, and general politeness.

On a desert-hot day in early August, when vast thunderheads were slowly rolling up on the far mountainous horizons, and the light stood universal in its brilliance, we came to the earth-made pueblo and found places to sit on the edge of a low rooftop with our legs dangling. One member of the party showed an extra keenness in the event. I was introduced to him and ducked my head in juvenile manners. They told me he was an artist—a painter, one of those who in such large numbers at that time came to make a

career of the landscape. But as time would reveal he painted like none of the others, whose delight in the picturesque he scorned in favour of the monumental and the ageless. His name was Marsden Hartley. I remembered his lively good spirits, the kindness he showed to me in my excitement over the event which was soon to occur in the earthen *placita* of the pueblo, his intensely light blue eyes like half-moons with the flat sides down. Their colour made me think of the stones worked into silver and worn by the Indians, and I recall how he pronounced the word '*turquoise*', giving it in French. Everyone had come in a picnic mood, but all were now subdued by the premonitory stillness of the pueblo—a sizable town where on that day more than a thousand people, Indian and white, must have been in attendance.

Suddenly the very air was shattered like glass when a great single drumbeat sounded, and out of the *kivas* at one side of the *placita* erupted lines of male Indian dancers, like some element of the earth forced upward to the surface, while at the same time, hitherto unnoticed, great ranks of Indian women came decorously in small padding footbeats from an open corner of the *placita* to join the men in forming a great massed design of bodies in the dance. All wore special costumes—the men largely bare, with pine boughs, turkey feathers, fox tails, and carrying gourd rattles. The women were like moving statues, erect and impassive under upright wooden tablets cut to fit their heads and ornamented with small feathers. They too carried pine boughs. Their legs were wrapped in white buckskin. The naked earth-coloured legs of the men and the white-wrapped legs of the women moved exactly together to the rhythm of a chorus of drums and chanters who held their station at a corner of the *placita*. The men's feet pounded, demanding; the women's barely shuffled, supplicating. The drums, the voices, echoed off the pueblo walls, and the dancers precisely enacted the rhythm. The rhythm was relentless, insistent, measured, yet penetrating as thunder. Every now and then without warning a sudden falter, a shift of body and sound, perfectly performed together by all the dancers—some three hundred of them—changed the rhythm in an extraordinarily complicated variation, and then once more the steady beat was resumed, pounding upon the earth to ask for fertility, as the gourd rattles simulated the scattering of seed and the down-sweep of rain. The women's pine boughs figured forth eternal life, and their head-dresses meant to be clouds which would fill the sky and bring rain

and renewal in the earth as they brought renewal in childbirth. Beat, beat, beat, it went; impossible to escape and to resist, and talking of it, you felt a human timelessness behind all acts of any being in his own time. Marsden Hartley leaned forward, his knees crossed, his elbow on his knee, his fingers curled against his rather sunken mouth, his *turquoise* eyes transfixed by the wonder of what we watched.

'Do you suppose it is something like that?' I mused aloud.

Christoph of course could not say; but he knew re-creation of primitive ritual was part of the intention of Stravinsky's amazing piece, and, unheard, but energetically imagined, it would bear for me through years some affinity with the substantive and intended magic of the dance at Santo Domingo.

Why not think so, Christoph remarked mildly, until you hear it some day?

My imagination had a fine festival in projecting the first performance of *Le Sacre du printemps* (it would be years before I considered it decent to speak of this work by its English title). There was surprisingly much evidence to feed my vision of it. Christoph handed me an issue of *The Dial* for January 1921, where I could read an account by Jean Cocteau of what happened after the wild evening at the theatre in Paris.

With Cocteau I rode in a cab containing Stravinsky, Diaghilev, and Nijinsky (who had choreographed the work) and drove through the Bois de Boulogne at two o'clock in the morning in silence. It was a fine night scented with acacia trees. Presently we drew close to the lakes in the great park, and Diaghilev, 'enveloped in opossum furs', began to murmur some lines in Russian while everyone else listened. He was weeping. Cocteau asked what we were hearing. The answer was 'Pushkin'. At a certain line Stravinsky and Nijinsky also gave way to emotion, and Cocteau begged to be told the meaning of what moved them so.

Stravinsky replied that the words were hard to translate—'really very hard; too Russian . . . too Russian', and went on to say that the line meant something like *'Veux-tu faire un tour aux îles'*, and I invoked Chardenal to understand that it meant an invitation 'to go to the islands', and they had all wept because one time, going to the islands at home, in Russia, the idea for *Le Sacre du printemps* had first come to them, and now after a performance amounting to failure and scandal and glory, it was the time to weep. Nobody had mentioned the scandal until then, and Cocteau declared that he

would never forget the 'great wet face' of Diaghilev, 'in the cab, reciting Pushkin in the Bois de Boulogne', and it seemed that I never would either, and it was decades before I read Stravinsky's own contradiction of the whole episode—he once told T. S. Eliot that Cocteau was 'a sincere liar'—and I read elsewhere that the uproar at the theatre was just what Diaghilev wanted, since the notorious would surely become the successful. Actually, Diaghilev, said Stravinsky long afterwards, was 'delighted'.

That pivotal event was described by many observers, with enlivening detail. If Cocteau was to be believed once more, an old *grande dame* of Paris thought the ballet had been mounted to make a fool of her, where she sat in her box. An observer closer to home was a young American musical critic who was present that night, and who, as early as 1915, had published several essays about Stravinsky in his book *Music After the Great War*. He was Carl Van Vechten, and it is quite likely that Christoph had his book, and that much in it which I now recall from my own copy of the first edition (which I obtained later) deepened my sense of affinity with Stravinsky and his world, and made me enter the atmosphere of the first performance myself. Nothing could have been more satisfying than the riot of that night, and I saw as historically alive for the first time a similar challenge and response which had taken place generations before, at the first performance of Victor Hugo's *Hernani* (which we were reading in French class). There, too, an opposition was exploded against established convention in art, and it was signalised as such when Théophile Gautier, in glorious defiance of the old, celebrated the new by wearing a red waistcoat with his black evening clothes at the première of *Hernani*.

The curtain had hardly risen, wrote Van Vechten, when the audience fell into partisan factions. I was sure which part I would have joined.

'A certain part of the audience, thrilled by what it considered a blasphemous attempt to destroy music as an art, and swept away with wrath, began very soon after the rise of the curtain to offer audible suggestions as to how the performance should proceed. Others of us, who liked the music and felt that the principles of free speech were at stake, bellowed defiance. It was war over art for the rest of the evening'—the seeds of a war which in my own terms were stirring in me—'and the orchestra played on unheard, except occasionally when a slight lull occurred. The figures on the

stage danced in time to music they had to imagine they heard and beautifully out of rhythm with the uproar in the auditorium.' That, I was sure, was what a great stage work should do to an audience. I felt Stravinsky's power seven years after the explosion described by Van Vechten, which gave me a feeling of being transported in place and time to the Théâtre des Champs-Elysées in 1913. 'I was sitting in a box in which I had rented one seat,' continued Van Vechten. 'Three ladies sat in front of me and a young man occupied the place behind me. The intense excitement under which he was labouring, thanks to the potent force of the music, betrayed itself presently when he began to beat rhythmically on the top of my head with his fists. My emotion was so great that I did not feel the blows for some time. They were perfectly synchronised with the beat of the music. When I did, I turned around. His apology was sincere. We had both been carried beyond ourselves . . .'

Van Vechten as early as 1915, then, stated forthrightly that Stravinsky was already 'the most vital of forces in the music world'. It was his opinion that the three great early ballets— *L'Oiseau de feu*, *Petrushka*, and *Le Sacre du printemps*—held 'more inspiration made manifest' than any other music recently heard in theatre or concert hall. He referred to the composer as 'this young Russian giant', and declared that 'his use of dissonance* is an art in itself . . . invention itself', adding that by 'writing a new language for it', Stravinsky had actually 'developed a new medium out of the orchestra'.

But there was no dogma to be attached to Stravinsky's procedures. Van Vechten quoted remarks by Stravinsky which expressed the composer's absolute freedom from fashion or the pressures of influence: 'I want to suggest neither situations nor emotions, but simply to manifest, to express them . . . Though I often find it extremely hard to do so, I always aim at straightforward expression in its simplest form. I have no use for "working out" in dramatic or lyric music. The one essential thing is to feel and to convey one's feelings.' What could more firmly support the vague desires of an artist hardly yet an apprentice than such a statement from a master?

* 'I adore dissonance,' said Stravinsky decades later in a film interview.

It was both luxury and bafflement to imagine how the Stravinsky works for ballet must look on the stage. Van Vechten spoke of the settings—'decorations in harsh and primitive colours by Roerich', citing the 'very beautiful green landscape for the first scene' of *Le Sacre du printemps*, 'and the grewsome [sic] setting, between somewhere and nowhere, of the second'; and he tried to evoke something of the dance-style of this work, which was staged by Nijinsky, already one of the three most famous figures connected with the Diaghilev company. He thought Nijinsky's choreography 'marvellously conceived', with each dancer, contrary to the ensemble convention of ballet, given 'a separate simultaneous task' —a procedure which must have been complicated in the extreme, as there were 'scarcely two consecutive bars [in *Le Sacre*] written in the same time-signature', and yet, said Van Vechten, he knew of no music 'more dance-compelling'.

Van Vechten wrote further about Nijinsky: 'The word "youth" expresses something of the wonder of this marvellous boy. He never seems to be doing anything difficult, and yet his command of technique is incredible. He always seems spontaneous, and yet I have been told that . . . he does not make the slightest movement of a finger which has not been carefully thought out. He seems to me the greatest of stage artists (and I include all concert musicians as well as opera singers and actors in this sweeping statement).'* It was essential, he said, to see Nijinsky in a variety of parts to 'get his true measure'. There was even a 'rumour that Nijinsky's element is the air'.

It seemed disgraceful that before 1915 'not a note' of Stravinsky's three famous ballets, or of his next work, the opera *Le Rossignol*, had been 'heard in New York, although Paris and London' were 'thoroughly familiar with them'. As for *Le Rossignol*, there had never been an opera like it; 'wonderfully beautiful', it continued to show Stravinsky's growth 'in every new work he has vouchsafed the public', and the conductor Alfred Hertz, hearing it in London, was so affected by it that he couldn't remain for the rest of the double bill on which it was presented, saying he had 'never been so moved, so excited before at the performance of a new opera . . . Oh!' he exclaimed to Van Vechten, 'if I could have the privilege of introducing that work to New York . . . !' In 1920 Hertz was conductor of the San Francisco Symphony Orchestra.

* Long later I came upon Sarah Bernhardt's remark when she saw Nijinsky dance *Petrushka*: '*J'ai peur, j'ai peur, car je vois l'acteur le plus grand du monde.*'

He was therefore an impressive witness in his statement to Van Vechten, 'I am considered a good musician. When I am conducting an orchestra, I can detect a false note in the furthest bassoon, or the nearest flute, but in the second act of *The Nightingale* I could not name a single note.' Opinions, descriptions, like these amounted for me to an encounter with Stravinsky even many times removed. There was, then, clearly a powerful new spirit abroad, and Stravinsky was its prophet, as articulate in words as in notes, for Van Vechten, in *Music and Bad Manners* (1916), quoted him as saying, '*La musique est trop bête pour exprimer autre chose que la musique.*'

Van Vechten attended later performances of the Russian Ballet season in Paris that year and at the curtain of *Petrushka*, he was given his first sight of Stravinsky, who was 'dragged on stage by Nijinsky'. The composer, he said, was 'very thin and short,* . . . pale, awkward, and timid'. He wore glasses which glared in the footlights and he seemed blinded, and he nervously fingered his lenses. He bowed—years afterwards Robert Craft said that Stravinsky, born to the traditions of the Mariinsky Theatre where his father was the leading bass singer, always bowed in the Mariinsky style. If this was also illustrated in the style of the dancers and of Chaliapin, it meant first a slow, noble, ocular survey of the whole house, starting with the top galleries, and coming in grand arcs to the lower tiers, the boxes, and then the pit, followed by a deep reverence, deliberately given, which conveyed both self-confidence and proud gratitude. It was a ceremony which had in its own right the quality of performance, and it shared in its smaller art the grand splendours so carefully devised and rehearsed in the entire repertoire.

In his curtain call, Stravinsky presented the first visual suggestion of himself which I read about. Van Vechten declared that his suit of evening dress was superb—'as irreproachable in fit and texture as that of Arturo Toscanini'. It was the first hint of the chic, air, style, very much *en dandy*, which seemed to me both appropriate and important in my image of him. The nature of his imaginative energy had to be visible in his outward style, and

---

* Stravinsky declared late in life that he was 5 ft 3 in tall, and weighed 120 pounds, and that these were his dimensions for fifty years.

evidently so it was, from the very beginning. Picasso drew him in 1917, and again in 1920. The portraits are of course clearly the same man; but the earlier one had a fastidious austerity which was particularly fascinating. A line drawing of head and shoulders—a sleek head, with strongly marked features of which the nose was the most prominent. He wore a rimless monocle in his right eye, which seemed proper to officers, lords, and geniuses. His mouth, a generously modelled flat oval, which seemed slightly pursed, was barely shaded by a closely trimmed moustache. The shoulders and lapel of his coat somehow suggested high tailoring. As a drawing, it was as simplified as possible, and yet one strongly felt the presence of both artists.

The later portrait was also a line drawing, showing Stravinsky three-quarter length, with the knees crossed, seated in a curious piece of furniture which suggested an officer's field chair. Again I saw the reposeful severity of the earlier likeness, but with a few differences—he was wearing a pince-nez instead of the monocle, and the closed lips seemed more protruded—the expression of one in thought, or of a musician listening to a musical phrase and apprehending it by mouth as well as by ear. The left ear was large. He was wearing a foulard cravat and a handkerchief was dashingly thrust into his breast pocket. Drawn loosely, his coat, waistcoat, and trousers yet suggested elegance; and it seemed plain to me that this elegance came from within, and always would, no matter what might be superimposed upon it. Finally, in the drawing, he held his hands with fingers interlaced. The drawing was made in the period when Picasso was engaged with classical female nudes to which he gave grossly exaggerated features, limbs and bulk, against which he played fanciful attitudes of movement or levitation, as though such heavy bodies were vessels of grace itself. Their hands, including fingernails, were always huge. So with the hands he drew in the 1920 Stravinsky portrait—but here the effect was different. The hands were in repose, they were exaggerated in order to portray the workman's strength which they commanded. The spread of the right hand was equal in vertical dimension to the whole head. Intentionally or not, Picasso here made an equation which went far towards capturing the essential nature of his subject. Since he could not draw the soul in line, he could suggest the powers of one whose capacity to construct was equal to his energy of mind. I found in some magazine a reproduction of this 1920 drawing, cut it out, stuck it to a piece of shirt-cardboard,

and fastened it to the blanket hanging on the wall of my quarters, such as all cadets used upon which to pin up their visual treasures, since it was forbidden to drive tacks into the plaster itself.

Small? Van Vechten had said so, and he must have been right, and indeed photographs of Stravinsky and Nijinsky together showed Stravinsky to be only slightly the taller. Yet in his drawings, Picasso saw him in his heroic dimension, and I added my own cubits to this. A hero who was also elegant—nothing could have answered more fully my own definitions. A portrait of the time by Jacques-Emile Blanche showed him wearing spats, leaning on a stick, sporting light trousers with dark jacket and waistcoat, and holding a topcoat thrown through the crook of his arm. Could the time ever come when such elements of style and manner might come within my own natural reach? It was not an idle speculation for me in youth.

In such examples began the iconography of Stravinsky, which, in drawing, painting, sculpture, and above all photography, grew through the century to immense volume. He was supremely photogenic, as the camera people would say, and this without his being conventionally handsome, or conforming to familiar ideals of physique. What invariably spoke was his personal expressiveness, which with extraordinary directness transmitted his state of being in whatever situation he was seen. This is another way of saying that his interest in all things was devouring, and his capacity to observe seemed without limit, far beyond Van Vechten's observation that 'Everything in the world of art is said to have awakened his curiosity . . .'. Worlds apart in degree, it was in kind the ruling concern of my life, and Christoph, seeing this, put whatever he could in my way to stimulate it.

Carl Van Vechten had one more early book which provided an arc between the military institute and New York for me. This was *Interpreters*, published in 1920. It was a collection of evocative essays about performers—Fremstad, Mary Garden, Farrar, Nijinsky, among others—and in the chapter on the great dancer I learned that the music of Stravinsky finally came to New York with the Russian Ballet in 1915, when *Petrushka* was presented, and again, in a later season, when *The Firebird*—'Stravinsky's

wonderful score'—had a performance. Van Vechten wrote with admiration of Olive Fremstad and Geraldine Farrar, but when he came to Mary Garden something like worshipful love came into his writing, and he gave himself—and me—the luxury of a wishful vision when he wondered why Stravinsky did not write an opera for her. It was the sort of external trifling with his own vision which any artist frequently had to endure, even as he wondered what people thought he was made of, that their ideas could possibly become his own. Even when accepting a commission for a work, Stravinsky prevailed in its concept, not the commissioner. Still, it was always a gesture of love and desire to share in the artist's work which prompted such suggestions, made as they were in a spirit far different from that which imposed assignments upon a schoolboy. I, too, daydreamed of ideal performances, creations, constructions, events, and atmospheres; and some of these had the power to remain as details in my education.

Finally, as I felt the personality and the effect of Stravinsky's work for the first time through Carl Van Vechten's responses, I still see on re-reading the essays of that observer how they remain the most perceptive of the earliest works of criticism in English about the composer. Others were to come who kept pace with Stravinsky's works as they appeared, and these, in their season, I followed wherever I could find them.

In my use of Christoph's issues of *The Dial*, I read Paul Rosenfeld's 'Musical Chronicle' with particular interest when he dealt with Stravinsky. Rosenfeld, as I later came to know, was a competently literate musician, and as a prose writer he had a following amounting almost to a cult. His style was circuitous, his perceptions sensuous, and his temperament, sustained by knowledgeability, dominated his analytical opinions. In other words, he was frankly subjective in his criticism. The elevated and allusive style of his musical essays seemed to suit the general tone of *The Dial*, and if I was not often given a direct sense of the music he discussed, I nevertheless received a challenging and interesting exercise in the art of mandarin prose-writing. He was perhaps more of an artist than an explicator, to use a word from the higher slang of the academy. To share his enigma with others without necessarily explaining it—this is the artist's task—no, a natural

Igor Stravinsky by Pablo Picasso 1920

purpose. I often thought Rosenfeld's critical comments had the double interest of confession and obscurity.

Still, it was also his duty to act as a reporter, and I felt his scorn when he complained in January 1921 that in Dr Damrosch's orchestral concerts Stravinsky was 'only represented by the early *Firebird*', and I shared his indignation a month later when he reported that in the season's first concert by the Flonzaley Quartet, 'the audience . . . expressed directly and flatly its dislike of the novelty performed, the Stravinsky *Concertino*'. The work was actually met with hissing, 'which increased in vehemence, drowning quite the laughter, when the members of the quartet made faintly as though to recommence the brief composition'. There was a fine stir about this, suggestion of a new 'scandal' in the career of the composer of *Le Sacre du printemps*. How I loved that particular use of the word 'scandal'. Previously, it had signified for me discreditable affairs of an individual nature, often involving sex, to be discussed just out of the supposed earshot of juveniles. But now! it meant a public sensation triumphant to the degree of its magnitude.

I could not of course hear the *Concertino*, and I hoped Rosenfeld would give me a sense of what it was like, and in a way he did, in describing what he thought of the work, but this was mostly in terms of attitudes towards the state of the world. The composition expressed 'futility', 'anger', 'boredom', 'the joke of it all, the work was a rasping, tired shuffle and breakdown'. Not only this, it was 'like a locomotive which has fallen off the track, making its wheels revolve in the air'. Rosenfeld was reminded of *Petrushka*, dancing again, but now 'seedier', and the *Concertino* was 'a piece of post-armistice existence'. He said it was 'a splinter of mirror in which there reflects itself sharply the disintegration of life in progress since the conclusion of the war'. It was an 'ugly, infinitely significant work', and he explained it by stating that 'The mortmain of weariness flung heavily on the budding bourn of life is but what men at all times have felt during the collapse of a civilisation.' Gosh. And then Rosenfeld went for the audience, the dull, inert, pork-rich creatures whose very monumental triviality seemed in fact to be the direct source of the composer's material. The essay turned into a social castigation of a concert hall full of Babbitts (we were all devouring Sinclair Lewis at the time), and somewhere in all that was lost the composer who had said with ironic precision to Van Vechten that 'Music is too stupid to express anything but music.'

Still, there was no doubt that Rosenfeld deeply admired Stravinsky and worked to convey his meanings by analogy, however thickly non-musical, much of which must surely have astonished the composer if he read it. In 1920 Rosenfeld published a collection of essays under the title *Musical Portraits*—the first book of his which I owned. In his piece on Stravinsky he declared that 'The new steel organs of man have begotten their music in *"Le Sacre du printemps"*. For with Stravinsky, the rhythms of machinery enter musical art . . . the spiritualisation of the new body of man is manifest.' It seemed at the time like a powerful insight, and I forgot (never having seen the ballet or heard the work) that it all had to do with the impulses of deeply atavistic folk propitiations of the mysteriously governed cycles of nature. Later, it may seem more pertinent to reflect that the rhythm of machinery is, above all things, regular, and that any deviation from a fixed beat is a signal of malfunction. But the prime characteristic of the rhythms in *Le Sacre du printemps* is its complicated irregularity, such as Van Vechten noted, and as the conductor Eugene Goossens cited in a typical sequence of time-values in bars reading '3/16, 4/16, 2/16, 5/16, 3/16, 5/16, 7/16'. It thus seemed difficult to confirm Rosenfeld's impression that in *Le Sacre* 'the music pounds with the rhythm of engines, whirls and spirals like screws and fly-wheels, grinds and shrieks like labouring metal. The orchestra is transmuted to steel . . . A dozen mills pulsate at once. Steam escapes; exhausts breathe heavily,' and so on. For the serious artist or critic there was always a danger in being self-consciously contemporary.

For myself, at the time, it was necessary to proceed with imitations of Eliot in poetry (some of which, my first published writing, appeared in Miss Monroe's *Poetry: A Magazine of Verse* a year or so later), and of the post-Impressionists and the Fauves in painting. Music I was unable to do anything about but listen. But the habit of doing so was already fixed, with the aid of what, until quite recently had been referred to as the talking-machine, or the graphophone. As the technique of sound reproduction improved with extraordinary swiftness, what had begun as rather husky, tubey, almost other-worldly notes, became a plausible approximation of performed reality at large for the huge world audience in the concert hall and opera house without stages; and its early marvel evolved into an indispensable form of musical document. The unprecedented achievement it was eventually to reach under

the guidance of Goddard Lieberson of Columbia Records was the recording of Stravinsky's entire major *oeuvre* conducted by the composer himself, thus establishing with final authority for his own time and for posterity his own conceptions of his work in performance.

The study of music (voice) brought me at the age of nineteen to the Eastman School of Music in Rochester, New York. These pages are not to be an extended history of my daily activities in Rochester, or of the nourishing friendships whose beginnings were valuable to my education, which during all my life has been derived informally. I need of that time only to mention Rouben Mamoulian, Vladimir Rosing, George Houston, Nicolas Slonimsky, Ernst Bacon, Otto Luening, Martha Graham, Anna Duncan, Guy Harrison, Lucile Johnson Bigelow, and, most importantly for the final emphasis of this narrative, Eugene Goossens, to express what has never lost savour for me as a cherished debt to my elders and betters for taking me seriously on evidence which was not highly visible at the time, and for receiving the contributions of my energy and temperament as ardently as they were offered in the work of the newly-formed opera theatre in Rochester.

Stravinsky was never far away. I encountered him as an inhabitant of novels—he was mentioned as a natural eminence of universal immediacy in the sophisticated world in the novels of Carl Van Vechten, which I read as they were then beginning to appear—*Peter Whiffle*, the first one; and *The Blind Bow Boy*, the second, in which The Duke of Middlebottom referred to Campaspe Lorillard, the central lady of the novel, as 'Zhar-Ptitsa', meaning 'Firebird', and I took it of course as a reference to Stravinsky's ballet, rather than to the Russian mythical creature on which the work was based, for without him, the legend would not have had general point for me. Though, to be sure, there was an exotic review of the arts called *Zhar-Ptitsa* which I bought whenever it appeared, for it was filled with writings and pictures which belonged to the world I was beginning to think of as mine, right there, within reach. Possessively I made a fanciful drawing of the Firebird passing across the sky like a long pavonine cloud.

The pervasion of Stravinsky was extended for me by a rich event which occurred early in the Rochester time—though matters went so swiftly that if now they read as in a synopsis, they felt so, even then, and so firmly did I discover, both inwardly and outwardly, that time was the least serious of limitations.

The art museum of Rochester announced an exhibition, with the artist in attendance, of the stage designs and paintings of Nicholas Roerich. Roerich! who had conferred with Stravinsky and Diaghilev about the décor for *Le Sacre du printemps* and which Van Vechten had seen and described. Our local Russians were at once alerted to the event, and were invited to the private view at the museum the day before the opening. I was somehow included.

First we met the artist. He was a rather short, stocky man, with a sallow bald head, a composed presence, with mournful eyes under a frown, a brownish-grey moustache and beard in Tibetan style. He wore a thickish tweed suit in the colours of heather. I thought he resembled Lenin, but this was heresy, for my 'Russianism', like that of all my associates, under Rosing and Mamoulian, our Russian directors, was imperialist and white, not to say refugistic. But there was nothing of the proletarian in M. Roerich's manner. In his receiving line he greeted everyone with aristocratic courtesy, if detachment, and then let us go to the exhibition. I cannot now be certain that the designs for *Le Sacre du printemps* were included, but their very climate brooded on the walls, for Roerich's vision was constant, and I recalled Van Vechten's ". . . very beautiful green landscape" for the first scene, and for the second, "a backdrop of steppes and sky, the *Hic Sunt Leones* country of old mapmakers' imaginations", as Stravinsky said. For the *Sacre* designs, as in the rest of the works about the galleries, in their muted sulphurous yellows, the smoky violets of vast distances, the swept landscapes of unexplored worlds, jewel-blue and lava-black, it was the imagination of an explorer at work, and indeed, Roerich had travelled to lost lands and returned an authority. He was of a calibre to sustain Stravinsky, and to him, 'painter, ethnographer, archaeologist, designer of Rimsky-Korsakoff's tomb,' wrote Robert Craft long later, 'Stravinsky confided his prefiguration of the new ballet . . . It was one of the most fortunate confidences of his life, for Roerich's knowledge, whatever it may have been, inspired Stravinsky and helped to sustain his vision. Roerich was the catalyst of the subject, an

incomparably more effective function than that of set and costume designer by which he is remembered.'

With mysterious fortuity, discoveries and approaches followed through my years in Rochester.

If Goossens was a presence of particular distinction and style, he was also a musician of highly schooled and used gifts. He had played violin under Artur Nikisch and Sir Thomas Beecham, he had been brought into conducting by Beecham, he was a serious composer, and most enlivening of all, he knew Stravinsky, had conducted all his major works, and was a figure in the determining circles of the contemporary idiom not only in music, but in literature and painting, in London, Paris, and New York. He was tall and as famously tailored for his concerts as Toscanini and Stravinsky, and he moved with the languid gait of an officer off-duty. Stylishly abrupt in speech, wittily amused at most matters which he noticed, he had the air of being tuned-out much of the time—he talked freely and fondly to me when I would ask to know about Stravinsky. He was an ambassador from Stravinsky's world—a member of it, and I drew closer than ever before to Stravinsky through him.

In later years, Merle Armitage edited a volume of essays about Stravinsky, which included a piece by Goossens, and Goossens published a volume of an autobiography. In much of what he wrote, Goossens gave coherent final form to the sort of information he let me have in scattered conversations in Rochester. I was most concerned with Goossens's musical references, and the figure who for me was their central one. In recalling my musical conversations with Goossens, I here combine my recollections with quotations from his later writings on matters which we originally discussed.

He first heard Stravinsky at eighteen, while playing in the violin section of the Queen's Hall Orchestra under Sir Henry Wood. He remembered how skilfully Wood guided the orchestra across the 'dangerous reefs' in such early works of Stravinsky as *Scherzo Fantastique*, *Fireworks*, and the *Firebird* suite. At a ballet performance in the Theatre Royal, Drury Lane, two years later

Goossens saw *Petrushka* and *Le Sacre du printemps* danced by the Diaghilev company and conducted by Pierre Monteux. Five years later, now himself a conductor, Goossens again attended the Diaghilev ballet, when Ansermet conducted *Pulcinella*, the *Rossignol* suite, and *L'Histoire du soldat*. It was a fulfilling satisfaction when in 1921 Goossens conducted *Le Sacre du printemps* in its first concert performance in England, and later many other Stravinsky works, which would culminate in his leading the first British production of *Les Noces*. He said that every time he conducted a work of Stravinsky's, he would 'sample it anew'. But, he said and wrote, the responsibility resting on the shoulders of the conductor of Stravinsky's works was a heavy one.

'On the one hand, we must avoid the devil of inaccuracy, and on the other, the deep sea of so-called "interpretation"!'

'But so difficult!' I would say.

'His sense of musical values must be unerring and his technical equipment vast.'

'Yes, but they all say that is true of you.'

'Yes, but above all, the conductor must be a wholehearted champion of the music. No mental reservations.'

'Have you talked with Stravinsky?'

'Igor? Of course. In his little studio over the Salle Pleyel in Paris. He has often said to me, "Either you feel my music, or you don't. Either its logic impresses itself on you, or it doesn't. Either you are musically and technically equipped to conduct it, or you aren't!"'

He said Stravinsky's insistence on following precisely the printed indications in his scores amounted almost to a mania.

'How is it possible to solve his technical problems?' I asked.

Well, granted that works such as *Le Sacre du printemps*, and others, presented 'more surface problems of a rhythmical nature than almost any music hitherto written', Goossens thought such problems would be quickly disposed of from the moment the conductor realised that, unless otherwise indicated, no deviation in tempo from the unit of rhythm could ever be tolerated.

'What music it must be to read and memorise!'

'I could memorise it. But I use a score.' Goossens squinted comically in recollection. 'Once one of my colleagues said he never conducted with a score, and asked me why I so often used scores at my concerts. "My dear boy," I replied, "I can read!"'

He came back to the subject and looked at me quizzingly.

'Why are you so interested in Stravinsky? He has hardly been played in this country. Have you heard him out West?'

'No. But I have always read about him.'

'You admire him. Impossible not to. His very first works made him the most discussed personality in music. He had the most challenging influence since Debussy. A genius of the first order. There are plenty of other moderns, so-called; but he has nothing in common with any of them. What he wrote at first may be rooted in Russia, but it was all arrestingly and uncompromisingly Stravinsky—which is to say unlike anything else. His craftsmanship and urgency of inspiration swept you along in a surge of dynamic realism. We youngsters imbibed draughts of this new creative tonic, and it went straight to our heads.' Goossens spoke not only as a conductor but as a composer. He shrugged. 'But we couldn't ape it, and it remains a fact that Stravinsky's would-be imitators fall by the wayside.'

All I could do at the time was stare mentally at imagined occasions.

'How was it when you gave the first concert performance of *Le Sacre du printemps*?'

'Ha. Twenty-five minutes of ensemble-cum-virtuoso fireworks more dazzling than London ever heard.' The orchestra of 105 players was hand-picked. Everyone was in the audience, including Bernard Shaw. Stravinsky was expected from Paris. He had not arrived by intermission time. 'I decided to prolong interval time, hoping that the boat train wouldn't have been too long delayed.' But the audience returned to their seats and after nearly half an hour Goossens felt he must return to the stage. Just as he raised his stick to cue the bassoonist for the opening statement, 'a movement in the dress circle caught my eye,' he said, 'and a trio of weary travellers—Stravinsky, Diaghilev, and Massine—crept into their seats. The suspense was broken.'

'How did it go?'

'The last explosive chord of the *Danse Sacral* had hardly erupted before the audience sprang to its collective feet and gave an exhibition of hysterical enthusiasm which put the fiercest demonstrations of the Parisians in the shade.'

Stravinsky was called to the stage and cheered and cheered again—a 'slight man of forty', said a London paper I have seen quoted, 'the most innocuous exterior to house such dark powers of wizardry'. Bernard Shaw, as Goossens quoted him, said, 'If it had

34

been Rossini, people would have said that there was too much "rum-tum" in it,' and Goossens said that Shaw asked him later,

'Why, Mr Goossens, when I bought a seat for your concert last week, did you make me pay a guinea for a shilling's worth of music and twenty shillings' worth of noise?'

'Does Shaw know anything about music?' I asked, not yet having discovered the volumes of *Music in London*, and in any case never having admired his self-serving intellectual showmanship. Goossens was his friend and probably made a soft answer, which I do not remember. I said something like this,

'If I could, I would go anywhere to hear Stravinsky.'

Goossens replied,

'But you will hear his music with our orchestra.'

So by a wide loop in my progression towards my main subject, the events in my life so far described brought me closer to the climate of Stravinsky as the prime creator of the twentieth century, and to my first actual hearing of his music.

It is not for me to discuss the music of Stravinsky, for two reasons. First, I do not think even the most earnest effort, of the most elaborate literacy, like that of Paul Rosenfeld, can through metaphor do more than refer to private excitement in another medium. One always returns to Stravinsky's own epigram about what it is that music expresses—music itself and only. Secondly, I am not technically competent to discuss his work in entirely musical terms—the only terms which 'interested' Stravinsky, as he remarked long later.

I can say only that, apart from the spell which it cast over my notion of what contemporary music was at its greatest, hearing the music of this master, about which I wondered so long in my absence from it, brought me a sense of fulfilment and completion I had never known before except from the noblest masters of the past, in particular Beethoven.

But there was one further and more immediate effect: the reality which reached me with the directness of an arrow from Stravinsky's works was one which made all extraneous notions and trappings seem very young and ready for discard. The exotic, the half-comic, half-earnest 'Russianism' and the other impersonations which seemed freeing to my youthful ardours, now were irrelevant.

35

My image of Stravinsky as a lord of world chic and Russian col-
loquialism vanished together. For the fact was, whatever his historic roots, his music seemed no more Russian, in the picturesque
sense, than Beethoven's seemed Teutonic. It was absolute in itself,
above national idiom, and its world in a particular sense was that
within the mind which produced it, whose amplitude embraced
for its purposes any manner or style which its musical ideas might
require.

It is, this, an impression which has abided and grown ever since
those Goossens concerts in Rochester, as Stravinsky evolved in his
work through phases which educated historians and trained critics
have chosen to label as 'neo-classic', or 'liturgical', or whatever
category seems to have come most readily to their fugitive needs—
particularly that one eager to note retrogression. Edmund Wilson
disposed of any puny sense of betrayal once and for all when he
wrote, 'It is likely to be one of the signs of the career of a great
artist that each of his successive works should prove for his admirers as well as for his critics not at all what they had been
expecting, and cause them to raise cries of falling-off.'* All the
while, this composer, who learned everything of importance about
his art all by himself, went on his way, fulfilling vision and sound
so that no matter what stylistic reference others tried to ally with
it, his music invariably received the life-giving touch that was his
alone.

Surrounded by all the disorder, the heights and deeps of theatrical occupations, the prodigality of my expenditure of young
energy, and the uncountable rewards of my daily association with
people of a wide variety of talents, this was a consummation of
experience and idea which beautifully answered all my years of
approach to it. By the reality of his music, Stravinsky himself
became at last real to me, without at the same time depriving me
of that sense of mythos concerning him which would continue to
interest the world for another half-century of his life.

It became increasingly possible to keep Stravinsky's music alive
in performances through recordings. The Victor catalogue listed
The Firebird for the first time in 1926 in a double-faced 12-inch
disc. Two years later Oscar Fried conducted it for Polydor. In
1930 Koussevitzky and the Boston Orchestra produced an album
of the *Petrushka* suite, with one side given to the *Apollo and*

* *The American Earthquake, a Documentary of the Twenties and Thirties,* Garden
City, Doubleday Anchor Books, 1958, p. 111.

Terpsichore episode of *Apollon Musagète*, and not long afterwards Albert Coates and the London Symphony Orchestra recorded *Le Chant du rossignol*. So far as I know, the first issue of the recorded *Le Sacre du printemps* came in 1933 from Victor by Stokowski and the Philadelphia Orchestra. It returned me to my first 'live' hearing in the Goossens performance in Rochester, and faintly, to my conjectured likening of the Corn Dance of Santo Domingo to the mass celebration of Stravinsky's timeless ritualists.

We came closer to the composer when Columbia issued six sides on which he himself conducted the concert suite from *Petrushka*, and when the same company gave us Stravinsky playing his *Duo Concertante* for violin and piano with Samuel Dushkin, for whom the work was written, playing the violin. We heard Vronsky and Babin's recording of the *Circus Polka*, and a suite drawn from the full ballet of *Jeu de cartes* with the composer conducting the Berlin Philharmonic Orchestra, and we heard him again as he conducted for Columbia the *Symphony in Three Movements*. Stokowski in the later thirties recorded the complete *Firebird* and the complete *Petrushka* with the Philadelphia Orchestra, and the *Capriccio for Piano and Orchestra* was played for Victor by José María Sanromá, with the Boston Symphony Orchestra and Koussevitzky, and it was Stravinsky himself with the 'RCA Orchestra' who first brought *Orpheus* to the phonograph.

The great ballets in these listings, and the operas as I later came to know them, fortify me to risk the remark that Stravinsky was an incomparable *stage composer*, in the sense of one fully alive to the particular sort of spell cast by the theatre—this, of course, in addition to his works composed with no pictorial action in mind. I never hear without that premonitory shiver with which we greet the first announcement of a mystery and its coming elucidation the very opening statements of all the stage works. As off-hand examples I think of the alien, enigmatic first song of the bassoon which opens *Le Sacre du printemps*; and the spell-casting harp figure whose descending notes at the start of *Orpheus* suffuses the theatre with a statement of the hunger and sorrow of the myth we are to see unfold; and the bright, commanding, formal brass fanfare before the first curtain of *The Rake's Progress*, which calls our wits from every-which-where to come to the play, out of house and land and square, and when we are there, the brasses are cut off now that we are captive, and we hear a piteous roundelay from gentle wind instruments which forecast the implacable folly to

37

come. I could cite any number—these only to recall for myself the independent creation of theatre itself in the sounds which announce the spectacle. Though I know nothing of the process of his work, it is as though he thought one way when writing for the orchestra pit and another for the concert platform, and I delight in his appropriatenesses—the one for evocation of visible events in which we are to see ourselves, the other for abstractions which evoke our other faculties; both in such personal style as to be unmistakably his.

To my great profit as both writer and reader, I found that Stravinsky was one of the most precise and original masters of language in his epoch. I have always taken pleasure from the writing of non-literary artists though it is far from a general rule that many of them have written with distinction, and when they have, it has been chiefly in spontaneous forms, such as journals and letters. Stravinsky belongs with the best of them—Mozart, Mendelssohn, Busoni, in their letters, and, in either journals or systematic treatises, with Da Vinci, Dürer, Schumann, Berlioz, Debussy, Delacroix, Reynolds, and the Americans Robert Henri and Ernst Bacon. His recorded words carry wit, erudition, linguistic power, and, to an almost confidential degree, personal character. '. . . My interest in words,' he stated in 1962, 'is not merely philological. I recognise that words are the very instruments of thought and that a large vocabulary permits the making of distinctions.'

I read his autobiography when it first appeared in English in 1936, and again in its new edition in 1958; and in 1947, his *Poetics of Music*, the Norton lectures he gave at Harvard in 1939 in French, of which I was never able to obtain a copy in the original language until the reprint of 1970. In my habit, I marked my copies, and I return to them often to see again what passages I would retain, certain that he is one of those rare writers felicitously able to put his absolute self upon the page.

I delighted in this autobiography, as much of whose forward impulsion came from its ideas as from its events; and in its 'aristocratic austerity' it seemed to me perfectly to complement as a work of literature the body of Stravinsky's music. Its closing remarks are as true of his whole career now as when he wrote them in mid-life:

'I live neither in the past nor in the future. I am in the present. I cannot know what tomorrow will bring forth. I can only know what the truth is for me today. That is what I am called upon to serve, and I serve it in all lucidity.'

In 1947, when Stravinsky's Norton lectures were published in English by the Harvard University Press, under the title *Poetics of Music, in the Form of Six Lessons*, I found his aesthetic principles stated in more extended and even more articulate form. It is always comforting to anyone who has worked continuously in any of the imaginative vocations to have precepts which he has gradually formulated for himself receive their general confirmation by a master. So much of Stravinsky's conviction about the nature and expression of the artist in music has application to literature that I have again and again revisited his words, for the double pleasure of his writing in and of itself, and the aesthetic creed which he enunciates. In open lectures and in work with individual students on countless occasions I have quoted him *in extenso*. His literary style has of course its direct affinity with his musical thought and the texture of its expression. It is immediately personal, its logic often finds statement through his ironic wit, its rhythm—the key to all readability—is like his own natural respiration, and his originality is as often related to his uses of the past as to the timeless ideas of his own present. Of his six lectures in the book, the third and fourth, *The Composition of Music*, and *Musical Typology*, can almost in entirety be entrusted to students of prose writing who understand analogy for their meditation as they consider their own efforts.

It is a small book, but it is too full of remarkable variety in subject matter and statement to quote extensively here; yet if there are certain threads which bind all the other ideas together perhaps they are those which Stravinsky spins out relating to the value of tradition, the essentiality of formal limitation as the principal instrument of the originating artist's freedom, the unworthiness of any sort of pretence in either making a work or presenting it, and the footlessness of being influenced by any current cult and its cant. Typical brief extracts reflect the power of the work as a whole.

'. . . I confess,' he writes, 'that I am completely insensitive to the prestige of revolution'—he, of all artists, who was first acclaimed as an overpowering revolutionist. But, he goes on, 'all the noise it may make will not call forth the slightest echo in me', and

we understand that it was not for the sake of revolution that he created new directions, but simply to fulfil for himself the music which came to him in his own nature. He was not preparing to lead anyone else. 'For revolution is one thing, innovation another. And even innovation, when not presented in excessive form, is not always recognised by its contemporaries.' He then astounds us by citing, as an example of one misunderstood in such a way, the composer Charles Gounod, and in his quotations from Gounod's critics we may hear clearly the sort of accusation to which Stravinsky himself was repeatedly treated in phase after phase of his always advancing realisation of renewed vision: 'They saw in Gounod "a symphonist astray in the theatre", a "severe musician", to use their own terms, and of course more "learned" than "inspired".' *Faust* was dismissed as ' "not the work of a melodist" '. After citing more shortsighted opinions such as strew the wreckage of criticism in all ages, he says, 'I am going to be polemical. I am not afraid to admit this. I shall be polemical not in my own defence, but in order to defend in words all music and its principles, just as I defend them in a different way with my compositions.'

If the best defence often lies in the attack, Stravinsky has bombardments for Wagner and his followers, and his preference lies clearly with the views and achievements of Verdi, 'at once modest and aristocratic'. He gives marks to Wagner for being powerful; but the famous concept of the 'Synthesis of the Arts' comes in for severe drubbing, and though the word is never used, the general complaint adds up to the self-enlarging vulgarity which was certainly visible in Wagner's life and which despite its lofty disguises of theory heaves forth in much of his music. 'How powerful this man must have been,' marvels Stravinsky, 'to have destroyed an essentially musical form with such energy that fifty years after his death we are still staggering under the rubbish and racket of the music drama!' Again he refers to 'the miasmic vapours of the music drama, the inflated arrogance of which could not conceal its vacuity', and, even more damagingly: 'Wagner's work corresponds to a tendency that is not, properly speaking, a disorder, but one which tries to compensate for a lack of order. The principle of the endless melody perfectly illustrates this tendency. It is the perpetual becoming of a music that never had any reason for starting, any more than it has any reason for ending.' This is a critical attack of such venomous acuity that its own energy approaches that of Voltaire in *Doctor Akakia*, and calls for reading aloud, to the same

tears of laughter that rolled down the cheeks of Frederick the Great even as the king knew he must take revenge upon his learned friend for the crime of *lèse-majesté*. As for the Wagnerian *leitmotiv*, it was 'a system that led Debussy to say that the *Ring* struck him as a sort of vast musical city directory', and for himself Stravinsky notes that the critical votaries of Wagner's device of identification 'let themselves be inveigled into musical tours conducted by the Cook Agency of Bayreuth'.

The sort of paradox in which Stravinsky took delight is illustrated in his quotation from Verdi—'Let us return to old times, and it will be progress.' Like all epigrams, it is but a text for a dissertation, and it is enlarged upon in various passages of the *Poetics*. 'Far from implying the repetition of what has been, tradition presupposes the reality of what endures. It appears as an heirloom, a heritage that one receives on condition of making it bear fruit before passing it on to one's descendants.' This is a far different matter from attempting to establish as a legacy a style invented *'pour épater les contemporains'*.

He speaks of 'a new age which seeks to reduce everything to uniformity in the realm of matter while it tends to shatter all universality in the realm of the spirit in deference to an anarchistic individualism . . . There are simple souls who rejoice in this state of affairs. There are criminals who approve of it.'

There is, then, a distinct relation between universality and order, and order implies a choice among limitations, which does not mean captivity or impotence, no matter what the vulgar and simple-minded of any recurrent *avant-garde* may proclaim.

'Which of us has ever heard talk of art as other than a realm of freedom? This sort of heresy is uniformly widespread because it is imagined that art is outside the bounds of ordinary activity. Well, in art as in everything else, one can build only upon a resisting foundation: whatever constantly gives way to pressure, constantly renders movement impossible.

'I shall go even further: my freedom will be so much the greater and more meaningful the more narrowly I limit my field of action and the more I surround myself with obstacles. Whatever diminishes constraint, diminishes strength. The more constraints one imposes, the more one frees one's self of the chains that shackle the spirit.'

Stravinsky thus enunciated the first requirement for the solution of form, which is the artist's highest inventive problem. As for the

substance, nothing could be more false in direction than the catchwords of cultism, in their current imperatives, to which the expedient second-rater is always scrambling to conform.

'Like every sort of evil,' states the *Poetics*, 'snobbery tends to give rise to another evil which is its opposite: *pompierisme.*' (In a didactic footnote the author explains that 'The word "pompier" originated with the resemblance in mid-nineteenth century pictures of the casques of ancient Roman officials to firemen's helmets. It is now applied to persons who represent pompous pedantry and officialdom.') He then proceeds with his demolition of cultural firemen: 'When all is said and done, the snob is himself nothing but a sort of *pompier*—a vanguard *pompier.*

'The vanguard *pompiers* make small talk about music as they do about Freudianism or Marxism. At the slightest provocation they bring up the *complexes* of psychoanalysis and even go so far today as to familiarise themselves, albeit reluctantly—but *snobisme oblige* —with the great Saint Thomas Aquinas . . . All things considered, to that sort of *pompier* I prefer the pure and simple *pompier* who talks about melody and, with hand over heart, champions the incontestable rights of sentiment, defends the primacy of emotion, gives evidence of concern for the noble, on occasion yields to the adventure of oriental picturesqueness, and even goes so far as to praise my *Firebird.* You will readily understand that it is not for this reason that I prefer him to the other sort of *pompier* . . . It is simply that I find him less dangerous. The vanguard *pompiers*, moreover, make the mistake of being contemptuous beyond measure of their colleagues of yesteryear. Both will remain *pompiers* all their lives, and the revolutionary ones go out of style more quickly than the others: time is the greatest threat to them.'

It is after all self-indulgence of the ego for its own sake which he attacks; and his assault extends also to performers.

'The sin against the spirit of a work always begins with a sin against its letter and leads to the endless follies which an overflourishing literature in the worst taste does its best to sanction . . . The Superfluous is refined upon . . . great pride is taken in perfecting useless nuances—a concern that usually goes hand in hand with inaccurate rhythm . . .'

Finally, as to the spirit of the work, and Stravinsky's religious response to it—daring in an epoch of chic infidelism with its complacent trivialisation of life—the *Poetics* concludes by saying

42

that 'music comes to reveal itself as a form of communion with our fellow man—and with the Supreme Being'.

An artist whose life and work rest upon a foundation so deeply serious as this could have no limits to the variety of his expression, from gaiety to pathos, celebration to wit and its tangents, grandeur and irony and every analogy for that precision which so rarely is general to life.

Through his music in its sound, and his thought through his words, it was possible, in the passing years, to contrive an inward portrait of him.

In 1954 I finally saw Stravinsky in the flesh. I had been in New York on publishing affairs connected with my history of the Rio Grande,* and now I was returning to New Mexico. Coming into the high-hooded Chicago station I always thought of one of the Monet paintings of the old Gare St Lazare—grey steam, violet air, dapples of sulphurous daylit city sky beyond the train sheds.

On this arrival, Monday, 25 October, I read in *The Chicago Tribune* that the London Festival Ballet company was appearing at the Civic Opera House and—my excitement was immediate— that Igor Stravinsky would appear in the evening of this day and the next as guest conductor to lead a performance of *Petrushka*. I at once rearranged my tickets on the Santa Fe train to leave a day later than I had planned, and waited for evening with the kind of visceral tautness you feel in childhood before a grand event whose very approach is hard to bear. The day went by in bookshops, the Art Institute, lunch at the Arts Club with Fanny Butcher, and a long walk along the lakefront with my *Doppelgänger*; for in most intense times, the powers of recollection always seemed most acute within myself.

The London Festival Ballet in that 1954 performance gave *Les Sylphides* before the intermission. The programme was to close with *Petrushka*.

On this night the immense auditorium was a great hive of honey colour and pale rose, in gold leaf and velvet, where the people glistened and turned in their hum before the dusking-out of the house-lights after the intermission. Followed the most

* *Great River: The Rio Grande in North American History*, 2 vols. (New York, Rinehart and Co., 1954; London, Macmillan and Co, 1955).

43

theatrical of all anticipations, which was the dawn of the footlights on the deep fringes and folds of the stage curtain. In the new darkness the lights glowed far away on the orchestra stands, and the conductor's desk with its open score was a glaring white amidst the subdued expectation in the house.

Though the auditorium was packed, I had been able to secure for myself a seat in the centre box. There was first a single hand-clap, then a few more in the first row, far away, as the low door under the stage apron slowly opened on a dim square of ochreous light, against which a figure moving with deliberate pace came in silhouette into the spacious orchestra pit at the station of the double basses, and slowly threaded the path between the first violin stands to the conductor's desk. This progress was assisted by an upsweep of applause into a great draught like that of air hauled into fire. Once at his desk, the conductor faced us, lifted his head, and then bowed once, deeply and slowly to the house, across the velvet orchestra barrier. The focused distance made him seem large, an impression heightened by his serious bearing. His face was pale, his glasses were fleetingly visible as they caught the light, his head was glossy and his features so strongly modelled that I felt power concentrated in that brief glimpse. He then turned to the score on his desk and after collecting the players with his eyes in quick turns of his head, he raised his arms and I saw his extraordinary hands. From even as far as my box I could see their workman's squareness, even, I could say, builder's—the manual power and nicety of hands long disciplined to the hard craftly aspect of an art. Against the now partially concealed desk, his black figure was lean and trim—was it the same tailcoat? It was remarkable how even in the stretched silence before the indicative upbeat the energy of his style could be felt. Then like a powerful breath in-taken his right hand broke the air—using no baton—in the silent upbeat, to be followed at once by a decisive downbeat; and the sparkling festival of the Russian village fair sprang alive in the horns and high woodwinds.

It was my first sight of Stravinsky. I have always been glad that it was in the formality of the theatre that I first saw him, a master at work in his own *métier*. I watched him as much as I did the stage, perhaps more, though the spell of the ballet was transporting, in the brilliant paints of Benois' setting, and particularly in a performance of the puppet Petrushka by the dancer Keith Beckett so beautiful technically and so affecting emotionally that

I have never forgotten any detail of it, and have always wondered why his career received no more celebration beyond England than it did. In any case, not to be stingy with response and word, the event was for me a historical epiphany, for which my slowly developing experience had at least in some measure prepared me. Happiness is as difficult to recall as pain. Usually we must do with the memory only of the occasion, not the sensation itself, when we have felt either. But sharply I remember both, as of that autumn night in Chicago, in that immense opera house, seeing him and hearing his work under his own hand for the first time.

Until then, Stravinsky had remained for me a strongly affecting abstraction—a construction, projected in vision, alive in my mind, commanding my ear. But now after the long convergence of events, my view of him became actual.

At the end of the ballet he came onstage with the dancers and stood in the centre of their brightly pied row to bow with them in his smiling, courtly, serious way, while the heavy, divided curtain flew upward and aside again and again; and I with the rest of the house stood and stormed him, feeling in an oddly egotistic and satisfying fashion that I now belonged personally to the foreground of his edifice of artistic meaning.

It was to be my fortune that within a very few years we actually met; and thereafter I was able to receive the further experience which enables me from this point on to turn outward, so to speak, with an attempt to reflect his actual presence.

Book 2

REALISATIONS

ONE Sunday in mid-winter 1956–7 the young conductor John O. Crosby was dining with his friend Mirandi Masocco in her house at Santa Fe. He was full of plans for establishing the Santa Fe Opera, tentative news of which had already reached the press and had stirred up that pleasure in anticipated disaster which belonged to the knowing segment of the local Santa Fe society. Crosby's determination was great, even though his imagination was at this point by turns elated and hopeless. Aside from great material problems, he wanted, if he could manage to open the new open-air opera theatre which he was building north of Santa Fe in the landscape towards Taos, to give a signal to the world that even if it was to begin modestly, the Santa Fe Opera would indicate its serious artistic purpose by including in its first season an opera by the century's most eminent composer.

Crosby was a citizen of both Santa Fe and New York and, after studying at Yale with Hindemith, and in Maine with Pierre Monteux, he was determined to make a career as a conductor and, further, as an impresario in the creation of a fresh operatic style of production, restudying the standard masterpieces, to discover them freshly, using young, personable, and dramatically skilled singers. Crosby wanted to combine this project with the American place he loved best—that South-western capital of forty thousand people, in its incomparable landscape, and with its varied cultural tradition. His ambition was to present *The Rake's Progress* as the highlight of a more conventional repertoire in the first season. It was, he believed, the greatest of modern operas. How could he hope to persuade Stravinsky that a new and untried company would be worthy of performance rights to his operatic masterpiece? 'If only,' thought Crosby.

'Do you want me to ask Stravinsky?' inquired Mirandi in her dauntless way.

Crosby could hardly believe that she knew Stravinsky well enough to urge the unborn opera company on him, but he assented.

Mirandi, after all, understood to a nicety the energies which gave Santa Fe its character as a sub-capital of the international

chic. The immigrant sophisticates of that old mountain city lived on the comings, the stayings, the goings, of the itinerant great, as well as on a fabric of local news which, the more intimate (read 'scandalous') it was, the richer assuagement it provided for emotional hungers which fed on fantasies if enduring realities were wanting.

She was in an ideal position to command this medium of power and satisfaction. She had an innate sense of the dramatic, she knew everybody, her spoken style was in itself extravagant and droll, though finally kind, and her daily post in her brother-in-law's shop (where she designed important jewellery), from which she could observe who came and went, gave her useful bulletins later to be released to her daily luncheon guests at her always-reserved round table at La Fonda. She was a model of style, with her cap of bronze hair; her immense eyeglasses with thick lenses which made a decorative virtue of her short-distance vision; her grand Roman nose; her wide cuffs of incised gold worn as bracelets, and her husky voice which would often break to emphasise a climactic point in her recitals. Her humour was equal to her courage, upon both of which she had often had occasion to draw in her life.

Her friendship with the Stravinskys went back to 1950. In the summer of that year, she received a phone call from the renowned duo-pianists Vronsky and Babin, who owned a house near Santa Fe. They were at the moment in Aspen performing in the musical festival honouring Albert Schweitzer on the occasion of the Goethe Bicentennial celebration, out of which grew the Aspen Institute and, later, the Aspen School of Music. During the many days of homage to Goethe, the Stravinskys, accompanied by Robert Craft, appeared in Aspen, and finding their old friends and compatriots Victor and Vitya Babin, who now were New Mexicans, they declared they wanted to see New Mexico, to meet Frieda Lawrence and Mrs Tony Luhan, and visit Santa Fe. Victor Babin asked Mirandi if she could meet the Stravinskys at Taos and take charge of their events.

She met them in Taos on 4 August for breakfast with Mrs Lawrence. They were 'enchanted' with Frieda, and talked the whole time about D. H. Lawrence, long dead. By noon they had moved on to Embudo, southward on the Rio Grande, to lunch with Mabel Dodge Luhan, with whom, said Mirandi, Stravinsky was 'not comfortable'. They soon left. Mirandi idly mentioned

that it was the day of the great festival of the Pueblo Indians at Santo Domingo—the Corn Dance.

Stravinsky immediately insisted on seeing it, though this meant a long drive for most of the hot afternoon. No matter. They arrived at the pueblo in time to see more than two hours of the dance, through a haze of dust raised by the dancers and hauled by the desert winds. Everything about the ritual 'ravished' Stravinsky— the dusty golden light which seemed to set the spectacle in another dimension of place and period, the chants of the Indian chorus, the extraordinary precision of the ensemble maintained by the three hundred men and women dancers, and above all the rhythms of the ceremony, characterised by its unexpected breaks, suspensions like held breath until the steady beat was resumed to pound the dancers' prayer into the earth to bring rain, fertility, life.

When I heard all this later from Mirandi, I remembered my speculations about *Le Sacre du printemps*, in 1921 during my schooldays, by which time I also had seen the Santo Domingo Corn Dance; and I asked her if Stravinsky had made any reference at the pueblo to his early masterpiece, with its intuitions about the enactment of myth, prayer, sacrifice. She answered,

'Yes. He said something about *reminders* and *recognitions*, as I recall it.'

Not to stretch a point, it was still a confirming hint of the unity in my sense of Stravinsky, far or near.

From Santo Domingo the party returned to Santa Fe, and late in the day though it was, they went for cocktails to the poet Witter Bynner's. His household was now shared by Robert Hunt, an old schoolmate of mine. They all made friends, and the Stravinskys so liked Santa Fe that they stayed a few days, were entertained by the painter Cady Wells, and by the Babins on their return from Aspen. Presently they motored westward to Hollywood by car, where, seven years later Stravinsky listened by telephone as Mirandi described the intentions of the Santa Fe Opera, including the director's great hope of producing *The Rake's Progress* in the first season.

'I am interested,' said Stravinsky.

'How marvellous. Then I will fly out to tell you more details,' said Mirandi.

She did so, taking along a set of blueprints for Crosby's opera theatre. They were modest predictions of the beautiful opera house of today. When he saw them,

'But the theatre is not even built yet,' said Stravinsky, 'and you want me to come?'

'It will be ready for the opening on the first of July,' promised Mirandi.

The Stravinskys had every reason to trust her. She had protected them from the more relentless and expert glamour hunters of Santa Fe. Her presence, part *gamine*, part woman of high style, and her darting realism of mind, amused them. She was the only living person privileged to address the composer, not as 'Maestro', or 'Mr Stravinsky', as everyone else did, but as 'Pussycat', to his evident amusement. She had been the guest of the Stravinskys in their box at the Metropolitan's unsatisfactory première of *The Rake's Progress* in 1953.

'So what do you think?' she asked now.

Stravinsky said he was gratified that a new company of young artists loved his work. To help them make a start in the world, he would agree to their producing his opera. More, he would ask Robert Craft to conduct it, and he himself would be present to supervise the production. Mirandi returned with her news to Crosby.

The Santa Fe Opera, then, would be able to take on life under the most auspicious possible patronage; for the Stravinskys were coming, *The Rake's Progress* would be given, and because of Crosby's love for the work, and the Santa Fe public's increasing devotion to it, it would remain as a repertory piece given every few seasons.

Faithful to a promise, Mirandi telephoned me at my home at Roswell, New Mexico, to tell me when the Stravinskys arrived at Santa Fe. We had discussed my desire to meet them. On behalf of her good friend J. B. Jackson she gave me an invitation to come to dine at his house in the country; a very small dinner for the Stravinskys and Craft later in the week. Would I come for it? There would be no one else, except perhaps two elderly ladies who had retired to Santa Fe after having served for many years as co-headmistresses of an exclusive girls' school in Pennsylvania. They lent tone to Santa Fe with gaiety and good breeding, and Jackson was fond of them for these qualities. He had charm, along with high intelligence, and it seemed appropriate that he should entertain the Stravinskys soon after their arrival.

The dinner party took place *al fresco*, curtained by vines, under the *portal* of Jackson's adobe house at La Cienega south of Santa Fe.

After the rest of the party was assembled, the approach of the car bearing Mirandi and the Stravinskys was announced by the barking and capering of Jackson's pair of Labrador retrievers.

The arrival had an imperially courteous air. They all moved slowly to us to be introduced by Jackson. They smiled and gazed with inclined interest at each of us in turn, they murmured compliments about the charm of the view and the simple setting for the party, and they were civil to the Labradors whose social gestures were full of thick thumping tails and generous salivation.

We were given drinks. In the subsequent preliminary constraints, I looked to describe to myself the Imperial Family—a nickname I later gave them, which caught on in intimate circles. Actually, the Stravinskys seemed to me, then and always, to carry an air of state wherever they went. One had a historical sense in their presence. There was nothing contrived about this—it was simply the effect of half a century of illustriousness which was like a natural climate for them to move in. Madame was Stravinsky's second wife, the first having died in the early thirties.* Robert Craft had joined them as musical aide in 1948 and rapidly became an indispensable family intimate—a stimulating companion in the wide-ranging intellectual atmosphere of the household.

In the gentlest way, Madame had the smiling assurance of a woman who has always been beautiful. She was tall, reminding me of Maillol's vision of womankind. Her elegance was highly personal, though not eccentric, and she moved with unemphatic grace in her rather floating garments against which large pearls and other jewels made light and colour. One saw first her great eyes, shadowed in blue, lustrous with humour and immediate opinion. Her hair was a subdued gold, retained in its sumptuous modelling by the sparest of black veiling with little black velvet dots in it. A stole of heavy satin lay about her shoulders. With her drink, she took a chair and I sat near her. She saw that I was dimmed by my sense of the occasion, and for my ease began to make a comedy of recent misadventures of travel in approaching Santa Fe. They had come by train, 'terrible', she could never sleep on the train, and even

---

* Stravinsky's children were all by his first wife. There were four, three of whom are living—Soulima, the pianist, in Illinois, Theodore, the painter, in Europe, and Mrs André Marion, in California.

reading, which she loved, was difficult because of the motion. The food was 'terrible', and her husband was made content only by very good Scotch which the steward could bring. But they were happy to see Santa Fe again, the beautiful—somehow she gave this word its primal meaning in sound—the beautiful landscape here, which they remembered from driving this way before. Did I live here? Where did I live. I was writer? She was painter. But not this: she gestured humorously towards the fine view. Did I know the painting of William Congdon? They had recently acquired a handsome Venetian painting of his—much gold leaf, umber washes, and incisements, in the style I recognised. In all this, it was the tone of her voice which moved me. She spoke with a Continental accent, not rapidly, in a dovelike sound which carried into her laughter, and she had a delicious way, like a girl, of under-lining certain words, often to indicate dislike in a mock petulance, with a downward shrug. Her expressions of liking were quiet, conclusive, and impressive.

Across the *portal*, Craft in his almost inaudible but precise speech was neatly parrying the assaults of the two elderly school-mistresses, who loved information, and knew, on most occasions, how to unearth it, and later, how to use it. They were always help-ful guests, for their spirits were high, and they enjoyed expressions of natural authority, either their own or that which they might meet in others. Craft was neatly made, pale in countenance, with dark hair, and eyes like cloves set behind black-framed spectacles. He had an engaging smile which he could combine with a little twist of frown which imparted social earnestness to the trivial, and helped to spare him thought, for which he had an abundant capacity, but only for matters of consequence. He wore a dark suit —blue serge or whatever—with a plain dark tie and white shirt. His hands were mostly in motion, shaping towards himself little hollow gestures of nervous preoccupation or of longing for escape.

Mirandi talked with Stravinsky, while Jackson, coming and going, an excellent and confident cook, saw to the dinner he was preparing himself. In his moments of appearance on the *portal*— we sat outside near the prepared dinner table—he joined any one of the separate conversations of his company, made with disputa-tious charm the proper dissent to advance it further, and retired within. When it was time to be seated at the table, he put me at Stravinsky's right, which I thought an act of fine generosity. Craft sat at Stravinsky's other side, and Madame was with Jackson at the

far end of the table, with the ladies, from whom the sound that carried was Mirandi's droll caw of affirmed amazement at what she had to report of Santa Fe in its ongoing restlessness.

It was a fine evening, the light of the nacreous sky lingered and an early twilight moon was already visible even as the western colour hung over the mountains. The food and wine were excellent and simple, in Jackson's informal habit, which helped me to recall that most celebrated persons disliked being made to feel special in private. I, therefore, concealing my elation and sense of great fulfilment, heard myself 'making remarks' to Stravinsky. In his style of listening much of his presence was revealed.

He had brought his stick to the table with him, and his glass of Scotch. He crossed his great-knuckled hands—those hands so knowingly exaggerated in the Picasso 1920 drawing, and the same which so powerfully had first held and then broken the silence in the Chicago opera house—on the grip of his cane, and he leaned and nodded just above the hands at me. I was astonished to see how short he was. It was as if the public man grew by cubits when needful, while in ordinary moments, the personal Stravinsky tactfully made himself smaller. He was now seventy-five, but age was the least relevant detail about him. He was nearly bald, but the few long pale hairs left to him were brushed straight back from his tall bony brow, until they joined a fringe of hair which stood away in a touching, rather childlike fashion, from his collar. His cranium was thus plainly and powerfully visible, and his ears, which were large, the very organ and symbol of his work, stood starkly like attachments against the angular, bony structure of the skull. He wore glasses, sometimes on the bridge of his nose, sometimes on his forehead, a habit he once said he had picked up from Rimsky-Korsakoff. A closely clipped pepper-and-salt moustache concealed nothing of his wide lips, which he pursed in listening. His nose made a commanding arc. Its nostrils were great entrances for the breath of life which he so abundantly drew. Trimly tailored in a dark suit, he wore a smart bow tie, and against the chill of the evening a French silk cardigan with bone buttons. When he showed a serious expression it was grave to a formidable degree. When he smiled, it was like an illumination, and when he spoke through the smile, his throat thickened and his eyes crackled with dark light, and his mood was captivating in its contagion. His virile voice was breathy and burry. The precision of his speech marked consonants with special value unless he was making a joke, when

he slurred all sounds in a running glee to express his delight in reporting or making a 'scandal'. A 'scandal', not meaning silly gossip, but an event, a matter, of mischievous outrage, often having to do with the inappropriate or the obtuse, delighted him.

Yes, I 'made remarks', and how he suffered them, I do not know, for on later occasions I often heard him dismiss with corroding scorn a footless conversation with even notable persons as mere '*bavardage*'—the syllables equally accented and dismissive.

What was worse, I 'made remarks' about music. The subject, nervously chosen by me for, I suppose, reasons which seemed suitable, was Moussorgsky. I blanch in recollection.

But with immense courtesy he suffered me. I had the feeling that Mirandi must have given me a good press. In any event, as he listened to my evaluations of Moussorgsky, I gathered that his views were not altogether favourable, for he listened in silence while I praised whatever works I knew by this earlier master—*Boris*, orchestral pieces from *Khovantschina*, *Pictures at an Exhibition*, some songs—and I mentioned how interested I had been by Oskar von Riesemann's biography in which Moussorgsky was described as a wonderful pianist and a remarkable drawing-room actor. Could Stravinsky have known him?

—No, before his time; but Moussorgsky had often been a guest at the Stravinsky family house in St Petersburg, and the elder Stravinsky had sung the role of Boris.

'I once possessed a copy of the Ur-*Boris*,' I said, 'without the professional polish given to the opera by Rimsky-Korsakoff. I prefer what I knew of the original score, though when I had heard the work given, it was in the Rimsky version, sung by George Houston, and again by Chaliapin. I thought it in any case a stirring opera full of splendour and pathos.'

Stravinsky made his remark about how Rimsky-Korsakoff had 'Meyerbeerized' the work. After making persuasive assertions, he had the habit of smiling broadly with closed lips, giving the hint of a nod, and leaning forward a trifle. The effect was that of a courteous punctuation to an opinion, whose demonstration was its proof—a Q.E.D. of sorts.

I do not remember further details of what we said about Moussorgsky, which went on a while, but Robert Craft told me later, after the first book he produced in collaboration with the Maestro, *Conversations with Igor Stravinsky*, that the passages about Moussorgsky on pages 44 and 45 grew out of this first encounter I had

with Stravinsky. In reading those pages I have the reassuring impression that my 'remarks' could not have been so fatuous as I suspected at the moment, for the printed opinions of Stravinsky were in tone and even in some detail more favourable towards Moussorgsky than those he suggested by silence at the dinner table.

It was a happy first direct encounter, and though I was unable to remain in Santa Fe for the whole season, and thus did not see the production of *The Rake's Progress*, as it was launched with modest resources and courageous imagination, I heard an appealing little story about it which Crosby told me later.

One night in a late rehearsal of *The Rake* when every crew member of the theatre was 'doubling' at various tasks (in contrast to the company's fully sophisticated and well-equipped technical department of today), Crosby, the general director, was on his hands and knees on the stage floor, working to attach some fabric or other to the framework of a piece of scenery. The Santa Fe night wind was capricious in that open-air theatre. He was having difficulty in both holding and fastening the cloth in place. As he worked, another pair of hands appeared next to his own, holding down the stuff for him. Intent, he took advantage of this help and tacked the material in place. Only then he really saw the extra helping hands. They were Stravinsky's.

Still, before I had to leave, I had further opportunities to see the Stravinskys, and my awe began quickly to give way to affection, which through the years was to grow into love; and on one occasion that summer I brought my copy of *The Poetics of Music* to be autographed. The author wrote, on the title page, *To Paul Horgan with all my 'sympathie artistique' Igor Stravinsky, Santa Fe, July, 1957*. My copy thus became a bookman's treasure, as well as a mark of professional and personal friendship, and I remembered that in 1910 Stravinsky had received Debussy's photograph with the inscription *à Igor Stravinsky en toute sympathie artistique Claude Debussy*, and I took pleasure in my alliance even so remotely with the arc of tradition through a felicitous phrase passed from one great composer to another and so to me.

In the winter season which followed, the première of Stravinsky's ballet *Agon* was to take place in New York. I was in town in the

late autumn and saw the Stravinskys and Craft at lunch and dinner during the rehearsal period of Balanchine's production. They were full of praise for the choreography devised by Balanchine for the twelve dancers, in which the spare musical configurations, in their interlocking intimacy, were so extraordinarily given physical form by the bodies of the dancers as they moved in and out of each other's limbs in formally erotic yet chaste bodily visualisations of the score. Stravinsky spoke of Balanchine's musicianship, making the point that he could talk with him in purely musical terms, not in dramatic or balletic analogies. Stravinsky and Madame attended many rehearsals, not only to see the work develop on the stage, but because they had to leave New York before the first public performance at the City Center.

'But why,' asked Madame in her voice which now and then suggested a flute in its lower register, 'no costumes! Nothing but those athletic black and white things, like underwear. That is good for rehearsal; but that has no charm for performance—' and she made a comprehensive and very feminine gesture of lifted hand in a stem-and-flower grace, and turned her head the smallest trifle, and her body, and in a second she created a sense of costume and illustrated such beauty of a theatrical purpose that I leaned back in my chair—we were lunching at the St Regis—and must have showed my amazement at her evocative style, for she wilted out of her pose, and laughed both to recognise my response and to further her point; and I realised that I had witnessed one of the countless occasions when both she and her husband spoke exactly what they thought, which was not often what others thought. Their frankness was sometimes a 'scandal', accompanied either by the most gifted sort of down-putting, or a delicate and piercing kindness; always derived from originality as well as vast experience.

But I went to the opening performance of *Agon* and sent a telegram to Hollywood, where they had gone, to describe the ovational success it had had, and also to pay my respects to the work, with its path of mystery marked by the most restrained of means.

In the first week of the following January—1958—Stravinsky was to conduct two concerts as guest of the Houston Symphony Society, whose regular conductor at the time was Leopold Stokow-

ski, but who was to be absent during this engagement. At the same time, Madame was to have an exhibition of her paintings at the Cushman Gallery in Houston, opening with a private view.

I telephoned to Mirandi from Roswell.

How would it be if she and I spent the time in Houston with the Stravinskys? We could all stay at the same hotel, I was eager to hear him conduct again, and I wanted to see Madame's pictures.

'Marvellous!' said Mirandi.

Would she sound them out to see if the plan would be approved?

'Marvy.'

Nothing if not efficient, Mirandi called me back late the same day. They were delighted. Reservations had been made for them at the Rice Hotel, and we must join them there. Unluckily Craft could not come, as he had recording commitments in Los Angeles; but if I was to be in Houston, I could be rather helpful. They would arrive 3 January, Friday, and we must all dine together that evening.

'Did you talk to him?'

'To both of them.'

'What did he say?'

'He said, "My God, what could be better!" '

'And Madame?'

'She said she had so-o-o much to tell me.'

'Is anything wrong?'

'Oh, yes, everything is *terrible*. Hollywood drives them mad.'

'But nothing really wrong.'

'No, they're fine.'

'It will be great fun.'

'The most marvellous.'

I arrived by train early in the morning of 3 January and went to the Rice Hotel, where I had a reservation for myself and another for Mirandi. I had been there once years before, and found the old 'leading' downtown hotel to be quite as it had been. We had all vetoed the new Shamrock Hotel, descriptions of which made everyone shudder. Moreover it was inconveniently located for Stravinsky's concert-hall purposes. Finally, the Rice was owned by Houston's leading young citizen, who had been a cadet at the military institute, where he had made a creditable record academically and in the military roster, for he had become a high-ranking cadet officer. He was a tall and knowledgeable young man who had succeeded to much of the commanding position held in Houston

and Texas in general by his late uncle, Jesse Jones, the financier and statesman who had served under Franklin D. Roosevelt in the Depression and in the Second World War. The nephew was called Johnny by his cadet and faculty friends at the Institute, and it was so that I addressed him when I telephoned him soon after my arrival, to say hello, and explain why I was in Houston.

He was warm in his greeting and at once activated his hospitality. He owned the *Houston Chronicle* and would send a reporter to interview me about my books. He and his wife would be delighted to let our party have the use of their box at the orchestra. He would send over a membership card in the Petroleum Club, situated on the top floor of the Rice Hotel, without which we could not order a drink with our meals. The card would also be good in the bar off the lobby. (In Texas one could order mixed drinks only in private clubs.) We would surely meet during my stay, and in any case he and his wife would be at the first of the pair of concerts. Was there anything else he could do for me in Houston?

'I don't know if it can be managed,' I said, but I had always wanted to see the Houston harbour, and the famous ship canal which had been created to connect Houston with the Gulf forty miles away. 'Do you happen to know how I can charter a power cruiser and a pilot to show me the shipping and part of the canal?'

'When do you want to go?' asked Johnny.

'Oh, I think Monday morning would be fine at any hour.'

'We have a municipal yacht which I'd like to put at your disposal, but unfortunately it's laid up for overhaul. But there is also a municipal tug, and I'll have it waiting for you at ten o'clock Monday morning'—and he named the location of the pier. 'If you don't mind, I'll also have the ship news reporter from the *Chronicle* go with you to explain things and get a story.'

My thanks were profuse.

Johnny waved them away over the telephone with statements of municipal pride in distinguished visitors, and assured me that I must let him know if the Stravinskys or myself should in any way need his services further. His feeling for amenity was not adequately described by terms like hospitable or helpful—he shared with the best of his fellow Texans a simple sense of obligation to be of use; and the fact that now in his maturity he controlled a number of instruments and sources of power gave him greater opportunity

to exercise that trait of character, which depended on more than wealth for its worth.

Mirandi arrived by aeroplane from Santa Fe by lunchtime.

'Are they here yet?' she asked.

'Not yet. Later afternoon.'

'Marvellous.'

We lunched. She was at her most animated. She was a mimic, but, like many such, had only one voice for all her variety of assumed characters. When she quoted Stravinsky or Madame, she made their accents sound alike, when actually they were subtly different. No matter. She captured their presence with accuracy and affection. I think no one loved them more than Mirandi. They had been very good to her. Madame had made a confidante of her, who felt deeply their real troubles—some physical and serious, such as the effects upon Stravinsky of one or more cerebral thromboses which he had suffered in recent years; some trivial but distracting, such as constantly beset illustrious people who had better things to do than behave like celebrities under pressure that never ceased. All Madame wanted to do was see to her husband's well-being, and keep on with her painting. All Stravinsky was interested in was composing and conducting concerts— and with that came repeated difficulties on a planetary scale, for his engagements took him everywhere in both hemispheres, and the preparations, the arrivals and departures, the inconveniences, the interviews, the odd assortment of orchestras—it was all 'terrible'.

Mirandi exemplified the concerned friend who in sympathy for the 'terrible' was yet able to find that narrow entrance into the comic which lay behind so much of the experience of the Stravinskys in their complicated life; and it was Stravinsky himself who was the first to see and in fact dramatise many an episode of self-comedy which others later reported around the world. He would often recognise and denounce, sometimes mightily with profanity, sometimes in a skewering phrase of hilarious precision, the element of the incongruous in so much that befell him and Madame. Beyond uncontrollable circumstance, there were countless other occasions for comedy which Stravinsky met with his own wit, in all its multilingual literacy. His humour was an equal ingredient with

his courtesy and his dignity in those aspects of his personality which one encountered this side of his genius.

So it was that so many stories about him, so many quotations from even his idlest discourse, were amusing, and even if they might be at his expense, as in the fastidious little eccentricities of approaching old age, they would elicit marvelling and delight. In his diminutive stature there was such amplitude of energetic spirit and style that if one thought of him as a small, frail titan, the very contradiction in these terms seemed appropriate to paradoxical aspects of life which both expressed and entertained him.

In Houston we were all going to miss Craft—Stravinsky had come to count on his presence so much that if on occasion we were all together except Craft, who was expected, the Maestro would look about and ask, 'Vere is Bōp?'

During this week in Houston, I would be able to perform some of the small duties of a factotum—reservations here and there, arrangements for limousines, various acts of protection, and the rest, in addition to doing what I could to give the sense of *entourage* and to offer myself in the role of responsive company if I could. What Craft habitually provided was of course what I could not— that was, a sense of the extension of the family household. His musical and intellectual, his spiritual, attunement to the personalities and presences of both Stravinskys was by now wonderfully completive of their sophisticated and cultivated interests. When in 1947 Craft approached Stravinsky by mail to ask certain directions about a work of the composer's which he planned to conduct with his chamber orchestra, their affinity in musical and intellectual matters was immediately established; and presently when Craft actually joined the Stravinsky ménage for good, it was to the advantage of both the younger musician and the older master. It seems to be generally affirmed that at the time when they came together in their close bond of professional association, Stravinsky, already illustrious, entering old age, securely the presiding artist of the century, was more or less at rest on his laurels, while other younger masters were coming to the fore in music, not to his displacement—nothing could effect that—but without much sign on his part of one of those astonishing new surges of power in fresh vision which had so often characterised his career. Now, somehow, Craft, erudite in all the literature of what was regarded as 'post-Stravinsky' musical creation, and with a mind as stimulating as it was penetrating, conveyed to Stravinsky a powerful new sense of

the contemporary. This, coupled with Craft's love and understanding of Stravinsky's work and its primacy, brought a remarkable renewal of all of Stravinsky's most characteristic originality and energy; a new phase of his work came into being, and his already extraordinary career had yet another dazzling extension. In a sense, Craft represented to him the challenging homage of the youngest generation of literate musicians; and, in his recognition of the fact that he belonged now not only to musical history but to the continued act of creating it anew in his own terms, which once again were beyond the conventions of even the new idioms, and deliciously infuriating to the critics, Stravinsky in the works of his last decade and a half, like a Tintoretto, a Beethoven, a Verdi, joined that line of artists whose late years engendered new flowerings as great as those of their early mastery—or even greater, in some cases. Craft's versatile intellectual powers were matched by his gifts as a conductor. His grasp of form, understanding of the roles of the various components of musical texture, his devotion to 'pure' readings, combined with that sense of taste which is never achieved through study, were all of a style to earn him the confidence of Stravinsky.

In another dimension, Craft was a valuable companion; and that was, as a relief from the generally vacuous intellectual and artistic atmosphere of Hollywood, where the Stravinskys had lived since the early 1940s, and where Craft had joined them, living in a house nearby on their property. Aside from Gerald Heard, Aldous Huxley, and Christopher Isherwood, they had, so far as I know, no close friends with whom to have even the idlest conversation. Craft provided habitual exchange of ideas on the levels of intellectual interest and taste which the Maestro and Madame required, ranging through a constant stream of the latest books in every conceivable subject matter, in four languages, provided they belonged to the highest literacy, and all the arts, and of course music in every deserving manifestation, even to the ultimate in experimentation. Hollywood society ordinarily did not provide responses in these fields, and I remember how I burst into laughter at Stravinsky's reply when I once asked him whether he found any amusement in Hollywood parties given by acquaintances in the film world. He replied that they were intolerably boring to him, and he referred to the most recent he had unwillingly attended, which was, he said, populated by 'forty-five pederasts and seventy-six miscellaneous idiots'.

They arrived in Houston late in the afternoon of 3 January, were duly photographed at the airport, and came to the Rice Hotel where Mirandi and I awaited them. Embraces. Mirandi kissed the top of Stravinsky's head with the greeting, 'Pussycat!' at which he beamed. We arranged to dine together when everyone was settled in and rested, with the aeroplane out of their ears. I said,

'May I take you to the Petroleum Club for dinner?'

'Petroleum?' asked Stravinsky. 'In Texas one even dines on oil?'

'No, it is a club in this hotel which is for oil millionaires.'

'Aha. That is better. We shall dine with millionaires.'

'But the point is, one has to be a member in order to order a drink in Texas.'

'But we are members?'

I explained about John Jones and the guest card.

'My God, what if there was no guest card!'

'No Chivas Regal, then,' I said.

'No, my God!'

For I had already assumed the pleasurable duty of seeing that wherever I was in attendance, as it were, his favourite Scotch was at hand.

So it was that at eight o'clock we met in the top-floor club, and our guest card was put to full use. The Scotch arrived, and very presently there was a congenial atmosphere. Like any city seen at night from a height, Houston was a great fancy of lovely lights. The Petroleum Club was almost empty, which was how we all preferred communal places. After a lingering draught of his second glass, the Maestro said in his best comedian voice, thickened not by liquor but by gaiety and drollery,

'My God, so much I like to drink Scotch that sometimes I think my name is Igor Stra-whisky.'

All punctually, we met in the lobby after breakfast the following morning. Stravinsky was carrying a great folio of scores of which I relieved him.

'Did you sleep well?' I asked generally, and Madame replied,

'No, he is not well.'

Her beautiful voice fell on the last word, and I recognised her habit of meeting distress with unqualified realism combined with objective devotion to her husband.

64

'No! Maestro!' I said, 'what is the trouble? Do you need a doctor?'

'But I must rehearse,' he replied, dismissing the doctor, and then with a smile as winning as though he was conveying good news, made a circular motion over his midriff, and said, '*C'est le bul-bul-bul.*'

'Digestive?'

'*Oui.* Up and down all night.'

'Oh! *Le bul-bul-bul!*' cried Mirandi. 'We call it the Santa Fe summer complaint.'

'Have you medicine?'

'Not for this. I need paregoric.'

'Then I must telephone a doctor and have a prescription sent,' I said.

'There is no time,' said Stravinsky. 'The orchestra is waiting. The car?'

'The car is out front.—We must do something. Let me try. We must wait just a minute.'

He nodded and they took a sofa in the lobby.

'You know?' I heard Mirandi say in her best foreboding voice, as I hurried away. 'Travel almost always does this to some people. Sick as *dogs.*'

There was a drugstore nearby. I went to the pharmacist and made a formal speech. The greatest living composer, I said, was the guest of the city of Houston and its symphony society. He was to give two concerts, his first rehearsal was this morning, the orchestra was at that moment waiting on the stage of Houston's Music Hall for him, and he was stricken with a sudden and most weakening dysentery. There was not a minute to lose, no time for a doctor's consultation, or even to telephone for a prescription. The situation was plain and surely understandable, and it was inconceivable that the pharmacist would fail to provide immediately the vital paregoric and bismuth.

He shook his head. Other remedies were available without prescription.

'Not strong enough,' I said, for I knew that Stravinsky meant exactly what he said when he specified paregoric, as he was famous for his medicinal expertise.

'Is it chronic?' asked the druggist.

'It comes on when least expected.'

'Who is he?'

'Igor Stravinsky.'

'Oh.' Impressed, the pharmacist looked at me levelly for a long moment. He was a mild and conscientious man and though music was not his passion he could feel urgent need on the part of others, and my will was pressing him in silence and anxiety. The moment was like a stop-camera suspension of life. Then he said,

'Where is he?'

'In the lobby of the Rice waiting to go. But he is weak. He is also elderly. His wife is with him and another friend. We are all going to be with him. He absolutely must give these concerts.'

'You realise you are asking me to break the law and traffic in opium?'

'I do, and I apologise very sincerely.'

'Well, I'll give you an eight-ounce bottle and ask you to give me your name and how I can reach you if anything comes up. I'll try'—he was mixing the anti-*bul-bul-bul* specific—'to get a doctor to cover this with a prescription by phone. I'll have it issued in your name.'

'Yes, yes, thank you, anything, fine, fine. I cannot thank you enough.'

In a moment with the life-saving bottle wrapped in a twist of blue paper in my clutch, I paid him and returned to the Rice lobby. The tableau at the lobby sofa had not changed. Stravinsky in his pinched grey felt hat which resembled F. D. Roosevelt's was withdrawn like a small bird in winter into the fluffed-out warmth of his large topcoat. Mirandi and Madame were conversing quietly. I rapidly approached.

'You have?' he asked when he saw me.

I held up the bottle.

His vitality returned instantly. With a surge of strength he stood, took my free arm, and we walked in the tempo of his limp— the right leg and his black walking stick—to the waiting limousine. Merely the presence of the remedy was enough to return his confidence to him. We all entered the car and as we moved off to the rehearsal, he tipped his head back and took a grand swig of the medicine, and like a connoisseur, wiped his lips, and smacked them as if to say, 'This is clearly a paregoric of the best year,' and put the bottle into his pocket. So far as I know he did not use it again, nor did he inquire how I managed to obtain it. He was often interested in—even fascinated by—idle information; but not when there was work to be done.

66

All traces of bleakness vanished from our party. At seventy-five he was again the source of strength for us all.

'Pol: you have the scores?' he asked, though he could see them where I held them on my lap as I sat on the *strapontin*. I showed them to him. 'Good!' He smiled with closed lips and spread his nostrils. It was the signal for a drollery on the way. 'How very tactful,' he said, 'of Stokowski to leave town for me.'

He said a word to his wife in Russian and she replied in kind. I understood later that they were confirming plans for the day. While he rehearsed, she was going to the Cushman Gallery to examine the hanging of her show, and she would return in the car to take us all to lunch. Mirandi was going with her, I with the Maestro.

'Tomorrow night,' she said to me, 'is to be private view. We must all go. It is black tie. There will be c-r-rowd, ter-rible.' She smiled, delicately shrugging her brows, and lifting her furs to her chin, looking calm and delicious.

The hall manager received Stravinsky and led us backstage to a plaster-lined dressing room with metal make-up desk and a mirror, a black leatherette sofa, a chair, and a small bathroom. Stravinsky asked me to hand over the scores to the manager who left to place them on the conductor's stand.

'How do you feel, Maestro?'

'For the moment, that is a needless question. Ask me after the rehearsal. I will now get ready—' This politely dismissive.

'I will be out front if you need me.'

'Thank you,' with a little bow.

I went to the auditorium. The orchestra under the work lights tuned and retuned their instruments, playing the Shah of Persia's music. There was a stack of programmes in the first row aisle. I took one and retreated to a third row seat. This was the programme for the pair of concerts:

BACH-STRAVINSKY	Variations on 'Vom Himmel Hoch'
STRAVINSKY	'Orpheus'
	Intermission
STRAVINSKY	'Scènes de Ballet'
STRAVINSKY	'The Firebird' Suite

67

Behind the orchestra were ranged on a bank of steps the members of a local choral society who had been prepared in the Bach variations by their own conductor. The rehearsal evidently was to proceed in the order of the concert programme.

There was an invigorating air of tension over the stage, waiting for Stravinsky. Many looks were directed at the stage side from which he would enter. The Persian cacophony continued and then as suddenly as though a baton had wiped it out, it ceased, as Stravinsky, hobbling as little as possible with his stick, wearing a grey cardigan, with a towel folded about his neck like an ascot tie, and his left arm aloft in almost a Papal gesture of benediction and greeting, appeared in the harsh and stimulating light of a symphony rehearsal. The players rose and applauded. He made his way to the central stand, faced them, and bowed deeply to left, to centre, and to right. His rehearsal etiquette was thus immediately established, to the visible pleasure of the orchestra. Then promptly to work.

In an habitual gesture, he licked the thumb and first finger of his left hand and turned the cover of the score on his desk. In a lifted voice, coloured by comradely humour, he said, making a pun on the title of the Bach chorale,

'Ladies and gentlemen, we will begin by coming down from heaven to earth.'

There was a ripple of appreciative amusement over the stage, and then, abruptly serious, he spread his arms, his strong square hands furled for the up-down beat, he created the new sort of silence required of the moment, and then broke it clearly and gravely.

His rehearsal manners were an effective mixture of strict professionalism and sympathetic courtesy. He was vigorous in his beat and in his cues, and he swiftly alternated his gaze from the pages of his score and the players. There was never in his conducting a flourish for its own sake. His score-indications had of course long been familiar to him and he built his fabric of sound out of the original auditory concept. His better-known works had for decades acquired a sort of 'public' sound—that patine of temperament overlaid upon them by the versions of different conductors in recordings and in concerts. All such was swept away when he

conducted his own works, and the result was that their anatomy emerged in their primal purity. Total logic was what he sought, never the momentary fragmental effect.

In the Bach variations, the local choral conductor had taken full advantage of the grandeur and beauty of the melody and all its aethereal changes; and he had taught his chorus to sing out in full voice. Had they been alone, this might have been musically acceptable as well as 'beautiful'. But in this instance, their voices dominated the orchestral fabric, which was a spare webbing of instrumental counterpoint; and the singers were intended to contribute an almost abstract other element*—to become in effect additional instruments in the same register of dynamic values as those in the instrumental writing. At their first young, full-throated entry, in the exuberance of hearing their fine attack, they submerged all else. Stravinsky stopped them.

'No, no, ladies and gentlemen, much less tone. *Mezzo-piano*. Beautiful ensemble you are giving us but too much sound. Please, again.'

Again; and they were still too loud. It required several tries, but at last there was the balance he required; and the exuberant young Texans found their proportion in a lovely performance entirely different from their first conception of the work. Their response to him was interesting. At first they seemed impressed by the public man, awed, but disregardful of the artist. He was celebrated, he was old, he was small and so 'foreign'-looking, he talked funny, he made no dramas of emotion in his face or gestures, he never 'lost' himself, he didn't pretend that the musicians were a collective instrument upon which he was playing. Curiosity and puzzlement seemed to hold the earnest singers as they regarded him. But gradually they seemed to forget their preconceptions, their previous lessons about what a conductor was, and entered into serious respect for the task in hand for its own sake, not their, or his, egotistic demonstrations; and I thought I saw affection begin to mingle with their musical concentration as this found its propriety. When they finally began to sing not like choristers but as integral elements of the overall sound he had brought to page in his

---

* Beautifully realised in a recording of the work brought to me from Paris in December 1958 by the Stravinskys when I met them on their arrival in New York. It was conducted by Craft for the series of Les Concerts du Domaine Musicale, and it bore the magisterial statement, *'Enregistré en présence d'Igor Stravinsky'*.

auditory imagination, their satisfaction was of a new and greater sort than that which they had first revealed. If he was exasperated by the slowness of their learning his requirements, he never showed it; but by his many demands for repetitions of their vocal lines, it was evident that he was for a long part of the rehearsal not pleased. When in the end he was satisfied, he radiated pleasure, and dismissed the singers with a long expressive shrug of thanks, lifting his arms, and showing his palms upward as if to say his gratitude in a silence more eloquent than words.

His deportment with the players was equally direct; professional, respectful. When he moved on to rehearse *Orpheus*—again, who can forget the immediate captivity of ominous pathos, beyond the pure musicality of it, in the descending harp figure which introduces both the beginning and the end of the work—he had on a number of occasions to halt the orchestra and instruct an individual player. Invariably, he spoke then in the warm voice of a fellow participant in a task of realisation by them both, and he would say,

'No, my de-ar,' and indicate corrections in beat with his arm and sound with his voice, using his rehearsal syllables which sounded like 'ta-rrrr-*ahhhh*', in various phrasings. I had never in countless rehearsals I had listened to heard a player addressed as 'my de-ar' by the maestro of the occasion; and it was clear that the Houston players, used to more majestic demeanour, were for the moment in love with their guest.

There were several other interruptions which gave everyone concern.

Twice during the *Orpheus* study and again in working on later pieces, Stravinsky halted the playing, and said with disarming candour,

'I must ask you to excuse me for a moment. I am in some pain' —a rustle of distress from the desks—'and I must go to the dressing room for a moment.' He saw the question on everyone's face, and he stated with a sort of sweet dignity which, like many of his most ordinary remarks, reflected a recognition of the human state with all its bothersome miseries, 'It is my 'ernia which is hurting me.' I had never known he suffered from hernia. 'There is an instrument of medical science which is calculated to confine this affliction; but sometimes when it loses its adjustment it becomes a torture worse than the disease. Excuse me.' He waved a smile at the orchestra. 'I must go to rearrange my truss.'

He left the stage. In the silence the concern of everybody was felt. I wondered if I should go to the dressing room, but thought not, since he had preferred to be alone earlier, even while merely changing to rehearsal clothes. Soon enough he returned, acknowledging with a smiling nod the relief on the faces all about. He resumed the rehearsal until the next interruption, required for the same reason. One could only think of the courage of so old and ailing a man to persist in his public work while suffering constant discomfort if not outright pain. I do not think it was simple illusion which made me feel that the musicians responded emotionally to him now, where before they had worked with him in purely professional gratification. Now his little habit of often clenching his left hand near his groin, or on his left hip, took on the meaning of an attempt to ease pain. But nothing caused him to restrain the austere athleticism of his bodily movement as he worked.

He expressed rhythm in every part of his frame. In his music the rhythms were so strongly marked, so frequently altered, not merely, as in so much music, a scheme of on-running pattern, that they required of him powerful and strict muscular movement. This was often—it seemed to me—reminiscent of the most elementary human use of the body; and I was often, sometimes with hilarity, otherwise with wonder at the great play and control of all common instincts in his creations, put in mind of those absently erotic and repeated self-levitations which you so often see in babies or very young children, and which bring to the adult mind reminders of copulative movements which associate pleasure and the making of life in our human/animal nature. I remembered an early statement of his to Paul Rosenfeld about the general place of rhythm in the scheme of compositional values: 'It is like this. It is like making love to a woman. . . .' Rosenfeld had also observed Stravinsky's fine politeness with players at an orchestra rehearsal of the New York Symphony Orchestra in the 1920s. Stravinsky, he said, on his arrival onstage, 'was an electric shock'. Giving his instructions 'in very correct English', he was 'abrupt, impatient, energetic, but never ironic either of himself or of his interlocutors; most exemplary in his relations with the players . . . A kind of interest radiated from him to the musicians, who began entering into the spirit of the animal comedy, and kindling him in return.'

At the end of the morning's work I went to the dressing room. I expressed concern for the 'ernia. He slapped the bothersome

71

thing away with a gesture, explaining that while an operation would dispose of it, his doctors thought that at his age the risks of any sort of surgery were increased, and that he would do better with a truss—a word which made him smile with distaste.

'And the *bul-bul-bul?*' I asked.

'There is now no occasion for it,' he said, and then admitted that before conducting, he often felt the same symptoms of intestinal flow—had in fact since his early youth been subject to the flux. If it was a matter of over half a century, then, I said, he made me think of Voltaire whose ill health began at nineteen and when his life ended at eighty-four it was not from illness but from exhaustion brought on by glory. In this there was the sort of encouragement which hypochondriacs live on, and Stravinsky, roughly wiping his face with his ascot towel—he was always very locker-room at rehearsals—made one of his affable silent bows of acknowledgment that one had said something worth hearing.

On the evening of that day I dined with local friends and met the Stravinskys and Mirandi for lunch on the following day—Sunday —when there would be an afternoon rehearsal, followed by Madame's private view at the Gallery. Stravinsky was always interested in the track ahead.

'So what is for tomorrow?' he asked.

'I am going to make a little cruise on the Houston ship channel' —and I explained about John Jones's further benefactions, this time involving the municipal tug, the harbour, the shipping, and the rest.

'No!' he cried. 'I must do this too!'

'But you have a rehearsal in the morning,' said Madame.

'Aha. You are correct, my de-ar. Could the amiable tugboat wait till the following morning, when there is no rehearsal'—for the first concert was to be given Monday night, and the next day would be free, with the second concert Tuesday evening.

'I should think so,' I said. 'I will ask.'

The tug expedition was rearranged by John Jones, and when I reported this to Stravinsky, he was as gratified as a child at a promise of a feast. In even so small a matter, the future interested him devouringly; his capacity for life always reached ahead; there was interest in the present, too, of course, and usefulness in the

past; but in all that was not yet accomplished was expressed, if it did not actually give him, his vital hold on existence. The final act of man's fate threatened him many a time in his life, and in his last years, the threats were again and again almost mortal, but repeatedly he turned them back with his astonishing recuperative powers, for more work, more life.

At six o'clock Sunday evening, we proceeded to the Cushman Gallery for Madame's *vernissage*. 'All Houston'—the expensively cultured sector—was there. Madame looked elegantly radiant. Her naturalness was as appealing as her unselfconsciously aristocratic bearing was full of grace. I often noted how on her entrance into any gathering her effulgence and style, her unhurried progression among people, her smiling luminosity, the pale light of her dark-lashed eyes under their blue-shadowed lids, seemed to bring responsive repose into the assembly; and I said to myself, She is like a moon-goddess. Tonight she was grandly clothed—pale furs, a softly folded dress of a dark colour and severe cut. She wore many rather miscellaneous jewels and these reminded me of an anecdote she told me of how once on tour with her husband she had met an old friend from Paris in a box at the Colón Theatre in Buenos Aires, who exclaimed, 'Vera! what wonderful jewels you are wearing. They are real?' to which Madame with simplicity, indicating one after another of her ornaments, replied, 'This one is real, that is fake, these are real, and that one, and that one are fake, the ear-rings are real—' and so on through the whole catalogue.

Her exhibition looked well, and though the rooms were not large, there was no undue sense of crowding. Drinks were at hand. While Madame received introductions, standing in the centre, Stravinsky, after shaking a few hands, looked about for a chair in a corner, went to it, with me trailing, and took his place in the most inconspicuous possible place. The occasion was Madame's event, and he wanted only to sustain her by his presence, and draw none of the usual attention to himself. I brought him a glass of Scotch and he said, without having to explain why, 'Pol, let us talk here', so that seeing him engaged, people who might otherwise have made a circle about him, detracting from the exhibition and its artist, hesitated to invade his limited territory. Mirandi knew people at the party, and made a fine jangle with her gold wristlets, and we heard her social laugh, the husky jump from a low note to an octave above, over the increasing clamour as more guests arrived, more

drinks were served, and more thermal conviviality of conjunctive bodies grew out of the occasion.

Madame's paintings were highly original—abstractions, yet with elusive reminders of familiar forms. Her application of pigment was technically exquisite—some areas of the surface barely brushed, others richly impregnated with dense colour as though a wing had dragged paint into natural imprints in some manifestation of anonymous nature—ripples in sand, or striations in long-seasoned stones, or the ghosts of leaves in sombrely glowing humus on a forest floor. The guests seemed impressed by her work, and the event had every mark of a distinguished and successful opening, including the rapid warming of the rooms, so that after about an hour, both Madame and the Maestro had had enough; and by a signal to Mirandi, Madame indicated that it was time to go.

The affability of their departure was even more flattering than the high style of their manner on arrival: they left each guest with the feeling that life was operated by an inexorable calendar far beyond their power to revise; that they were as subject to its exigencies as anything in astronomy; and that in taking leave, they regretted more than anyone what must seem like early deprivation. It was all so courtly and final that nobody suspected what must have been the Stravinskys' fact the world over—that casual encounters with strangers however attractive and worth knowing could not lead to anything, and that if fortune dictated that eminence should belong to one and not another, then there was hardly any personal responsibility involved, and once good manners had been exercised, there was little need to protract any occasion.

In brief, we left, went to a pleasant dinner in the splendid emptiness of the Petroleum Club, with more cocktails, and wine later, while over us all, for Madame's sake, remained a warming glow at the enthusiasm which her work had brought forth in the interested people of Houston.

In the morning there was another rehearsal, much like those of Saturday and Sunday. Monday afternoon was given over to rest before the first concert. I went anonymously to bookstores. The day seemed at moments to approach the evening concert with unsettling swiftness, and at others, to drag alone at an exasperating

and ominous pace, both conditions producing hollow nervousness even in myself, who had but to carry scores and extra towels, and a small bag containing perhaps an extra shirt, and, surely, assorted medicaments whose presence in the dressing room would be a comfort, even should no dosages be required.

The management had provided a box for Madame, Mirandi, and myself. I went backstage with Stravinsky while Madame and Mirandi remained in the auditorium. He was somewhat abstracted, his concentration already forming for the work ahead. His movements as he adjusted his professional possessions on the make-up counter, his neatness in all things, were executed as slowly as in a dream. It was no time for small talk, but tension is contagious, and I relieved mine by remarking on the fine cut and fit of his tailcoat.

'Thirty-five years ago or more,' he said, smiling broadly, 'I had it made in London'—the same tailcoat, surely!

He wore a soft white shirt with collar turned down, and a white tie. Dimly away was the sound of the orchestra already on the stage, tuning and riffling.

'Pol,' he said, 'please, come back in the intermission to keep the door. Not to see anyone during the intermission.'

Yes, of course, I said to myself. At the interval, he must lie down and rest on the couch, and perhaps change his shirt. I promised to return during his curtain calls, and as I made to go and join Madame and Mirandi out front, he divined my emotion for him, and he took my shoulder and pulled me towards him, and silently and lightly kissed me Russian fashion on first one cheek, then the other. I felt on my face a mist of cold perspiration among the barely visible crystalline points of his beard, not shaved since morning. I felt remote compunction, betrayal, in leaving him to await alone yet another call into the concert lights.

It was always interesting to listen to one of his performances in the company of Madame. She responded to the enthusiasm aroused by his very first visibility—everybody applauded fame; but something about his frail, determined manner as he would enter the stage (until the very last concerts, without his stick, though he needed it for real confidence at every step) immediately touched the feeling of the audience; and when he turned to bow to the applause, his concentrated gravity brought surges of another sort of response. Everyone moved from the anticipation of the concert-goer merely expecting entertainment to the awe which accompanied

75

attendance at a rite of high consequence. Madame did not applaud, but at the reception he received, she smiled sideways with calm pride. When he began to conduct, I could feel her acute attention for any sign of fatigue, strain, or discomfort. There was always present an element of risk in his public appearances in his last decade, for the two strokes he had suffered during the fifties, one in Berlin, the other in Bologna, left him, he once told me, with no sensation at all in his right leg, foot, arm, or hand—though amazingly he did retain muscular control. It was astonishing to me that he could continue with his public engagements under these conditions, and when I wondered—I think to Craft—whether the strain on him might not be too great, I was assured that the doctors encouraged Stravinsky to give concerts, as the exercise was good for his muscles and his circulation. Still, strokes sometimes occurred in sequence, and I myself felt uneasy as I was lofted in spirit by his music brought into the air by his own vision and hand.

His workmanlike rehearsals had produced excellent results. The Bach variations proceeded in the stately balance he had laboured for, and the ceremony between orchestra and chorus was beautiful to see as well as hear. The meeting of two masters in the work was a lesson out of *The Poetics of Music*, when in our very presence, we heard how 'tradition . . . appears as an heirloom, a heritage that one receives before passing it on to one's descendants', for if Bach was there, so, too, and unmistakably, was Stravinsky.

He left the stage and it seemed to us he was gone a fairly long time, and Madame gave me an inquiring look. I was about to go to the dressing room for news when he reappeared, and it later turned out that he had needed to rearrange his hernia appliance, which had slipped—a tedious process, as it meant undressing and dressing almost entirely. But when he lifted his arm for *Orpheus*, his power was all present, and for the duration of that score I was concerned with nothing but the work itself.

He received so many calls that I was in the dressing room for many minutes before he returned. He came in, seized a towel, and began patting his face with it, while in pantomime he instructed me to lock the door. White with perspiration, he was catching his breath in long draughts through his nose. His little chest rose and fell like the top half of a pair of bellows. I believed he should lie down. I offered him a fresh towel which he took. Someone knocked and I opened the door a slit and said that Maestro Stravin-

sky asked to be excused from seeing anyone, and then I locked us in again. He was rapidly coming down to ordinary respiration and I suppose heartbeat. I felt it suitable to say, now,

'Well, Maestro, when I hear you conduct, I feel that not only do most conductors do things that are quite unnecessary, but are often actually harmful.'

He threw down the towel. He took my shoulders and declared in a voice of high glee,

'Pol! I h-h-ate interpretation!'

I delighted in his vehemence. I laughed—I had not before heard him actually state this famous position. In the context of that dressing room, I could not fail to have a fleeting thought of its absent resident.

'The concert is wonderful,' I said, 'and the *Orpheus*!'

He had no need to hear superlatives from me, but he saw my excitement, and pulling me to the dressing table where duplicates of the evening's scores lay, he opened to certain pages of *Orpheus*, and began to explain to me the musical anatomy of certain passages. This inversion. That progression. Variation of a phrase prominently heard earlier in a different scoring. To the grasp of these abstract niceties I was inadequate but this did not lessen my fascination with the fact of his demonstration. His animation was as fresh as if the work had just been composed, and despite my inadequacy in technical matters, I received a direct and powerful demonstration of the primacy of form among all the elements of creation in any art. At the same time, in my hinterthought, I was nagged by other questions—the couch; a quick shower or sponging; a fresh shirt; at least attention to the 'ernia and its retainer. But before there was time for anything else, even for finishing the elucidation of the *Orpheus* score, there was a tap at the door, and the call boy said, 'Ready, Mr Stravinsky, please,' and the intermission was spent. It had been spent for me, for my interest, in response to my great elation at the performance.

'Is there anything I may do for you before I go out front again?'

'No, thank you, my de-ar,' he said, 'but come back immediately, we will all escape.'

And so we did, after a performance of *L'Oiseau de feu* which rose to a thundering climax more theatrical and audience-rousing than I had ever heard, all despite strict canons of taste against 'interpretation'. Stokowski could not have produced a more overpowering crescendo than that with which the composer himself

closed the piece. Houston leaped to its feet, and later, backstage, crowded the cement corridors; but with self-accusing charm, Stravinsky, wearing a great fur coat (sables? martens?) like the one which had belonged to his father, the pre-Chaliapin Imperial Opera *basso*, made his way past hands which pulled at him, and the voices of patronesses hoping to halt him with fascinating anecdotes—'heard you conduct in Paris in 1922'—'met you and your chawaming waf on the *Ile de France* and we all had a drink together'—'Ah just cain't stay away tomorrow naght, Ah'm comin again, mystro'—and we at last were encapsulated in the limousine and on our way to the Rice Hotel, and early bed. Nothing much was said in the car. Stravinsky descended into stillness and I felt that some dissatisfaction was at work in him. He would have supper sent up by room service. As we parted he politely said goodnight. Mirandi and I stayed a little longer in the bar. We reviewed the evening, and then I said,

'I would love to do an opera with him.'

'He says he will never do another.'

'I know. I've heard that. But I have the perfect libretto subject. So far as I know it has never been used.'*

'What is it?'

I told her. It was about the Emperor Maximilian and the Empress Carlota of Mexico, and their brief, ill-gotten, and tragic reign. I saw it all—the ironic contrast between the diamond glitter and Strauss waltzes of Hapsburg Vienna, the handsome young archduke and his marriage to the beautiful princess of Belgium, the offstage rumble of power politics (I thought of *Boris Godunov* as a political opera, and this could be another), and far across the ocean, the troops of Napoleon III faced by the inscrutable, primitive jungle forces of the Mexican Indians, all anonymous but for Benito Juárez, who looked as if he were carved out of weathered lava. Imagine the immediate juxtaposition and at moments the actual simultaneous overlay of Vienna court waltzes and the half-remembered gigantic Aztec war drums whose tympani were made from stretched and sewn skins of giant serpents. Then, of course, Vienna transplanted to Chapultepec Castle, and the sudden signs of the regime rent in two, and the despair of the Emperor and Empress. Appeals to Europe by courier, in vain. The French losing in Mexico, Maximilian's throne cracking. The Empress, going to Paris, appealed to Napoleon III for help, who was inertly

* I was wrong. Darius Milhaud had already used it.

78

unresponsive. In final desperation she went to Rome, to beseech Pius IX for his intervention. But he too was powerless.

'Imagine the scene,' I said, with due employment of operatic licence. 'The Pope all in white, nothing about but dark red velvet and some shadowy murals high up, and a standing chandelier, and Carlota in black, begging in an aria for the rescue of her husband's empire, and, in being denied, going mad, then and there, in the Pontiff's presence! It is a scene for Callas.—They had to send for doctors, and keep the Empress overnight in the Vatican: the first laywoman ever to spend a night there since the Borgias—at least admittedly. Then back to Mexico, the last battle, the Emperor's betrayal and surrender, and finally, his execution at Querétaro. He and three of his generals are murdered by the firing squad on a little sandy hill outside the city. He bestows gold pieces upon his executioners, and takes his place without a blindfold. I see the stage —huge, it must be as large as the Metropolitan's—with nothing but that low little mound, and a vast, yellow sky, and the few ragged soldiers and their tatterdemalion officer, and facing them the beautiful, elegant, golden-haired prince, and when the muskets fire, a sudden crash of tropical Mexican rain falls densely out of the sky, obscuring everything, and the snake-drums and crashes of strange metal now triumph in the orchestra, and the curtain falls together as fast as possible.'

     God   mar-
'My   how   vellous,' cried Mirandi, in her husky social cry like that of a tropical bird which knew how to make her interval of an octave. 'Have you told Stravinsky about it?'

'Oh, no. I could not. It would have to reach him indirectly, to give him a chance to show interest, or reject the idea, without any awkward face-to-face discussion.'

'Do you want me to mention it?'

'If you like, and if you think there might be a proper moment.'

'Oh, I will.'

Nothing came of it, except for a passage two years later in *Dialogues and a Diary*, when Stravinsky said to Craft, as they were flying over the Mexican deserts for concerts in Mexico City,

'The moon must be like this, only with more face powder,' and then went on with a direct echo of my 'libretto', to speak about 'the possibility of an opera on the subject of Maximilian and Juárez', but dismissing it with the remark that he thought it would have been 'ideal for Verdi in his *Don Carlos* period. Imagine,' he

said, 'the scene of Carlota going mad in the Vatican, and the finale with Maximilian tipping the soldiers who are preparing to shoot him.' My hope and the subject were ended by the Mexican steward's announcement that 'Men and women may use the lavatory indistinctly'. I remained grateful to Mirandi, and still felt that a melodramatic subject could be treated in a fresh idiom however splendidly Verdi might have done it.

After an early lunch the next day, Tuesday, 7 January, we came to the municipal wharf. There was the tug, awaiting us. It was a grey-painted wooden vessel, with its bow up-sloping, its pilot-house and mast and rudimentary funnel leaning back, its afterdeck open, and a comfortable cabin with padded benches. The *Chronicle* ship news reporter was awaiting us. He was a friendly young man who saw us aboard, introduced us to the pilot and the engineer, who comprised the whole crew, and held himself ready to 'explain things' on our voyage.

In clear weather but with a slow cold wind, we began edging out into constricted waterways lined with moored freighters from around the world. Houston industry crowded the waterfront on both sides of the harbour, which soon gave way to a winding channel. Our progress was slow until we entered a clear straight path. Though we were all warmly dressed, we felt the cold; but the interest of our various separate observations made it a happy trip.

Stravinsky standing on the narrow starboard deckway, wearing his fur coat and the Roosevelt felt hat, overwhelmed the ship news reporter—who came to instruct and remained to listen—with, I could assume, discussions of such appropriate topics as the shipping industry's relation to the balance of trade, the economic implications of an inland harbour rising to the status of the nation's third greatest seaport, the optimum in tonnage likely to be adopted as the most profitable in seagoing cargo vessels, the relative dangers of an oil cargo which might ignite, a metal cargo which might shift, and a grain cargo which might expand and burst bulkheads if not hulls, and such.

Madame was occupied in taking photographs of ships that were tied to the shore, and an occasional one we might pass. She was as interested as her husband but her feeling for the events was

Caricature of Eugene Goossens, by Paul Horgan, 1925

Igor and Vera Stravinsky at home in Hollywood, 1957

visual, and she remained alone in the afterdeck. She had a capacity for silent absorption of anything which interested her; and now she was taking mental impressions with a painter's eye of the whole scene—the flat land almost at the level of the water, the long winter striations of the Texas sky, the black, rust, white, and wooden colours of the dozens of ships with their fluttering house flags, the pale flesh colour of the earth where it was exposed at the water line, the obsidian dark grey-green of the channel water, the far hang of industrial smokes over and beyond Houston.

Mirandi was in the pilot-house animatedly conversing with the pilot, and I was in the bow, making rapid pen-scratch drawings of some of the ships and fittings along the shore. Presently I felt cold and went to the cabin, and Mirandi called me to say that the best view was from the wheelhouse. I joined her there. The pilot, a cheerful middle-aged Texan, when I asked him if there might be any chance that I might steer the tug, said,

'Sure enough.'

We had turned around by then and were heading back to Houston—an hour and a half down the channel, and so back. At our speed, it would have taken three hours to reach the open Gulf of Mexico. There was not time for this—or, actually, interest. We had all seen enough, and though it was interesting, the voyage became in the end monotonous. For me the high moment was to take the wheel and feel the response of the rudder. We were glad enough to disembark, with handshakes all around. Once in the car, we admitted that we were frozen, and Stravinsky said,

'Whisky!'

We were soon settled around a large uncovered table in the hotel bar-club with drinks before us. In the early moments of recovering from its chill, we said that the little voyage had been fun, and I was charged to relay thanks to John Jones, which I did later in the afternoon. In the comfortable silence which followed, I was amused to think of the variety of our characters, and I said, feeling a little uneasily like a gamesmaster on a cruise ship,

'Everyone has a single word which is most characteristic of him. One he either uses frequently, and so gives us his most consistent view, or one that others use about him.—Mirandi, do you know what yours is?'

'Tell me.'

'You say "*marvellous*" all the time.'

'I do? How marvellous.'

For if Mirandi said 'marvellous' habitually it was because she really saw almost everything as a marvel, whether trifling or great, and so announced it in the italics of her speech.

'So, what is mine?' asked Madame, indulging our nonsense.

'Your word is *"terrible"*,' cried Mirandi with gaiety.

Madame thought about it, and then smiled judicially as if to say that her use of the word was if habitual entirely accurate.

That left Stravinsky. I turned to him and said,

'Maestro, I don't think anyone but yourself can settle on any one word which will do for you. Have you a word? What is your word?'

He diminished himself towards the table edge with an expression of abstruse mischief. The gleam of a Cagliostro came into his eyes. He made a mysterious glance around the table and said,

'Ha! A vord. I have a vord. I vill give you my vord.'

With that he moved everything aside that was on the table—glasses, a dish of pretzels, Madame's scarf, Mirandi's gold cigarette box; and once he had a clear plateau, whose dimensions under his spell seemed to grow into a great plain, he slowly began to build something invisible which, so great was his power of magic, rose before our eyes. He reached far out on every side of the table top and with selective care scooped and patted unseen particles of matter towards the centre, scowling like an adept in the performance of an arcanum. He kept muttering, 'Vord, aha, I have a vord, *ja*,' and he worked the unseen substance until we saw a pyramid take shape in our persuaded imaginations. One great hand after the other raised the table top to an imaginary peak in its centre. It was like seeing the volcano Paricutín emerge before our eyes. His power as a magus was as great as all his other powers. 'Vord, *ja*,' and his modelling of the structure became grave and elegant as he completed his task—critical adjustments here, a smoothing there, 'My vord, aha, I have my vord,' an incantation, and when he had stretched our suspense to the utmost, he made a breathy chord of his voice and cried,

'*Here is my vord*,' and he began now in gleeful haste to tear away and scatter to the floor the invisible stuff he had so convincingly built up, 'my vord is *merde!*', and so broke our spell. He joined in our laughter, but so fastidious was his power of illusion that he himself was subject to it, and not until he had swept away every imaginary grain of the *merde* from the table top did he stop his work. Then, with comic exactitude, he restored Madame's scarf,

the various glasses, and Mirandi's gold box to their proper order, with a little bow, and the game was over.

The second concert was another success. The Stravinskys never discussed how things went in performance—he had another way of admitting to feeling about that as I later discovered. We again had to fight our way out of the Music Hall, for by word of mouth the first night had brought out even greater enthusiasts for the second, and the Maestro would have been detained for an hour or more if he had not with brief self-deprecating bows insisted on making his way to freedom. The next morning, with triumphs secure over the liquor laws of Texas, the *bul-bul-bul*, the always unpredictable problems attending work with unfamiliar orchestras, the gallery-going public of Houston, and the ennui attending endless unpacking and packing, the concert troupe—for so I regarded the four of us—scattered variously homeward.

There were no works by Stravinsky in the 1958 season of the Santa Fe Opera, but the opera orchestra gave a series of symphonic concerts and Craft conducted one of them (20 July), when he led the *Danses Concertantes*, and also the *Begleitungsmusik* of Schön-berg and the *Eroica Symphony*. He also conducted at the opera, and the Stravinskys came for part of the season, staying at La Fonda. They attended Craft's rehearsals and performances at the opera, made themselves sociable in Santa Fe, and I had the appeal-ing duty (I was now a member of the opera board and in a year or so became chairman) of doing what I could on behalf of the opera management for the comfort of the Stravinskys—taking them in my car where they wanted to go, lunching and dining with them when they were lonely; in the course of which it was myself who was the more rewarded.

Among the pleasures was that of making certain that Stravinsky had a sufficient supply of Scotch on hand; and since in New Mexico one could buy miniature bottles of various brands of liquor, I bought one day a couple of cases of the miniature Chivas Regal bottles, which would be handy to carry about on errands, or to take to the opera theatre for convenient nips against the

evenings when they were cold. A few days after I brought the little bottles to the Stravinskys' suite, I found that the Maestro had arranged the whole twenty-four in military formation on the windowsill—a company at drill, with a commander out front, and a sergeant bringing up the rear, and in between, perfectly aligned ranks of squads. He smiled with me at the orderliness represented there, and I recognised his persistent trait of severe neatness. His desk was so kept, and his travelling possessions. For her part, Madame, who needed the company of many books wherever she was, used one of the beds in her bedroom as a book table, and had a couple of dozen crisp new volumes stacked there in rows.

They—we all—missed Mirandi that summer, for she had married and moved to Hollywood, where her husband, Ralph Levy, the film producer, writer, and director, had a busy career. But the Stravinskys looked forward to having her as their neighbour, for the Levys had bought a house whose property touched along their own, and for many years Mirandi was a daily visitant, a repository of frequent woes which to be endured must be shared in review. The friendship begun in 1950 was already almost twenty years old, and it would persist and grow deeper.

Stravinsky composed daily at a muted piano—he could not work if he thought he was being overheard. In other hours he and Craft worked on the first of their extraordinary collaborative volumes which was already in galley proof for publication the following year—1959. Material for a second volume was already taking shape, and they asked me to find a title for it. Of the suggestions I submitted they chose *Memories and Commentaries*. I proposed also that they would be well-advised to become the clients of my lifelong friend and agent, Virginia Rice, which they did, to everyone's satisfaction.

Sometimes Stravinsky could not be found. He enjoyed wandering away from the hotel without explanation. He could not venture far—his lameness was a deterrent, but he ignored it as far as possible, and one day it turned out that one of his favourite—and private—diversions was to wander up and down the aisles of the Woolworth store on the plaza a long block from the Fonda. It is not known whether he ever made any purchases, but the profusion of trifles, the various ingenuities of merchandising visible there engaged the forefront of his attention. But who knew, while he was drifting along the bins at Woolworth's, or was subjected to any other trivial instant, how much he was occupied behind what he

was gazing at? He never missed a detail however small of immediately observed life; but there was also that sense of greatly larger affairs which concerned him in mind and in perception by sense. No one I ever knew was always more 'present'; and yet no one more removed from the interest of the foreground on behalf of what really at the moment furthered his inner formulations.

For one had the sense that he was at all times most deeply alive and questing in relation to his work, and if he began to take a shine to me, I think it occurred when in one or another of our conversations he learned that I spent the morning hours of every day, no matter where I was, at my own current piece of writing. (The discipline which governed my life dated from the time I returned from Rochester to New Mexico.) Once he knew this, he was, evidently, concerned that it be inviolate; and almost invariably, when we met after a separation of some portion of the year, his first question was, 'Pol: you are vorkink?' and when I was able to say yes, his smile broadened and he nodded sagely at the first lesson of professionalism, which was to say, anti-trivialism.

This concern, which I was grateful for, was one day broadened into another dimension of those who make works. (He was sparing in the use of such words as 'creator', 'creative', 'artist', and in once referring to himself as a 'maker' he swept aside much false glamour which the press and the facile amateur had long attached to the evolvement of works in the arts.) We were driving back to the hotel from some errand, when without preamble he gave voice to the train of his hitherto silent thought, along these lines:

'What anyone thinks of one's work cannot change it. Nothing can be said which can make it any better than it is, or any worse. It is simply itself. What is inherent is the point. This is the real point about paying no attention to the views of critics. One should pay attention only to one's own vision, desire, and practice, in one's efforts to make a work of art. Who really knows how good it is? If we think of time, and its evaluations, still, the work will be what it is. The future will know if not the present. One should *make* without thought of value judgments on the part of others.'

This made explicit for me what I had long felt vaguely to be true, and it fortified my own view that vanity and a spirit of competitiveness in the arts, and the attendant scramble or even hope for a critical vogue, were not only childish—they were idiotic and unbecoming.

85

'Therefore,' he concluded, 'the only answer is to work, and if there are opinions which seek to influence, discredit, or even for the wrong reasons, to praise, one must say only, *Thank you very much, go to hell.*'

With this one of his favourite expressions, which he could deliver either with inexpressible drollery or irritable contempt, he now gave a charming, affirmatory smile, which in no way relieved his statement of its seriousness. I was grateful for it, have quoted it often to colleagues (including my students in writing), and have felt lucky that I had never belonged to any prevailing literary cell such as those which clustered about various intellectual or ethnic neighbourhoods of New York and certain academic cliques, where reputations were made according to powerful if fugitive conformities. Sometimes asked if I did not feel a sense of exile, living in New Mexico, so far away 'from things', I always replied that what I felt was a sense of independence; and if further asked if I did not think I paid a penalty in critical popularity and thus a lack of either an élitist or a huge public, I could only say that chance, over which I had no control, and the mode, in which I had no interest, played as much part in achieving a position of current vogue in letters as merit.

In the winter of 1958–9 an idea for the extension of the opera's cultural meaning to Santa Fe was put forward by Dr Eric Hausner, a much beloved citizen of the town. It was to invite Stravinsky, during his summer visits, to conduct various of his works on religious themes in the Cathedral of St Francis at Santa Fe, to which the people of the city would be admitted free. Crosby was at once attracted by the idea, recognised that its fulfilment must depend technically on use of the opera's resources, and delegated me to carry it forward in discussion with the next authority on whose decision all possibility rested.

This was the Archbishop of Santa Fe, the Most Reverend Doctor Edwin Vincent Byrne, who for several years had shown me kindness, particularly in connection with my research for a biography* of his predecessor, Juan Bautista Lamy, first vicar-apostolic, bishop, and archbishop of Santa Fe, about whom Willa Cather

---

* A work in progress, interrupted for the writing of the present book.

wrote her appealing lyrical novel *Death Comes for the Archbishop*. I requested an audience—the word is more apt than appointment or interview, for Archbishop Byrne, though personally a humble man of intense spirituality, held a princely view of his office in the apostolic succession, and in official matters comported himself accordingly—and was granted a day and hour.

He received me in his office in Cathedral Place overlooking the now bare spaces of Archbishop Lamy's famous garden, which had been allowed to die. Byrne was a very tall, uncorpulent man, with a wave of silvery hair surmounting a fine-skinned pale face. His eyes were veiled behind large rimless spectacles, and he had a curious trait of rarely looking into one's own eyes, but rather across one's left shoulder. Yet he seemed to perceive, and more than that, to feel, all that one bore in word and perhaps in thought withheld. He wore the prelate's long black cassock piped in red-violet, with its little capelet, and the full-length row of red-violet silk buttons. In working hours, he did not wear his great silken sash of the episcopal colour. His pectoral cross was hooked into a breast buttonhole and provided a useful object to finger in thought while framing an answer. Under his cassock he wore an old pair of khaki G.I. slacks—he had been a Navy chaplain—and its edges, and the silken buttons and the black cuffs of his habit, were threadbare. I recognised his lack of private vanity; and otherwise his neatness was exemplary. With animation in the breathy high register of his voice, which sounded as though rimmed with candied sugar, he greeted me warmly and directed me to sit down. He then asked paternally if I were still writing. I recognised this for what it was —merely a way to open our conversation, and said yes, and then he waved me to proceed with my purpose of the moment.

As I unfolded this in a carefully rehearsed statement, he listened acutely, while his pale eyes rested on a point of concentration in the middle distance beyond my left ear.

Here, I stated, we had all this splendid and ardent young talent in the artists of the opera; and again coming to town for the season was the composer Igor Stravinsky, everywhere acknowledged as the greatest of the age, who was, both personally and in many of his works, revealed as a man of deep religious commitment. Here, too, we had one of the truly historic cathedrals of America, in a city famous the world over for its cultural awarenesses. Would it not, I suggested, citing Dr Hausner, be a beautiful event if each year on a Sunday evening, under the patronage of His Excellency

the Archbishop, Maestro Stravinsky could be persuaded to conduct, in the cathedral itself, with the assistance of vocal and instrumental artists of the opera, one of his compositions on religious themes? The idea, I hastened to state, was not original in a strict sense, for it had happened that in 1956, the then Patriarch of Venice, Cardinal Roncalli, now in 1959 gloriously reigning as Pope John XXIII, had invited Maestro Stravinsky to present in the Cathedral of San Marco the world première of his latest work on a religious theme, the *Canticum Sacrum Ad Honorem Sancti Marci Nominis*, for solo voices, choir, and orchestra, and Maestro Stravinsky had accepted. The event had made both musical and ecclesiastical history in our time. It would seem that the Archdiocese of Santa Fe might have a correspondingly significant opportunity. Such a concert would of course be free to the public —a commercial motive would be impossible, and full decorum (ladies covered, no applause) would be expected of the audience. If the Archbishop looked favourably on the idea, and in fact authorised the opera to extend in his name such an invitation to Maestro Stravinsky, the matter would at once be taken forward again.

The Archbishop mused briefly aloud.

'Stravinsky? He *is* the foremost of composers today?'

'Oh, yes, Your Excellency. It would be like having Beethoven in his own time.'

'Ah. Beethoven. Indeed. Yes.' He laid his eloquent slender hands on his cross. Its amethysts returned light. 'And Venice. Pope John. There is, then, in fact, a precedent?'

'I should say the highest, Archbishop. And of course nothing like it has ever been done in our country.'

'Yes. Of course the highest.'

Decisively and suddenly he looked me square in the eye and the impact was strong.

'We shall go ahead,' he said. 'An *American* precedent. You may be confident of our fullest assistance. A beautiful proposal. I shall hope to meet Maestro Stravinsky.'

'He will surely want to call upon you, sir'—and I gave my fullest thanks and left to report to Crosby at the opera. In due course word went to Stravinsky in Hollywood, he agreed to the plan, which included performances by Craft of appropriate works, in each concert, by other composers, to be followed after the intermission by one of Stravinsky's sacred pieces under his own hand. It was a

good day's work by everybody, and it resulted in some of the most beautiful musical events of recent years.

Though again there was no work of Stravinsky's on the Santa Fe Opera schedule for 1959, Craft was engaged to conduct a production—the first in the United States since one given by the French Opera in New Orleans a century before—of Donizetti's *Anna Bolena*. He arrived ahead of the Stravinskys to begin the musical preparation of the work, which was to be directed for the stage by Bliss Hebert. All went well until Friday, 26 June, when Crosby was obliged to telephone the Stravinskys at Hollywood that on the preceding day Craft 'fell and dislocated his elbow', and was in the hospital. It seemed that at a break in rehearsal with the orchestra in the theatre Craft in high spirits at how well affairs were moving vaulted the barrier between pit and first aisle. His foot caught on the rail, he put out his right hand to break his fall, and, actually, put his right elbow out of commission. It was an event to upset the strict routine of the opera, and Crosby's sympathy for the victim was salted with administrative irritation, for his roster of conductors was not yet large enough to 'cover' any of them who might not be able to appear. Craft was taken to St Vincent's Hospital, x-rayed, equipped with a plaster cast on his conductor's member, and he was ardently attended by a sumptuous mezzo-soprano of the company. She readily assumed the spiritual costume of an inflexible Florence Nightingale, which he perhaps did not find so becoming as her incarnation as a romantic, and more comfortably intermittent, companion.

It was clear that Craft would not be able to conduct the Donizetti, and Crosby was fortunate in having as stage director for the work a man who was also an able musician; and, to finish this part of the story, Hebert took over the conductor's desk, to the cheers of the company at the opening performance, and gave an excellent reading.

On the following Monday I met the Maestro and Madame as they arrived at Lamy from California on the 'Super Chief'. They were in a state of great concern over Craft, and were eager to go to him at the hospital. On the way into Santa Fe I asked if we should not pause for a moment to see the guest house set aside for them at Witter Bynner's place in town. This had been arranged

by their Hollywood neighbour, Mirandi Levy. As it was on the way to the hospital, they thought this was a sound idea, and we pulled into the stockade of lilacs and other dense shrubbery of Bynner's corner in College Street. Up stone stairs, ornamented with Chinese ceramic lanterns and stone dogs, we came to the adobe guest house. As an old friend of the establishment, I had stayed there, and its cool, inelegant interior, with abrasive Navajo rugs, stretched-leather Indian chairs, its approaches by devious paths and odd levels, its typically Santa Fean quaintness consisting of Indian, Spanish, and Mexican objects whose prized antiquity was matched by rude workmanship, and its strange remoteness from ordinary amenities—all this had never bothered me; but I could know by their faces and their low-voiced exchanges in Russian that the arrangements did not strike the Stravinskys as ideal. They gently quizzed me. About servants? Oh, there was a staff, headed by Rita Padilla who had been with Bynner for years. She possessed assorted nieces of ages from ten to fifteen who scampered with shrieks through the housework. Rita was the cook. Would there be a cook for the guest house? No, it was not likely. There was a phone? Yes, a private one. They looked at the kitchen, the old bath, the two comfortless bedrooms. A few bags were silently deposited against their return, and tonelessly they asked to go to the hospital.

I drove them there and we found Craft's room. He was propped up in bed with his cast on a lap pillow. Cordilleras of books flanked him. There was emotion close to tears at their reunion and I left, saying I would return in an hour to take them back to their guest house.

I idled away the time, wondering how the Stravinskys would manage in the guest house. Bynner and Hunt were the utmost in conviviality and warmth, but they stayed up all night, slept till noon, lunched at two, dined at nine, and were besieged by people. The kitchen was empty except at mealtimes. Privacy would be intended for the guests but I knew from experience that it was impossible to detach the life of the main house from that of the guest house. In his sense of social realism, Hunt had said the whole plan was a mistake, but Mirandi in her fond exuberance had thought to do everyone a huge favour—Bynner the prestige and joy of having illustrious and fascinating tenants without rent, the Stravinskys all the excitement and gaiety of the household and an authentic Santa Fe house in which to live like natives.

When I returned to the hospital and knocked at Craft's door, I entered to find a tableau of such woe that my heart fell like lead. There were signs of tears on Madame's face. Stravinsky was diffidently ingratiating over what I would soon hear. Craft was nervous and circuitous in stating the case which they hated to bring up but must.

In brief, they had talked everything over all the time I was gone, and with every apology for seeming ungrateful, they begged to be delivered somehow from staying at the guest house. This request in all its anguish came forth by fits and starts, small overlappings of blurted comment and hope: something about the place was cold and comfortless, it was too remote, they needed room service day or night, they could not see themselves 'living with' anyone else, even such charming hosts as Bynner and Hunt, and on, and on. Stravinsky grasped my wrist with great power and implored me to find them other quarters. The intensity of their concern was so strong that I wanted to take them in my arms and comfort them. I had to say,

'The only place would be the hotel again, but they are booked to the roof. I was told yesterday there was no room for someone else I tried to make a reservation for. But let me try. I will see the manager myself.'

'We shall wait here?'—eagerly.

'Do. I'll come as soon as I can.'

'Will Bynner be offended?'

'Never. The last person to be offended. Though he was delighted to welcome you, he would want you to be free and in comfort, wherever.'

'And Hunt?'

'He in fact did not think from the beginning that you would be happy there.'

'Ah!'—relief began to show, mingled with the uncertainty of finding a roof elsewhere. I left them and went to the hotel. There I saw the manager, a sensible and considerate Irishman, who somehow felt through me both the exalted misery and the imperative necessity of the situation; and by a dazzling play of solitaire with his reservation cards in their slots, he found a two-bedroom suite for the Maestro and Madame, who could occupy it immediately.

I hurried back to the hospital with my good news, and was rewarded by joy like light as it broke over all their faces. I was embraced, I was their deliverer, and before dinner they were

safely transferred, bags and all, to La Fonda. Craft remained in the hospital, and when released he would return to the room given him for the summer by the two stylish schoolmistresses in their beautiful hillside house, where, to their witty indignation, his angel of mercy would continue to administer to him—'with the *door closed*', the ladies announced over Santa Fe, their sibilant delight over imagined dalliance as energetic as their definition of decorous hospitality.

It was characteristic of Stravinsky's strict professional discipline that he was ready to take the first cathedral rehearsal on the evening of the day—29 June, 1959—on which he arrived. All was serene. Craft was not seriously hurt, the hotel suite was a great relief, and the cathedral event interested him. The concert was to take place Sunday, 12 July, and the works to be given were first, Bach's cantata *Trauerode*, which by then Craft would be able to rehearse and conduct even with his plaster cast, and Stravinsky's *Threni*, which he himself would conduct.

He had asked in advance that a quiet place, to be equipped with a muted piano, be found near the Fonda hotel. Extending my grasp of favours, I had asked the Archbishop's chancellor if there might be such a room in the little adobe building at the far side of the garden where Archbishop Lamy had had his private chapel. There was, and it was placed at Stravinsky's disposal. No one else would have the key to the room while he was in Santa Fe that summer. I liked the idea of such an association between Lamy and Stravinsky, even remote as it was.

The cathedral had been built to its 1959 condition in 1885, when for lack of funds Lamy had been forced to suspend work. It was a simple structure, reminiscent in style of the churches of Lamy's home province of the Auvergne. It was not a large church—it seated perhaps 1,200 people, and its plaster arches and vaults in the Romanesque style were far from lofty, yet some grace of proportion was there, and despite banal decorations in stencilled patterns on the walls and columns, and in the mass-produced plaster statues, the inner volume of the church had a noble simplicity reflecting the nature of its builder. In the choir loft in addition to the pipe organ was a harmonium made in Paris by Debain, whose label described the maker as '*inventeur de l'har-*

monium', and '*Fournisseur de S.M. l'Empereur*'—Napoleon III.

When Stravinsky conducted the first reading of *Threni* that evening, with the singers and orchestra players ranged in the sanctuary before the high altar, we all discovered how beautiful were the acoustical properties of the church. Without damage to the precision demanded by Stravinsky they added an almost imperceptible linger of sound after each note, which suited the grave splendour of the composition, with its sung lines, its occasional spoken or whispered texts, and the brief marvels of punctuation in refrain—'Aleph', 'Beth', 'Res(h)'—by declamatory voices and instruments which followed each lamentation of Jeremiah. The singers felt the extra musical dimension given by the transepts, vaultings, and aisles, and rose with the work as it unfolded for them.

The Archbishop was not present—we had an appointment to pay a state call upon him in Cathedral Place at four o'clock on Thursday, 9 July. Meanwhile, the work would go forward in cathedral rehearsals, with photographers coming and going, a handful of opera people, Madame, myself, a few others, present, depending on the commitments of the musicians at the opera theatre. One thing everyone noticed—how Stravinsky, in passing the altar, or a shrine, or a side chapel, always showed piety and decorum, making a little genuflection and crossing himself in the Russian manner, touching the right shoulder instead of the left at the word 'Holy'. This church, a poor Romanesque exercise in adobe, plaster, and native sandstone, was a far cry from Saint Mark's of Venice, but it was sanctified, and it represented much that was meaningful to Stravinsky, to whom religious traditions were in no way inconsistent with various other determining strands of his character—his aristocratic worldliness, his ironic vision of much that animated human affairs, his entire unorthodoxy as an artist combined with his awareness and use of a strict cultural heritage, his often scandalous wit. In other words, religion, for him, took its place in this world as well as the next; and in this he had intimate knowledge of an elevated example.

For one afternoon—it was Tuesday, 30 June—during the rehearsal period of that summer, he and Madame went with me to see Bynner and Hunt late one afternoon. There were other guests and lacking a chair I found myself settled on the floor facing Stravinsky who sat in a low Victorian chair which suited his short stature. I told him of my first interview with the Archbishop, who

93

so appreciated the precedent set by Pope John for secular concerts in cathedral churches: otherwise—I shrugged in doubt at what our local chances might have been.

Stravinsky inhaled with his wide, closed smile at what this made him think of, which he then told me in detail. He and his wife had been in Rome recently, the Rome of his old friend the Cardinal Patriarch of Venice who now reigned in the Vatican. One day, conducting an orchestra rehearsal for a concert of his works in the palace of the Santa Cecilia musical society in the Via della Conciliazione near the Vatican, Stravinsky felt someone tugging at the leg of his grey flannel slacks. Busy with the orchestra, he ignored the distraction. It came again. He glanced around. Below him at the stage apron was someone in red-violet over black—a monsignor. Stravinsky halted the orchestra for him.

'He said,' related Stravinsky, 'that the Holy Father wanted to see me.'

Stravinsky lifted his arms and replied,

'But I am rehearsing.'

Yes, yes, of course—but as soon as he was finished, he was please to come to the Vatican. Pope John had read in the papers that the Maestro was in Rome and desired very greatly to see him again.

'I am very appreciative, but you see how I am'—Stravinsky indicated his locker-room rehearsal clothes of slacks, wilted shirt, cardigan, towel—'and I beg to say that I cannot dismiss the orchestra to go and change.'

No, no, replied the chamberlain, he was to come just as he was as soon as convenient after the morning's work. The Holy Father would understand. It was not to be a state audience.

There was nothing for it but to finish the rehearsal, dry off with the towel, restore himself with Scotch, and go to the sacred palace. There he was received at once with an embrace from his old patron. They were of the same height. Stravinsky's leanness accentuated the Pope's great girth. They were in a private parlour of the papal apartments. Together they crossed the wide floor and settled into gilded armchairs in a window embrasure for a gossip. It was animated.

So, what was the latest in the world of art? asked the Pope. For example, what was Picasso up to now?

Stravinsky told him whatever he knew.

And what were the most fascinating recent books? asked the

Pope. And who were the interesting new artists?—naming several
he was aware of himself. He thought highly of Giacomo Manzù,
of course, who was doing the great new doors for the Holy Year
entrance to St Peter's. Then there was Giacometti in Paris. And
what of the new musical noises that were being made with laboratory appliances—and so on and so on, questions and answers in a
steady flow about the most current cultural matters whose precise
words are lost but whose extraordinary range of knowledge and
interest revealed Pope John as a worthy partner in conversation
with his visitor. I can now imagine—for I saw the Pope later that
year in two general audiences in the same day—the heavy, wide
face with its small smiling eyes, and the great Punch nose, and the
mouth with its almost purple lips expressing delighted good will
which composed the rapport between the two friends. Stravinsky
had no idea of how long actually the conversation lasted, but surely
almost an hour, when he became aware of a slight opening of the
tall gilt-and-carved door and a discreet red-violet signal without.
It was time to make way for another visitor. He rose. With a sigh
the Pope stood up with him, and linking arms, slowly walked
Stravinsky, with respect for his limping pace, across towards the
door. Halfway to it, said Stravinsky, the Pope halted them both
and said,

'Maestro, please: do me a favour.'

'*Mais certainement, Saint Père.*' (The whole interview was in
French.)

'Yes,' said the Pope, 'when you are in Rome next time, *call me
up!*'—with a hint of droll reproach that he had had to discover
from the papers that his friend was in town.

Stravinsky now made comic sounds in his throat and repeated,
'*Call me up!*'

He promised to do so—as if there were the smallest chance that
a telephone call would ever be allowed to reach His Holiness, and
they resumed their progress to the door. Once there, the Pope
faced Stravinsky and touched his shoulder and said,

'And please: dear Maestro: one more favour.'

Stravinsky bowed agreement with whatever it might be. Pope
John said,

'May I have your autograph?'

As Stravinsky bent to kiss the Fisherman's Ring, Pope John,
with his left hand, lifted his white *zucchetto* in homage to his
visitor, who, almost dismayed, murmured that of course he would

send the autograph. In Santa Fe Stravinsky was still moved by the gaiety and sophisticated simplicity of his friend.

As in all other matters, the Stravinskys were connoisseurs of hotel life, and had long mastered the art of being publicly conspicuous without in any way acknowledging the fact. From the Paris Ritz—their favourite—to the Trianon Palace at Versailles, and the Hassler in Rome, and Claridge's, to God knows what in between in both hemispheres, they put up with the suspended sort of existence that must be led by professional nomads. La Fonda in Santa Fe, while it had many pleasant features, also had small disadvantages. For one thing, to get to the main floor public rooms and to the outdoors, one had to come along a very long corridor from the elevators to the lobby; and here there were constant ambushes by typical hunters. Stravinsky had to move slowly, with his cane, and when I accompanied him he invariably took my arm for support. When I saw someone gleaming from the gauntlet of chairs and potted oleanders (deadly nightshade itself) I would try to plot evasive action; but if we were halted, Stravinsky was polite, even to such as the breathless lady from Texas who said she just had to shake his hand, and having done this, sought to detain him with *ba-var-dage*—'Oh, Mystro, don't you just *love* this darlin lil ol *ho*tel? Ah think it's just s'cute Ah could eat it up, and ennyhow, Ah just think Ah'm goin *buy* the whole *darlin* lil ol place!'

He never made unnecessary comment, and we would pass on from such arrests to idle talk in which his words were breathily spaced because of the exertion of a long walk.

Almost every noontime he lunched in the charming patio which La Fonda had at that time not yet destroyed. I was invited several times a week to lunch or dine. One example or two of the frequent times will do here.

On 9 July, the day we were established at the patio table he liked best—it was shaded by an ancient cottonwood tree. He sat wearing his forty-year-old beret which Picasso had given him. Madame did not always accompany us—sometimes she was not hungry, sometimes she was painting in her room upstairs (Eleanor Bedell gave two one-man shows of her paintings in Santa Fe), or making collages, or threading tapestries after her own abstract designs. When Craft was rehearsing at the opera, he would be

Stravinsky in his library, Hollywood, 1963, with Robert Craft

Stravinsky conducting the first rehearsal of *Oedipus Rex*, with Paul
Horgan as the Narrator, Santa Fe Opera, 1960

unable to join us. It thus came about that I was fairly often alone with Stravinsky. Having finished my morning's work, I was happy for his company and a good lunch.

He invariably ordered a Scotch, to be followed by jellied madrilene and a spare dish. His social sense was great, and if a passing vagary of health, or a stupid letter, say, had upset him, he strove to conceal a state of irritability. As he himself once said, 'I am much more in certain mood than anyone,' by which he meant 'more moody', and Madame once said, 'He is difficult with himself,' and added, 'He does not want to show that he has emotions.' He would sit leaning on his black stick, whose handle was carved to fit his right hand. It remains a positive cast of his grip. Sitting with lips closed, yet smiling widely, nostrils distended, he would often make a quick inhalation, like an accented upbeat; at the same time raising his little shoulders, and into this limited gesture he could convey a wonderful range of expressivity. As he grew older, he tended to use words less, and gestured indications more; but his communication never ceased. I rarely saw him in an abstracted or absent mood—until the end. He was afflicted with some allergy which kept a slow but persistent flow at the tip of his nose; and he touched this delicately with Kleenex now and then to dry it up. Almost bald, his head had a beanlike contour which like an infant's was both touching in its exposure and impressive in its integral form. With waiters as well as importunate hunters, he showed the same royal sort of courtesy, and I thought this politeness was the other side of his medal of personality—that caustic brilliance and sarcasm which could operate when there was anything worthy of calling it forth. In conversation his voice rarely varied in volume, maintaining a slightly breathy, husky tone, but his articulation was slurred only when he sought his droll effects, and his sibilants were given extra force by what I took to be false teeth. His general style, which for almost half a century had reached me first through print and recording, and now through personal presence, was concentrated, impacted, densified, to the greatest degree. In all its expressions, from the idlest personal in conversation to the utmost significant in composition and performance, there was a total absence of vulgarity. To be with him was to be conscious that one was within the field of energy of genius, even during its lapses into restful triviality. I think at times he may have found my company somewhat trying, for the tone of my response to him; for in his presence I often

found it difficult to release to its fullest, for whatever that was worth, my own intrinsic personality—and it would be just that sort of release which would have engaged him most in anyone. Even with the growing familiarity of years, I never lost something of awed restraint; but it was one of his powers that he never needed explanations—he could feel what one felt, and if there was something genuine behind it, he was aware of that, too, and accepted what could not easily find expression when he knew it to be compact of both respect and love, with a pinch of intelligence thrown in.

Samuel Dushkin, the violinist, who was his friend and colleague for decades, made with fond penetration a statement of what I had come to know for myself:

'. . . Among friends, his personal charm was evident at once. It was not long before I realised that he was not only capable of giving tenderness and affection but seemed in great need of them himself. In fact, I sensed very soon something tense and anguished about him which made one want to comfort and reassure *him*. The Stravinsky I had heard much about and imagined and the Igor Fedorovich I met seemed two different people.'

So to me: the illustrious, formidable master of damaging wit and terrifying honesty—even of detached Olympian vanity—was only a public façade, as it were. I had nothing with which to match his brilliance and erudition, not to say experience; but I came to love him so wholly that he took this for its value, whatever, and gave back to me a sense of intimacy, polite and formal, yet lovely and warm.

As our lunch progressed, I said,

'One thing I've been wondering about, Maestro—you prefer not to dine before conducting, and the hotel dining room closes at nine o'clock on Sundays. May I arrange for a supper for you and Madame and Bob, and perhaps one or two others, in a private dining room afterwards? For one thing, we could have a drink then, which one cannot do publicly in New Mexico on Sunday.'

He made a comedy of exaggerated astonishment at the law, and then said,

'That would be ve-ry agreeable.'

'I think one would be expected to invite the Archbishop, if you agree.'

'By all means.—There is one other thing: singers do not like to

98

eat before performing. Perhaps you could include my soloists.'

'Of course. They'd be delighted to be with you.'

As we idled our way through lunch, I mentally rehearsed the staff work for what would be needed for the Sunday night post-concert supper. It was soon clear that if the singers for *Threni* were to come, then so must the artists who were singing with Craft in the Bach *Trauerode*. It followed, then, that if solo singers needed to be fed, so did choral singers. Further, it would be a solecism to omit the distinguished choral conductor Miss Margaret Hillis, who was preparing the chorus, and, too, the opera *répétiteurs* who had worked for weeks on the programme. It was taken for granted that Crosby and his generous and appealing parents be invited; and my thought naturally progressed to the notion that if the chairman of the board was having the Stravinskys in for a little post-concert snack, various other officers of the board and benefactors of the opera must be included lest I alienate good will by segregating the illustrious ones from bridling common folk. The opera's lean budget had no item to cover such an event. It would in all respects be my personal responsibility. So be it. As for arrangements—it was not for nothing that I had served rather more weighty matters during four years as an officer of a special staff division in the War Department in the 1940s war. It was clear that invitations for all participating artists must go up immediately on the opera bulletin board, others be phoned the same afternoon, and the hotel forces be mobilised to manage in private what it would be too late to do after nine o'clock Sunday in public—the simple necessity of providing Stravinsky with a double Scotch and a bite of roast beef after his performance. All this resolved upon, I was able to enjoy our lunch *à deux*, during which people came and went, received his bow, and he no more felt the eyes of others who could not help staring at him than if they had been that other medium of mechanical curiosity, the camera lens. He wandered in and out of comments about our current concerns and now and then by a ricochet of interest produced pronouncements, some of which he smiled away as trivial but useful socially. These never had an air of being chiselled in stone—they were flying chips of his unresting cerebration.

'The productions of Wagner at Bayreuth clearly demonstrate that he is a bore.' When I assented as expected, he added with his little slump of posture to serve as an accentuation, 'But Wagner is a *professional*, not an *amateur*,' and with an inclination forward

—his labour-saving Q.E.D.—he made clear that because of this he could respect a bore who was not an amateur.

This led him to a word concerning banalities in music. Much in the music of Gounod, Puccini, Tschaikovsky, were *young* banalities, and thus deserved no respect. But in the case of Tschaikovsky, if his banalities persisted, they deserved respect because in time they became *mature* banalities.

As for Puccini, he said the violins in *Madama Butterfly* drove him mad. 'If I ever have to listen again to these—' a heavy exhalation suggested psycho-catastrophe. He liked *La Bohème*, and thought it Puccini's best work. I quoted to him the famous witticism, 'Wagner is the Puccini of music,' which drew silent agreement. By tangent from *Madama Butterfly*, he observed that the 'Japanese language is not a language—it is a habit', which, somewhat mystified, I accepted on faith.

Habit and derivation were not the same. It was Bellini from whom Chopin derived. How on earth, I wondered. Yes, Bellini's scores were transcribed for piano and played in Polish drawing rooms, where the youthful Chopin heard them, and developed his melodic style which was so clearly an extension and elaboration of a virtuoso vocal idiom. Yes, I thought, any coloratura could sing the waltzes, for example.

A comfortable pause in which thought drifted evidently through phases relating to how innovation, experiment, originality, or whatever, came to be, and he presently said,

'Berg, Schönberg, Webern and I—we are all old men: *but we are sure!*'

I don't remember whether I asked him what he felt about the young men who, with a claim to erasure of the past and premature finality in the future, were experimenting with computer and other electronic devices of the laboratory. From other utterances of his which I have read on the subject, I think his answer would have been, with a comic glottal thickening of his voice, the familiar,

'Thank you very much, go to hell.'

At four o'clock promptly on the same day we arrived at Archbishop's House in Cathedral Place.

I was long used to Archbishop Byrne's combination of the

personage, the ceremonious priest, the saintly ascetic, the effective administrator, and the innocent in matters of contemporary culture. Many persons saw only the grandeur of bearing by which he sustained the historical significance of his office, but I was always moved by his sense of style, with which he often combined a lively charm, and he could also on occasion take part with robust gaiety in informal gatherings. People who thought he gave himself airs forgot that he was accustomed to the adulation of natural courtiers like the lesser clergy, officially awed nuns, Catholic widows, and parochial schoolchildren. It was inevitable that men of eminence in various pursuits of life came to believe that vast wealth, or high rank in the military, or the government, or the university, or the Church, conferred upon them authority not only in their specialties, but in all matters.

A nun housekeeper admitted Stravinsky and me and showed us into a spotless parlour arranged in that mixture of lower class self-respect and old-fashioned comfortless taste so characteristic of American prelatic residences—lace curtains, gilt wicker taborets with vases of artificial flowers, plush and mahogany armchairs too heavy to be moved, a machine-tapestried sofa with three doilies pinned in a row at head level, life-sized hand-coloured photographs of previous prelates and one of the reigning Pope, a gas chandelier converted to electricity, and a crucifix on a wall. For all its massive clutter, there was no sign of amenity for the mind—no books, no periodicals, no works of art, or any decorous ease for the body.

After a moment, the door opened and the Archbishop entered, smiling energetically, striding rapidly within his cassock—an unfrayed one, with full sash—and with his arms outstretched. He wore his red-violet *zucchetto*.

'Dear Maestro Stravinsky,' he cried, in tones of jubilee, and Stravinsky began a genuflection to kiss the prelatic ring, but Byrne arrested the gesture, raised him, and conducted him to an armchair at right angles but some distance away from the one he thereupon occupied. He acknowledged my presence by waving me to a third chair, equidistant from the others, so that we were all related but removed from each other in a triangle which made easy conversation impossible.

'Thank you,' he said to me, 'for bringing Maestro Stravinsky together with us. I am honoured.'

'Yes, Your Excellency.'

Stravinsky bowed over his stick.

'And I too, Archbishop.'

The awkwardness in the room was almost palpable. Stravinsky, used to the most sophisticated company to be had on earth, was yet respectful of the station and person of a provincial metropolitan prelate in the full splendour of his state garments, and he now applied that protocol which must leave to presiding rank, as with royalty, the initiative in conversation. Therefore, after a pause,

'Indeed,' said the Archbishop. 'Yes, indeed. We are very proud to have your wonderful music heard in our cathedral.'

There seemed nothing to reply to this. Stravinsky, with a serious smile, bowed from his chair. It was suddenly evident that his host was somewhat nervous and at a loss. I cudgelled my brains for suitable small talk. I said,

'We are finding the rehearsals very beautiful, Excellency. The acoustic in the cathedral is beautiful.'

'Very beautiful,' murmured Stravinsky.

'How beautiful, then,' said the Archbishop, running his thumbs up and down under the heavy gold chain of his pectoral cross. 'We are all looking forward most eagerly to your concert Sunday evening.—You are comfortable in our little garden house, at your composing?'

'Yes, thank you very much, I go every morning.'

'Yes, we have seen you crossing the garden.'

Stravinsky's face became expressionless. He disliked being observed in connection with his work.

'You have been to the opera?'

'My wife and I go on occasion.'

'On occasion. Yes.'

A silence fell.

But it was comfortable after the stiffness of the conversation, and I saw Byrne at last look directly at Stravinsky, and Stravinsky return the look, and in that moment, in an exchange of simple reality, both men came to be fond of each other, and I went easy within myself.

The final compliments and observations which followed were informal and natural. As the Archbishop stood to terminate the interview, he came and put his arm around Stravinsky's shoulder, towering above him, and walked him companionably to the door, and when they said goodbye, it was with warmth. Stravinsky bent to kiss the ring, he was not allowed to, and as he did so, the

Archbishop put his left hand for a moment on Stravinsky's head—
a gesture more of affection than of official blessing. If Byrne was
out of his depth in matters of modern music, he was a man who
felt greatness when he saw it, and if Stravinsky had a formal
respect for an exalted state of holy orders, he knew a man of
spiritual certainty when he met one; and in the end the audience
was a success. To those of whom he might appropriately expect
sophisticated response and did not receive it, Stravinsky could
show indifference. The Archbishop represented something else,
to which Stravinsky in all sincerity paid reverence.

Unhappily, during the time when the details of the cathedral
concerts were being worked out, their originator, Dr Hausner, had
died very suddenly; and when the first such concert was given on
Sunday evening, 12 July, 1959, it was dedicated to his memory.
The event drew great public response. Anticipating crowds beyond
the cathedral's capacity, the opera management had set up loud-
speakers outside the cathedral; and people thronged the surround-
ing streets as far as the plaza to hear the performance whose
printed programme read:

THE SANTA FE OPERA
presents

A CONCERT OF MUSIC
ON SACRED THEMES

under the patronage of
HIS EXCELLENCY THE MOST REVEREND
EDWIN VINCENT BYRNE, D.D.,
ARCHBISHOP OF SANTA FE
THE CATHEDRAL OF SAINT FRANCIS
SANTA FE, NEW MEXICO

JULY 12, 1959—8:15 P.M.

The audience is asked to withhold applause.
Ladies are asked to wear head coverings.

This Performance is Dedicated
to the Memory of

ERIC HAUSNER, M.D.,
1905–1959

*Who not only generously supported the Santa Fe Opera
in all its activities and needs, but who also originated the
idea of presenting this Concert of Sacred Music in this
historic cathedral.*

PROGRAMME

I

Johann Sebastian Bach

SACRED CANTATA No. 198
'TRAUERODE'
(Ode of Mourning)

SARAMAE ENDICH, *soprano*
ELAINE BONAZZI, *alto*
NICO CASTEL, *tenor*
PETER BINDER, *baritone*

Soloists, chorus and orchestra of the Santa Fe Opera

Conducted by
ROBERT CRAFT

(MARGARET HILLIS, *Choral Director*)

Musical Preparation: BLISS HEBERT and JOHN MORIARTY

II

Igor Stravinsky

THRENI: LAMENTATIONES
JEREMIAE 'PROPHETAE'
(Lamentations of the
Prophet Jeremiah)

MILDRED ALLEN, *soprano*
REGINA SARFATY, *alto*
FRANK PORRETTA, *tenor*
NICO CASTEL, *tenor*
ROBERT RUE, *baritone*
ANDREW FOLDI, *bass*

Soloists, chorus and orchestra of the Santa Fe Opera

Conducted by the Composer
for the first time in the United States.

(MARGARET HILLIS, *Choral Director*)

Musical Preparation: BLISS HEBERT and JOHN MORIARTY

I brought Stravinsky to the sacristy where the artists were assembled; and I heard the programme from a side chapel. One can

only say of it that it reached splendour in every respect of the works given and their performance. To labour this would do no service to the occasion. What I can report is a moment of the intermission which had its comedy.

Madame appeared at the concert in full beauty. She was grandly jewelled, she wore a stiff satin cloak of red-violet which reached the floor like a coronation vestment. It came from a famous Parisian couturière. During the concert she sat in a place of honour in the front pew to the left of the centre aisle. In a corresponding place to the right of the aisle the Archbishop was disposed in his own full-length cape of red-violet which was matched in colour by Madame's.

They had never met; and at the intermission, when people stood chatting quietly, without applause, he went to introduce himself to Madame, who came forward to receive him in the centre aisle. As I had long known, he had no small-talk, however earnestly he worked to produce it. After their greetings, there was an awkward pause during which the beautiful lady smiled inquiringly at him, and he nodded silently towards the middle distance. Finally, Madame, with luminous mischief, broke the silence, saying,

'Archbishop, do you know that that is Schiaparelli "Shocking Pink" you are wearing?'

Politely he showed interest of a cultural nature.

'Oh?' he said. 'Indeed?' He clearly had never heard of Schiaparelli, as heaven knew he had no need to have done. 'How interesting. Yes.'

'You see?' said Madame, extending her lucent satin towards his own silk. 'We match exactly.'

'Ah. Ah yes. I see we do.'

Fortunately just then the orchestra began to return to their racks in the sanctuary, the intermission was over, and the conversation ended cordially as everyone resumed their seats.

After the concert it fell to me to bring Stravinsky from the sacristy to his hotel room. While the supper guests would be gathering downstairs in the private hall, he must change from his concert clothes, deal with perspiration, and come down off the heights which every artist must do through some distraction or other after a performance.

We made our way without being halted from ambush and reached his room, adjoining that of Madame. She was downstairs greeting guests, and in fact was standing with the Archbishop and other leaders of the evening in a receiving line.

'Is there any way I can help you, Maestro?' I asked.

He replied in a husky voice that all he needed was to change, thank you very much. I did not know whether to go or stay, as he roughly but slowly took off his tailcoat which he threw on his bed with energy behind which I could now read discontent—'very much in mood'. His face was white and sweating. All his features seemed pulled by the force of gravity. He seemed to be in a private rage. He ripped off his white tie and began to deal with cuff-links. The first one he tried to remove resisted him. He tugged at it, he made subdued sounds like a kind of growling, which may have been slurred profanity, in what language I could not detect, and finally when he had the link free he threw it as hard as he could into a corner of the room. With one arm now free he started to tear at the other cuff.

'Should I—' I began, but looking at me with an expression of profound misery he shook his head and I saw that what I had read as anger was rather more like almost mortal disappointment. He said,

'It is never good enough!'

I asked a silent question and he went on,

'The performance. Never!'—he threw the other cuff-link away and I noted where.

'But I thought it wonderfully beautiful!' I said. 'I have not even been able to tell you how beautiful.'

Now fumbling with shirt studs, he shook his head.

'Oh my God, the mistakes you did not hear!'

It seemed to me that he was too distressed to bother with the supper party below. Wondering how to suggest tactfully that his meal should be brought up to him, I drifted to the corners where the cuff-links lay, gathered them up, and set them on his dressing table. His knobby fingers were trembling as they worked at the shirt studs. I understood at last that he was suffering from a state in which I saw him several later times. I fancied that it was not unlike the let-down after love when in the height of consummation all faculties are merged beyond thought, but which later fall separate as thought returns, and with it, all feeling spent, a sense of entrapment in the limitations of life so lately transcended. By

analogy, there occurred to me: '*Post coitum omne animal triste . . .*'
A surge of compassion beyond presumption went through me but
I knew of no way to reassure him. The studs finally came free and
with his shirt hanging wet and loose he looked at me. No even
invisible state of another ever escaped him, and he said,

'Pol: you are very kind,' meaning 'kind' to feel as I did, and
turned to go to the bathroom for fresh heavy towels.

'I will wait for you in the hall,' I said, he nodded, and I left him.
To court a cliché quite deliberately, I will say that my heart was
heavy for him, who had the world, and who found that in no
particular did it precisely and beautifully correspond to the world
of his private vision. A failure in any detail of his concept or its performance was a failure in totality. I remember now how short of
speech and abrupt in separation he had been after the first Houston
concert. I wondered why he ever accepted ordeals which failed so
wholly to bring him satisfaction. Perhaps I should go below to
bring Madame—and as I was in the very thought she turned a
corner distant in the corridor and came towards me, radiant and
yet purposeful.

'How he is?' she asked in the inverted English which she sometimes used when preoccupied.

I explained what had gone on. She shrugged.

'Always it is the same. I will go [to him].'

'Shall I wait?'

'No—they are looking for you. I will bring him.'

She entered her own room with her key and shut the door.

I found the supper room thronged and full of convivial noise.
Everyone had a drink in hand but the Archbishop, to whom I paid
respect, and then circulated to greet our other personages. I had
asked for a small table to be set up for the Stravinskys, Craft, and
the Archbishop, at one end of the room, just enough to seat the
four of them, while the rest of us all would find places at random
at many other tables placed about the room. I was talking to someone above the noise when a sudden silence fell to be followed by an
explosion of applause and I turned around to see Stravinsky and
Madame in the high doorway at the top of the few steps which led
down into the supper room, and in him I saw a master of trans-
formation.

With his arm linked in hers, he was smiling widely, not quite
bowing but inclining himself forward, taking in the whole room.
He looked fifteen years younger. There was colour in his cheeks, he

was nicely brushed and combed, and he was dressed with utmost smartness in a dark suit, a pale shirt, and a polka-dotted bow tie. The two of them came down into the room and made a progress through the crowd, lingering for a robust handshake here or there, until they came to the Archbishop, where they paused to make reverence, but instead the Archbishop and Stravinsky found each other's embrace and the crowd applauded again. Mirandi, referring to *Threni*, that most complex of works, embraced Stravinsky and said, 'I loved it, it's so catchy, I hummed it all the way over here.' Her jape raised his spirits even further. Then to table, where Scotch and the rest awaited. The world with all its imperfections was restored to purpose. Stravinsky's exhilaration reached and lifted everyone—there must have been eighty or ninety present—and the party became a success.

Before it was over, he beckoned to me and said, holding on to my sleeve,

'Pol: you will lunch with me, tomorrow, alone?'

I accepted, said goodnight, escorted the Archbishop to the door, and so home to bed.

No less courteous than usual, he seemed somehow not quite engaged during luncheon the next day. With coffee at the end, he was able to bring himself to speak of why he had invited me to lunch alone with him.

He made rather a speech, and with a number of unaccustomed halts in it he got around to the point with troubled delicacy. It took me a little time to enter the penetralia of his ellipses, but what finally came clear was that the party the night before had been delightful, but also, he could guess, very expensive.

(Good God, what can I say if—if—I thought.)

He had not considered in the beginning that so many people would be involved. The drink and food were very good, but one knew how these things mounted up.

He was not looking at me while voicing these facts, but the notion, at once grateful and impossible, that he might be thinking of sharing the expense made me shrink within.

'Pol: I want to help you in the matter of the party.'

He looked at me and saw my mixed anguish. I could not conceivably take any money from him, and yet his thought of my

possibly strained resources was touching. He saw that he must persuade me, if he could, and he said,

'I do not see why you should bear the whole cost of it without relief.'

I certainly felt nothing so bridling as foolish pride at the idea he was circling in on, but I could not help feeling, and showing, I suppose, that it was not possible after the fact to let him split the bill with me. He knew what I was thinking. A master of the unexpected in all ways, he said with the most grave tone of admonition,

'Now I will help you: you can claim a deduction on your income tax for the cost of the party.'

My relief was difficult to conceal, and so was my mirth. My first thought was that I had seen a virtuoso performance of the Stravinsky thriftiness which was so celebrated in his lore; and even if I had, my second thought was that no man who had suffered the privations he and his family had been forced to endure during the 1914 war in Swiss exile, when friends actually gathered money to help them survive in the most modest circumstances, should be easily laughed about if in later prosperity the habit of his caution with money should persist. My third thought was, I feel, closest of all to the fact; for I think he was ready to say in effect that we should each pay for half of the party when he saw my distaste for the idea, and with a rapid shift of mind offered instead the consolation of tax deductions, thus sparing me any fumbling efforts to refuse with grace his original scheme.

I thanked him heartily. At once his humour brightened, and he drew from between the pages of a book he carried a typewritten paper which he had signed. For Crosby had asked me to extract from the Maestro a statement endorsing the opera—one which we would be free to use in publicity. Stravinsky had told me to write anything I pleased—he would sign it. I found it a delicate task to concoct sincere praise of the opera company without putting extravagances into Stravinsky's mouth. After some labour, this is what came forth:

> In the Santa Fe Opera, the United States has a vital cultural resource. Here are young artists, creating productions of opera with fresh imagination, delightful musical talent, and a serious respect for the ensemble. My work has been presented by this

company with taste and skill. I wish for the Santa Fe Opera a long future of prosperity and further artistic achievement.

In high spirits, relief, and gratitude, our lunch *à deux* ended— '*À bientôt, à bientôt*'—and so, presently, did the season. Before we parted he autographed my copy of the *Threni* score: 'To you, dear Paul Horgan—nobel [sic] witness of these Lamentationes Jeremiae Prophetae in July 1959 in Santa Fe, N.M. from your sincerely devoted I Stravinsky.'

Our next encounter came in London in early November of the same year—1959. Motoring in Europe with my Roswell friend and neighbour, Edward Bisett, who was taking a long vacation before moving to New York, I had worked at archives in Paris, and across France, and down to Rome, in search of materials for my biography of Archbishop Lamy. Bisett had met the Stravinskys in Santa Fe; Madame had spoken of his intelligence and pleasing manners; it would, I knew, be a comfortable meeting all around if we should join the Stravinskys in London to hear a performance of *Oedipus Rex* at the Festival Hall on 9 November, with the composer conducting, and Jean Cocteau, the author of the text, as the narrator. To simplify our convergence, we all agreed to stay at the Ritz in Piccadilly.

After vicissitudes of air travel too tedious to recite—the two-hour scheduled flight turned into a ten-hour endurance—Bisett and I arrived from Rome in the early black evening of 7 November. The Stravinskys were already in London but we did not see them until the next day, Sunday, when we met them in the round lobby of the Ritz as they returned from a rehearsal at the Festival Hall. Since Santa Fe they had spent a month in Venice, and had toured in Italy for concerts at Naples and Bologna in October. I now had what I hoped would be an agreeable surprise for them.

For my second move in London had been to telephone to Goossens, whom I had not seen since an earlier stay in England in 1955. If I could arrange a party, would he dine with us all on the present Sunday evening? He was elated at the prospect of seeing Stravinsky, and I felt particular pleasure in being the agent of bringing them together again—one my cherished old friend, the other a beloved friend recently materialised in the flesh after a lifetime of interest in his work and image.

'Goossens? In London? Now?' exclaimed the Stravinskys with pleasure.

Yes, I hoped we would all dine at the Berkeley in the evening. The Stravinskys and Craft were not engaged, and I was therefore charged to convey greetings and anticipations of Goossens, who some years before had been knighted for his services to music in Australia. He was happy to hear that we would all be able to come together for that Sunday evening.

Meanwhile, Madame, Bisett and I went during the afternoon to the Royal Academy to see a copious retrospective exhibition devoted to the paintings and drawings of André Dunoyer de Segonzac, whose work I had admired ever since encountering it in reproduction decades before in *The Dial*. The exhibition was too comprehensive to see with full enjoyment in one visit, and we three went again a day or two later while Stravinsky and Craft were busy with other matters.

Our dinner Sunday evening was an intimate and convivial event. Stravinsky and Goossens had not met for decades, and now spent almost the entire meal in a duet of reminiscence and reminder, with Craft as an occasional contributor to the musical shop of the two old friends. Bisett had fallen under Madame's spell, and the other three of us had easy talk in the climate of her knowledgeable gaiety.

London, after Paris, must have been the great city most

hospitable to Stravinsky, and it was Goossens who had in the early years done the most to prosper the Maestro's works there. In September 1921, writing the 'London Letter' in *The Dial*, T. S. Eliot said that 'Looking back upon the past season in London . . . it remains certain that Strawinsky was our two-months' lion . . .' and referring to a certain concert, added, 'Strawinsky, Lucifer of the season, brightest in the firmament, took the call many times, small and correctly neat in pince-nez. His advent was well prepared by Mr Eugene Goossens—also rather conspicuous this year —who conducted two *Sacre du printemps* concerts, and other Strawinsky concerts were given before his arrival. The music was certainly too new and strange to please very many people; it is true that on the first night it was received with wild applause, and it is to be regretted that only three performances were given.' There were also ballet performances, and Eliot found the production unsatisfying, saying that 'in everything in the *Sacre du printemps* except in the music, one missed the sense of the present'. He then went on to add that 'Whether Strawinsky's music be permanent or ephemeral, I do not know; but'—it was a non-musical misfortune that Eliot joined in with the naïve fallacy concerning Stravinsky and the machine age—'it did seem to transform the rhythm of the steppes into the scream of the motor horn, the rattle of machinery, the grind of wheels, the beating of iron and steel, the roar of the underground railway, and the other barbaric noises of modern life; and to transform these despairing noises into music.' While this seemed to carry gloomy appreciation, there could have been small consolation in being approved for the wrong reason, and on the whole it was probably more satisfying to Goossens—Stravinsky probably never heard of it—who when conducting *Le Sacre du printemps* with the New York Philharmonic was told that the president of the orchestra, a certain Mr Flagler, characterised it 'after the concert as "obscene music" '.

The history of Stravinsky's grotesque treatment by critics is a rich subject which could engage a whole chapter in the life work of such a connoisseur of musical invective as Nicolas Slonimsky. In his autobiography, Goossens had a fine contribution to such literature. He was arranging what he called 'a mighty concert' in the Queen's Hall for a day in June 1929. 'I had collected a hundred and ten of London's best players . . . and decided on a trip to Paris to persuade Stravinsky to take part in the concert as soloist. I found him in his little studio in the new Salle Pleyel, practising

the piano vigorously with the aid of some iron dumb-bells which, from time to time, he would lift over his head and then slowly deposit again on the floor.

' "What are you using them for?" I asked him.

' "For the development of the forearm," he replied, and added:

' "I find this additional muscular strength very helpful in playing my music."

'I then asked him to play his piano concerto at my London concert in a month's time, to which he agreed, after some discussion about terms.'

At the concert, then, Stravinsky did play his *Piano Concerto*—a first performance in London. 'The hall was sold out and the enthusiasm overwhelming,' reported Goossens. He then went on to quote extracts from the leading London newspaper critics in their reviews of the concerto. Once again the professional music commentators lagged after the prophetic value of Stravinsky's music by decades or perhaps a generation. Richard Capell of the *Mail*, said Goossens, found the work a 'Parisian freak', and 'unimportant but rather stimulating, ugly but not odiously ugly . . . the best of what the jazz-mongers of the day would like to do if only they had enough intelligence and technique . . . It is probably rather like Bach as Bach seems to wireless listeners who hate the name Bach and want nothing but coon songs.' The critic of the *Evening News* said of the concerto that 'To the initiates, or propagandists, it is no doubt a miracle of beauty . . . The plain man would call it a hoax.' The formidable Ernest Newman of *The Sunday Times*: 'The pleasure of seeing the composer of *Petrushka* again was equalled only by the pain of hearing the composer of the *Piano Concerto*. It was sad to think that the one-time man of genius had degenerated into the manufacturer of this ugly and feeble commonplace'—and this, quite aside from the concerto itself, given as an opinion in 1929, before the composition of *The Symphony of Psalms*, *Perséphone*, *Symphony in C*, *Orpheus*, *The Rake's Progress*, the *Requiem Canticles*, to cite only a few later masterpieces. To return to the concerto, the *New Age* critic wrote, 'Of the incredibly, lamentably feeble and dreary display made by M. Igor Stravinsky and his piano concerto, it is difficult to write adequately.'

Much in their common past to grow hilarious over, much in the current scene to exchange views about: I heard no detail of their conversation, but in Stravinsky's burry gaieties, Goossens's elegant and original rhetoric, and Craft's neat discernments there was

much camaraderie throughout the Sunday evening dinner; and when we took to the outdoors afterwards for a stroll along Piccadilly, Stravinsky and Goossens walked ahead of us arm in arm, in the comfort of technical and personal understanding; and I suddenly recognised that Goossens was the only conductor out of the great many whom I had discussed with Stravinsky about whom he had never said an adversely critical word, while of the others (including even such as Pierre Monteux and Ernest Ansermet who had consistently devoted themselves to his work) he made remarks ranging from the grateful to the profanely furious to the sardonically dismissive.

The evening ended with an agreement to meet once again, all of us, before the Stravinskys' few days in London would be ended.

The professional purpose of the London episode took place the next evening—late, at an odd hour. It was to be a B.B.C. concert of *Oedipus Rex*, broadcast from the Festival Hall. Because Otto Klemperer was conducting at the usual evening concert time a performance in his Beethoven series with the Royal Philharmonic Orchestra, the Stravinsky-Cocteau event in the same hall was scheduled for 11 p.m. immediately following Klemperer's.

Bisett and I brought the Stravinskys and Craft to the stage entrance as the Klemperer concert was ending. I caught a glimpse from backstage, where we had to wait until the concert was over and the hall emptied for the next audience. Klemperer, seated in an odd sort of armchair, was producing a performance of much splendour from the players, with the most unlikely gestures—he was like a wind-tortured old tree with crippled limbs, bending and swaying under a power greater than himself yet which he seemed to control. His face was runnelled with a sort of impassive anguish. When it was over, he lurched to his feet to acknowledge applause, and then marching like a man with heavy weights on his feet left the stage. After return calls, he disappeared. Stravinsky in his own dressing room did not see him. The hall rapidly emptied, and a new audience—the B.B.C. concert was sold out—entered. Bisett and I had been given seats out front and there we now went. I was to hear my first live performance of *Oedipus Rex*.

It was a concert production, with no attempt at staging. The chorus was ranked above and behind the orchestra against the

exposed square organ pipes of the stage wall. Places for the soloists were set facing the conductor's stand. A chair for the narrator was to the stage right of this, and some twenty feet away, in its own zone of stardom. It would be occupied by the writer of the text —both sung and spoken—of the work, M. Jean Cocteau, who had had a long if intermittent association with Stravinsky. I did not see them together backstage before the concert, if they actually met then.

They entered the stage together, Cocteau preceding the composer. As the applause swept forward from the house, Cocteau, a short, slight figure, in French evening clothes, grandly swept his right arm in an arc that matched the spatial curve of the hall, and turned his body half towards the audience, his head with its silvery antennae of hair lifted as if to tune in on glory while walking to his chair, where he stood and faced the farthermost rows; while Stravinsky, on his way to his own station at the podium, proceeded without flourishes to take his place. He bowed to the orchestra, then turned and bowed once to the audience, while Cocteau made several acknowledgments, with arms extended in magnanimous grace, of the continuing applause. This was ended when Stravinsky in a brisk gesture turned to Cocteau and faced him without expression. It was clearly a cue for the performance to start, as usual, with the first words of the narrator. Cocteau resigned his affair with the audience in order to practice his art.

The stage directions of *Oedipus Rex* state that the 'speaker expresses himself like a lecturer, presenting the story with a detached voice'. Cocteau placed one foot ahead of the other, raised his head, and pointed at his listeners with his right hand, index finger extended, and declared in a dry, didactic declamation,

'*Spectateurs: Vous allez entendre une version latine d*'Oedipe Roi . . .'

The effect was that of an irritable schoolteacher admonishing a dull class. Stravinsky stood motionless, his hands folded in front of him. At Cocteau's last syllable of introductory text, Stravinsky brought into the air the first great chord of the musical text, launching a precise performance by orchestra and singers. The same could not be said for the narrator's part. The work has six passages for speaker alone, when the singers and orchestra fall silent, and the synopsis of the proceedings is recited before each new musical chapter. For his passages, Cocteau rose from his chair, and when the music resumed, he sat down to interest

himself cordially in the entire detail of the Festival Hall—the boxes which protruded from the walls like drawers pulled half open from a piece of furniture, the ranks of seats which rose in three levels towards the rear wall, the side doors where standees clustered, the faces in the rows near the stage. He presented a presence of animation, and seemed to be fulfilling a duty which called upon him to be seen, as though this, rather than the musical statement unfolding behind him, were the purpose of the occasion. He was in his own glory and it consumed his whole attention. Twice during the performance, lost in the calm rapture of his open fame, he missed his cues; at which Stravinsky, first waiting politely for him to stand and speak, then felt obliged to touch his hand sharply to the score and face him to bring him out of his trance. With no mark of discomposure, Cocteau would then come to his feet, resume his scolding gesture, and give his words. It was clear that the composer was annoyed by the destructive indulgence of the author's vanity.

There is only one place in the score in which the speaker's words coincide with statements by the orchestra. This occurs when the narrator declares, '*L'assassin du roi est un roi.*' The last four words, as I was to learn later, are to be given equal emphasis while the orchestra sounds under them with four accented eighth notes in 9/8. Cocteau ignored the requirement, and left Stravinsky to bring in the orchestra without him after the text. As far as Cocteau seemed to be concerned, the precision and indeed the whole musical aspect of the performance were incidental; and as the attenuated, quiet farewell to King Oedipus moved to the work's conclusion, in chorus and orchestra, '*Tibi valedico, Oedipus, tibi valedico*', with long-held notes, followed by an eloquent full bar of silence before two last measures of curt, accented chords in the bass, which call for bated breath while the work reaches its final silence, Cocteau was on his feet, leaning up on tiptoe, wafting his gratitude by sweeping his long, taut-fibred hands from his heart to the house. At this, though the music was not over, the audience concluded that it must be, if the celebrated narrator was soliciting their applause. They at once gave it, while, unheard, Stravinsky gravely brought his work to its close, in what rage I could imagine.

There were many calls. Stravinsky, ignoring Cocteau, bowed once and disappeared. Cocteau returned to his own happy obligations on the forestage several more times, and the concert was over.

Bisett and I went backstage. Stravinsky, Madame, and Craft

were in their dressing room. We passed Cocteau on the way. He was surrounded by admirers, proceeding with him to his own dressing room next to Stravinsky's.

Visitors had to be received, but we were all soon on our way out of the hall, into a car, and on the way to the Caprice restaurant, where I had reserved a table for supper. If Cocteau's exhibition was referred to at all, it may have been in a growling series of remarks in French made by the Maestro to Madame. I know he did not speak to Cocteau after the concert, whatever exchange they may have had before.

There was a sombre atmosphere in the car as we rolled across Westminster Bridge expecting uplifting drinks and hot food. The hour was now after midnight. We were all hungry, not having dined beforehand. As we came to the Caprice a block from the Ritz, we saw that there were no cars near to it, and that the entrance was dark. I leaped out and went to the doors. A man was there superintending a cleaning crew within. The restaurant was closed.

'But I have a reservation—'

He was sorry, but the restaurant had closed at midnight. We were too late.

London seemed deserted. We dismissed the car, walked to the Ritz, went up to the Stravinsky rooms, and ordered drinks and sandwiches. It was a gala that failed.

But not, of course, in the ultimate values of the score of *Oedipus Rex*. It was good to recall then, as it is good now to revisit the actual text of, Goossens's view of this music, and the great companion pieces of its period in Stravinsky's canon, in which Goossens speaks of

'. . . The extreme economy of statement to be found in the later works'—Goossens is writing in 1951—'from the composer's pen. There is as much scope for real expression in a performance of *Apollo*, *Oedipus Rex*, the *Symphonie des psaumes*, *Perséphone*, as in the "Berceuse" from *The Firebird*, but there is absolutely no room for sentimentality: a commodity as foreign to the work of Strawinsky as it is essential to a drawing-room ballad . . . Writing as a conductor . . . I emphatically protest against the later work of Strawinsky being dubbed the desiccated, tenuous, devitalising thing it is represented to be by so many of the knowing ones . . .

No musician can deny the mastery with which the composer has set down, clearly, precisely, and uncompromisingly that which is as logical and outspoken in content as anything I know of in music.'

A play starring Michael Redgrave and adapted from Henry James's *The Aspern Papers* was running in London. On Tuesday evening we were all present. Our seats were not all in one location, but we met in the intervals. The play and performance as such were not distinguished, but had an entertaining effect which, however, was not acute enough to offset the particular tone of response which habitually came forth when the Stravinskys were not critically satisfied. It was an air suggesting a miscarriage of justice. The less than first-rate was a swindle. Monosyllables of disinterest met the spectacle, except from Craft, who had the knack of softly uttering damaging opinions through gleaming smiles. The play— James's story—set going for me reveries about Lord Byron and the destruction of his manuscript autobiography in the first floor fireplace of John Murray's in Albemarle Street—that sacrificial furnace of nineteenth century English letters. I also remembered references in James's letters about the early London seasons of the Russian Ballet, and—it is of course a remote connection but one which amuses me—after seeing *L'Oiseau de feu*, Henry James, according to the last volume of Leon Edel's great biography of him, took to referring to Edith Wharton as 'The Firebird'—a nickname which suggests to me more of the exotic and colourful than I previously associated with the imperious and busy satirist of that thin imitation of the real, the Old World thing, which New York and Newport and Lenox called Society—Mrs Wharton's American orbit.

After *The Aspern Papers*, Bisett gave a supper party at the Savoy Grill, and there was suddenly, without direct contrivance by anyone, that sense of simple contentment which on occasion can enfold a small group of convivial people, even when one of them— Stravinsky in the instance—is a famous figure subject to recognition in public places and forced to ignore it.

We said goodbye that evening—the Stravinskys were leaving for elsewhere in the world before returning to New York in December. A day or so later Bisett went to travel on the continent. I remained

in London to correct proofs on my current novel*—a large one requiring weeks—and in that time Goossens asked me to lunch with him on 1 December at the restaurant Quo Vadis.

'I am asking no one else,' he said.

We met, he was in his most amusing form, we reminisced about Rochester, he spoke of his delight in being with the Stravinskys again. It was the last time I saw him, for he died a few years later; but I am happy in the remembrance of his fond high spirits that day, when his humour, his acumen, and his breadth of intellectual allusion all partook of his distinction of presence. Two days later Bisett and I embarked on the greatest of all liners, the *R.M.S. Queen Mary*, for a wildly rough and inspiring winter crossing to New York.

Later that month—19 December—the Stravinskys arrived in New York, to stay at the Gladstone Hotel. I asked by telephone if I might call to welcome them, and was received at a quarter to five. They had been there only an hour or two, but already the sitting room of their suite was like a luxurious disaster area, with the contents of luggage exploded over furniture and floor, as searches for immediate necessities had been conducted. Among these was a gift for me—that recording of the *Canticum Sacrum* and the Bach variations made in Paris which I have mentioned earlier in connection with the concerts in Houston. Also unpacked were several drawings of Stravinsky by Giacometti which in their string-like tangles of line, in what was obviously anguished effort to capture a likeness, seemed to me unsuccessful, though because of his eminence and personal appeal the artist's work was shown and handled with respect that afternoon. I could not but agree with Giacometti's own judgment, when in a film documentary showing Stravinsky sitting for him, he examined and condemned one of his own drawings. *C'est abominable,*' he cried. I was asked to remain for an early dinner downstairs *en famille*. Plans for the coming summer at Santa Fe were under discussion with Crosby. The Stravinskys and Craft expected to return to the opera, if dates and repertoire were satisfactorily worked out. We would all be joined together again there.

---

* *A Distant Trumpet* (New York, Farrar, Straus and Giroux, 1960; London, Macmillan, 1960). When on its publication I sent Stravinsky a copy, he wrote—red ink on his calling card—'Dearest Paul Horgan, so many thanks for your Trumpet, even for the distant one. Love IStr Hollywood May 7/60.'

Once home again in California, Stravinsky and Craft resumed work on their series of volumes and on 28 January, 1960, Craft sent me one of his highly organised postcards in writing so minute that he could deal with many matters in little space. 'A favour,' he wrote. 'You named vol. II—*Memories and Commentaries* . . . Would you think of a title for vol. III? It must be announced on the jacket of vol. II. It consists almost entirely of pieces like the *Sacre* piece, on Stravinsky's own music, but there are other sketches of people, and musical talk as well; also, a journal which is full of informal remarks of I.S.'s ("Taste is a moral category", etc.). Quite different from vol. 2, as 2 is from vol. I . . . The Stravinskys send their most affectionate greetings as do I.'

The matter of the title was a pleasing task, and I thought about it out loud one evening while dining with Donald Berke in New York. I had several notions for the solution, but none seemed much good. Finally, pressing towards a meaning the precise expression of which eluded me, I asked Berke, himself a musician,

'What is the terminology for that sequence in which a musical proposition is stated, and is followed by a factoring out of its given elements?'

'Yes,' he replied. 'Exposition and development.'

'That's it!'

'The title you are looking for,' he said, 'is *Expositions and Developments.*'

He was right. I immediately wrote to Craft suggesting the phrase, and he answered promptly (16 February, 1960):

'Your title is *exactly* what we need—the musical connection is a stroke of genius, and the idea that it is a *continuation* of something is conveyed also. But the actual substance of the book is precisely what your title says—the Maestro joins in sending you *mille grazie.*'

Now that the title was such a success, I did not feel I could accept thanks for it; and I wrote again, stating that I did not deserve the credit, and naming Berke as the one who did, describing how he had arrived at the proper phrase. I hoped that when the book came out he might have a copy inscribed by the authors with acknowledgment of his contribution to the volume. Craft (21 February, 1960):

'Of course I will get the maestro to inscribe a copy of the book to Don Berke as the onlie begetter of the title—do tell Don that we *are* grateful.' In the same postcard he added, 'Mr S. is in full swing on his new choral pieces, and he has also finished a *Gesualdo Monu-*

mentum—instrumentations and additions to several madrigals . . .'

Later, in August/September, there was a strenuous Latin-American tour in the course of which Stravinsky and Craft would conduct in the principal capitals of the Southern Hemisphere. Madame wrote me a postcard from Chile—'We miss you! Your company was always so necessary for us. Here we change every 5 days the city, the food, the orchestra, the friends, it is very fatiguing. With love . . .' The tour had a cumulatively disheartening effect on her husband, for the orchestras were not what he was used to, and towards the end of the tour, one concert was such a disaster in performance that, I was told later, he retired to his bed for twenty-four hours in mute reproof of the world.

In one of Craft's 1960 postcards, he had written, 'We are all more excited about Santa Fe this year than ever before.' At the moment, I did not know that I was to be alarmingly involved in the coming season of the Santa Fe Opera.

One day later in the winter I lunched with John O. Crosby at the University Club in New York. As chairman of the board of the Santa Fe Opera I had more than ordinary interest in his plans for each season, though I was necessarily careful not to intrude suggestions upon him, for I believed that board members should exert no effect on the artistic direction of the opera, and felt I should, despite my own experience in the opera theatre in a previous generation, set a proper example by listening to but never proposing ideas for repertoire, casting, and so forth, to the general director. Actually, I always felt I would have been more useful to him in some capacity related to the stage side of the footlights; and my natural interest lay far more with matters of production than with the administrative mechanics and fund raising of the board, where I had little of practical value to offer. But I believed so fully in Crosby's purposes and achievements that against my own sense of inadequacy I accepted re-election as chairman for many years, while the hard practical work of the board was carried on under more able presidents and other officers and members. Crosby, knowing my love of opera, often kept me informed of coming events in the company, and I was much enlivened at lunch that day to hear him say something like this:

'We are giving two Stravinsky works in the coming season

[1960]. A new production of *The Rake's Progress*, and a Santa Fe première of *Oedipus Rex* in a double bill with *Gianni Schicchi*. The Stravinskys and Craft are returning to us. Craft will conduct *The Rake*, of which the Maestro will supervise all full rehearsals, and he himself will conduct the *Oedipus*.'

'It sounds splendid.'

'I have a request to make of you,' said Crosby. In the preparatory months of wintertime, free of the hourly pressures and responsibilities of a summer opera season in progress, he was always outgiving, enthusiastic, full of optimistic charm. He now let this free in my direction, his eyes shining over the rims of his glasses, his fixed smile gleaming.

'Well,' I replied, 'if there is anything I can do for you, of course:'

'I want to cast you as the Narrator in *Oedipus Rex*.'

I was shocked into silence. My amazement delighted him. He had more for me.

'It seems particularly appropriate to everyone,' he continued. 'A literary man, an artist identified closely with Santa Fe, a professor used to lecturing—it all fits perfectly.'

'But I have not done anything in theatre in years and years.'

'But this is a non-dramatic role. And furthermore'—he paused and his persuasive appeal brightened even more—'Stravinsky himself asked for you especially, and I thought it such a good idea that I agreed to take it up with you. May we announce it with the rest of the cast?'

With the sensation of drowning slowly in glory, and filled with premonitory qualms, I heard myself accept the assignment. Two things about it, after all, gave me pleasure. The first was that Stravinsky had asked for me. The second was that by agreeing to do the role of the Narrator, I became, in however small a way, a member, instead of merely a spectator, of the Santa Fe company.

When the Stravinskys arrived in Santa Fe on 6 July, 1960, I was in Chicago to give a talk related to my 1960 novel. Two days later I was back in Santa Fe, and on Saturday afternoon, 9 July, the first orchestra rehearsal of *Oedipus Rex* with full cast was held at the opera theatre, with Stravinsky conducting. It was a typical July day for Santa Fe—far thunderheads, unremitting heat, light 'like a diamond', as the Spaniard said four centuries ago in New Mexico

—and the most terrifying honour of my life was about to descend upon me.

I had rehearsed the text with the stage director of the production, Hans Busch, and it was arranged that I appear from the wings for each of the Narrator's episodes, to stand at the side of the stage apron. I was not obliged to memorise the text, but devised for myself a quarto book with cardboard pages from which I could read the ominous information of the libretto 'after Sophocles'. The narrative passages were in English, while the text of the opera itself was in Latin. Stravinsky declared in a film interview that in *Oedipus Rex* he used a Latin text for the first time.

'I asked Cocteau for a very banal libretto,' he said, upon which Cocteau brought him in due course a libretto 'which was Wagnerian.'

'But,' ironically protested Stravinsky. 'I needed a libretto for *everyone*,' and sent Cocteau away to write another text. This was 'a little *less* Wagnerian', but still insufficiently so, and again Stravinsky rejected the poet's work.

'My dear,' said Cocteau as Stravinsky comedically quoted him, 'it is a pleasure to work with you—I will make another one.'

His third attempt was 'an Italian libretto', Stravinsky accepted it, and set to work. The original text in French would be translated into Latin for the musical fabric of the opera. The Narrator's passages remained in French—and later were given generally in the language of the country of production. My lines, accordingly, were in English, translated by e. e. cummings, and the Narrator was to deliver them, as the stage direction stated in the score, as though by 'a lecturer, in a detached voice'. I remembered Cocteau's shrill didactics in London, and, as rehearsed by Busch, I was prepared to speak without dramatic inflection of any sort.

I felt under-rehearsed—but worse: I was unconvinced by what I had to do. This is a poor situation for anyone caught in public performance. I reflected later upon an exchange between Stravinsky and Craft about the use of music and spoken text together. Craft asked for the composer's general view of this medium, and Stravinsky replied, 'Don't ask. Sins cannot be undone, only forgiven.' I don't think I went that far—but the more I played the Narrator in rehearsal and performance, the more I felt that in this particular work a spoken text was unnecessary; was a distraction from the magnificent musical scenes as they explicitly unfold in tragedy; and I concluded that the device of the narration was

attached to the libretto by Cocteau merely to provide himself with a public vehicle in the first performances with Stravinsky. General evidence suggests that Cocteau hoped all his life to be professionally within Stravinsky's inmost regard, but never quite was. Perhaps the *Oedipus Rex* narration would inextricably link them. But remembering the London performance, in which the speaker did little to cement relations with the composer, I thought that in the end Cocteau's device, touching in its hunger for association with the Maestro, was unavailing.

Still, when at rehearsal the moment came, and I had to step into view to open the work with the Narrator's first words, and saw Stravinsky, wearing his famous beret, a white shirt, a pair of reading glasses, and grey flannel slacks; and the full orchestra in the pit, and, on the stage, the chorus arrayed for its first tremendous utterance, I was almost muted by a sense of occasion. I managed to utter my first paragraph and retreat from sight with the first buccinal pronouncement, *double forte*, '*Kaedit* nos pestis*', to try to breathe down the beating of my heart.

On my cues, I returned to view, and Stravinsky had nothing to correct me for until the passage 'The assassin of the king is a king', the last four words of which, as we saw in London, must take on musical beat exactly consonant with what the orchestra does at that point. I read the line, 'like a lecturer', with ordinary emphasis, giving little value to the two connecting words, 'is a'.

'*No!*' cried Stravinsky in a powerful tone. 'Pol! Equal value: *kink is a kink! Hrá-rá-rá-rá!* Please: again.'

We repeated the passage. It was in the repetition that I learned my lesson, for he stopped the rehearsal and again, now with heavy emphasis, illustrated what must be; and on the third try I had it. We proceeded. My words and the four equally stressed eighth notes under them were in proper accord.

The first run-through ended with no more instructions for me until we were finished. An intermission was called and I came down to the theatre arena. There Madame met me, coming rapidly down the aisle, smiling seriously but kindly.

'No! Pol!' she said. 'You should be more *h'ham!*'

'Oh?'—and I cited the stage direction which I had been rehearsed to observe.

'No, it is all wrong. You will try.'

I thanked her, feeling more inadequate and unconvinced than

* So spelled in the full score.

ever about my whole share in the proceedings. I sought out my director, Busch, and repeated Madame's injunction, and asked when we could rehearse again in private, to achieve more dramatic expression. Understandably, he was furious. Who after all was directing the production? Why did everyone have an opinion? What were all previous rehearsals supposed to serve if everyone who came along had a different idea? There would be *no* change of style at this point. I was doing everything correctly. Let me continue to do so, composer's wife or no composer's wife. I was caught between two powers, and was more discontented than ever. My state of feeling must have registered in my performance; for with the exception of Madame, and one other, in the entire company and administration, no one ever in any way mentioned to me my participation in what was after all a great artistic enterprise, in which I was proud to be involved because of Stravinsky, though I wished I had had more help in realising my role more interestingly. I will cite the other exception presently, coming to a moment after the performances of that summer were over.

The next morning, Stravinsky and Craft met me at my request to discuss revisions I wanted to make in what I thought was an almost schoolboyish translation of the narration passages. They accepted my changes, improving several of them, and at the dress rehearsal the next evening, I felt somewhat better about what I had to declaim. I saw Madame in the theatre; and with her deeply in mind, I let myself respond more theatrically to the Narrator's lines, using more voice, ranging through more varied inflections; and at the end, she came to me and said,

'Pol! That was much better tonight!'

My discouraged awe was somewhat lightened by her approval, and when the opening night, Tuesday, 12 July, came, I was resigned to my work in greater composure. The company gathered backstage. That sense of ritual which descends upon a theatre company about to make its collective revelation of a work for the first time was heightened by the deep shade through which in the darkened open stage the singers went to their places, dimly perceived by the audience; and when I heard, backstage in my own shadows, the public-address speaker make the announcement, 'Mr Stravinsky to the pit, please', I shivered for the world sound of it, as well as the inexorability of the endurance immediately upon me. I knew when, climbing from under the stage and between the music stands of the pit, he came into view of the

audience, for the applause rolled over him like surf; and then the stage manager touched my shoulder, I stepped forth, 'my' spotlight came on, and we were ready to begin.

But not until a small ceremony was properly performed. Stravinsky looked up at me gravely. The whole significance of my publicly performing a work of his under his direction came freshly alive in me; and without having planned to do so, I bowed deeply to him before my first line; and from his lighted desk he bowed seriously to me in return. I then read my opening text, and on my last phrase his arms went up, and exactly as I finished, he proclaimed the first music.

The second and last performance of the work that season took place two nights later, during which a distant storm blew closer, yet without producing rain—only great rolls of thunder after godlike revelations in lightning. Donald and Patricia Anderson, from Roswell, were present, and assured me that the statements of the storm fell over the theatre at precisely the appropriate moments in the narrative passages to produce the most foreboding possible effect.

It was a work of such exalted intensity that the artists were all drained by it, not least the conductor. After the first performance I was witness to a heart-wrenching reduction and yet another of those reassemblies of self of which I had had glimpse after the cathedral performance of a year ago. But this time there was fullest revelation of what meagre, almost one would have thought what entirely insufficient, physical means were available to Stravinsky for the public acts of transcendent evocation he was capable of.

After the first *Oedipus Rex*, then, and the calls, the breathless descent backstage, the courteous gasps in bidding goodnight and making thanks to various artists, we hurried down the hill behind the stage to my car to go to the hotel where Stravinsky could refresh himself and change. Craft and Madame remained in the theatre for the other half of the double bill—*Gianni Schicchi*, with José Ferrer making his operatic debut in the title role. They would meet the Maestro later. I now went with him, and Hans Busch accompanied us, for he wanted to be helpful. Busch, a large blond man handsome in the heroic German style, was gentle despite his

size, and sensitive as the artist son of the eminent conductor Fritz Busch. We drove rapidly to the hotel, ascended to Stravinsky's room, and I saw that the *omne animal triste* was already upon him. 'Performance is always for me torture,' he declared in the film which Rolf Liebermann made about him; and a weighted silence held us all.

Once upstairs, in the mirrored lights of the bedroom, we saw how exhausted he was. As usual, cold sweat made him pale. He was breathing audibly. He was lost in a depth of spiritual discomfort no one else could measure. As if we were not there—Busch and I—Stravinsky began to undress, slowly, precisely. No outbreak; only misery and exhaustion. He laid off the tailcoat, the tie, waistcoat, shirt; and with tactful kindness, Busch received each of these articles in an entirely impersonal manner while I stood by, feeling I should not be witnessing so intimate a toilette, wishing I could be of help, yet incapable of making a single move, even of departure. Busch steadied him while he stepped from his trousers. Busch handed him a towel and Stravinsky slowly and absently rubbed himself dry. And then I could not believe what I gradually saw.

His body was so ravaged by ailments and age, so bandaged for the 'ernia, so like the tiny, vulnerable body of a hurt and splintered bird, his arms were so small, the bones of his shoulders and the small arch of his chest so meagre, that I almost expected to see the heartbeat through his skin and its pathetic garment—a knee-length silk singlet with a ribbed pattern running vertically and covering his undertrunks, yet revealing contour—protuberance or cavity—beneath. Divesting was in this case like the removal of ritual garments after a rite. Can I make anyone see the pathos and courage of that combination of the most frail and barely fleshed bone with the abstract wonder of spirit and mighty strength which it housed and could summon into effect when work was to be served? Seeing him exposed in the poorest stuff of physical life, I could only bitterly bow my head before the old truth in all its ragged glory which said that the spirit of man was unconquerable so long as breath was left to him.

With the most careful modesty he turned away from us as he had to lift his singlet and open his trunks to reset the dreadful truss. This retained the fabric of his intestine which would otherwise escape from the abdominal wall; but in his preoccupation he innocently forgot that he was facing a long mirror where helplessly

and in fascination one could see exposures of apparatus which he so delicately hid from view. His thick hands worked at straps and buckles, equators of elastic, and pads for retention; and then he drew the trunks together and the singlet down and eased a breath of relief. I was aware that he must, then, have scarcely a single moment of physical comfort, even in his moments of most contagious sociability and charm.

Then for the first time he acknowledged our presence, though to be sure he had not missed any implication of our being there; and by small degrees, his energy began to return. It was as if his psyche with all its awareness had shifted back to this world of other beings from another where he lived alone. He opened chests of drawers, selected a shirt, he chose a dark suit from a closet, took up and critically compared two bow ties, pointed to a pair of suède shoes which Busch bent to bring him; and, item by item, the tiny, crackable, twig-made figure began to disappear under the smartness of each added garment; and as this happened, the inner mood began to change its shape also, and looking at himself in the glass, he fastidiously brushed his hair straight back in his lifelong habit, he judged his countenance at various angles, and saw how it became its famous best in distinction and expressivity; and when he tied his tie it was with a flair worthy of a Regency beau. He stepped into his shoes and Busch to spare him knelt to tie the laces. Stravinsky thanked him with a touch on the shoulder. He assumed his jacket, set a silk kerchief in his breast pocket, and then turned, and with a sort of rationed smile, made a quick little bow, accompanied by a swift in-drawn/out-blown breath, and, armoured by chic and restored good spirits, he looked all of a sudden astonishingly fit and ready for anything.

With a grainy little laugh he said, like an officer and a prince,

'Gentlemen, it is just time for a small glass of Scotch,' and forthwith produced Chivas Regal. In bathroom glasses we silently toasted each other; he took up his stick, smoothed his hair once more before the mirror, and we went off downstairs like three tomcats on hind legs setting out for the evening.

Who could forbear?

After the last *Oedipus Rex* performance of the season, I brought him my score with a request that he merely sign it. Knowing

better than anyone how inadequate my narration had been, I hoped to spare him any comment.

'Please do not bother with a sentiment,' I said. 'But I would much love to have your name in my score.'

He took it and wrote (the other exception):

'To the very dear Paul Horgan/my very sincere thanks for his/ wonderful narration in our Santa Fe performance of Oedipus Rex/Cordially/Igor Stravinsky/Santa Fe/July/1960.'

On the following Sunday evening—17 July, 1960—the second of the annual cathedral concerts was given. The programme read:

THE SANTA FE OPERA
presents

A SPECIAL CONCERT

under the patronage of
HIS EXCELLENCY THE MOST REVEREND
EDWIN VINCENT BYRNE, D.D.
ARCHBISHOP OF SANTA FE

Symphony Number 38 in D Major (Prague)
WOLFGANG AMADEUS MOZART
Symphonie Concertante Opus 84   JOSEPH HAYDN
Conductor: ROBERT CRAFT
Symphony of Psalms   IGOR STRAVINSKY

CONDUCTED BY THE COMPOSER
THE SANTA FE OPERA ORCHESTRA AND CHORUS

The audience is asked to withhold applause
Ladies are asked to wear head coverings

THE CATHEDRAL OF SAINT FRANCIS   JULY 17, 1960
SANTA FE, NEW MEXICO   8:15 P.M.

Again I brought Stravinsky to the sacristy where a discarded episcopal throne stood in mid-floor. There he sat in his concert clothes reading the scores of the *Prague Symphony* and the Haydn *Symphonie Concertante*, and conducting each work with reduced but expressive movements, while Craft, in the sanctuary with the orchestra, admirably led the actual concert for the full audience.

I watched the pages over Stravinsky's shoulders. With the smallest flexings of knuckles, shoulder hunchings, inhalations on certain accents, finger pointings to an imaginary orchestra seating ranged before him, Stravinsky 'gave' the music for himself—and incidentally for me; and I was confirmed in what I had long believed, that the conductor's plastic expression of the music was an excellent way even for the amateur listener to discern its fabric and eventually perhaps to come to a realisation of its greater form; and for a lifetime this had been my justification for beating the measures while reading scores in listening privately to recordings.

The orchestral tone under Craft's precise musical justice was enriched by the acoustic of the vaultings and the sense of removal we felt in the vestry; and I recalled with satisfaction the experience of the rehearsals I had attended during the week, when the old church of my long-gone historical friend Lamy served so new and unexpected a purpose. There was always a scattering of a few people for the rehearsal sessions. I listened from many different positions—the choir loft, with its old French organ, the transepts, the side aisles; and there always seemed a particular pleasure for Stravinsky in working in a holy edifice. He was as ever entirely given to technical work—his sleeves half-rolled back, his collar open, his flannel slacks a trifle drooped, his voice vigorous and sure in his vocalised illustrations to the players, and his mood full of paternal gaiety, so that the young musicians had many an occasion to laugh at his original turns of wit as he gave instructions.

Again I had noticed how as he moved about the cathedral during rehearsal breaks he always half-genuflected and crossed himself when he passed a side altar, or the large crucifix at the chancel rail, or the high altar, where during rehearsal and concert the Blessed Sacrament was removed and the tabernacle door left open. His respect and decorum for the outward symbols of faith were unselfconscious, humble, and sincere. 'What exquisite spiritual manners,' I said to myself as I observed all this, for of course his Russian Orthodox faith did not receive correspondent recognition in the theological conventions of the Roman Catholic Church—an always odd circumstance in my eyes, since the Roman rite permitted inter-communion with the Greek Orthodox Church, which in turn gave the same ecumenical honour to the Russian Orthodox: a curious metaphysical disavowal of that piece of learning retained from cadet days which stated that things equal to the same thing are equal to each other.

Meanwhile, the wonderful variations stated in the solo violin of the Haydn went forward, there, out of sight in front of the high altar; and Stravinsky brought the work to a fine conclusion in his pantomime performance of the work. The intermission came, a soft murmur rose from the standing audience, and very soon it seemed the orchestra and chorus were filing back to their places for the last half of the concert.

Presently the full apparatus was ready; the opera's stage manager came into view from the narrow passage leading from the sacristy to the volume of the cathedral along which the celebrant always went out to say Mass, gave a signal, and I helped Stravinsky out of his throne and walked with him to the entryway.

At a certain point he disengaged himself from me: he did not want to be seen receiving aid from anyone as he came into public view. I halted and watched him go slowly but smartly forward. In the wall of the passageway at elbow height in a position to accommodate the priest just before he entered into the sanctuary for Mass was inset a stoup for holy water. It caught Stravinsky's eye. He paused briefly and dipped his fingers into it. It seemed to me the ultimate gesture of religious tact, that in a Roman cathedral, and just before entering upon a complicated and exhausting performance, he should reach to bless himself, and I thought of devout bullfighters making the sign of the cross asking God's protection before courting danger. But Stravinsky could never be counted on to do the expected thing. He deeply wet his fingers in the holy water and just before coming into view of the expectant performers and listeners, he smoothed his hair with it.

In a moment, after a held hush, '*Exaudi* . . .'

The Stravinskys and Craft wanted to see more of the extraordinary country around Santa Fe but the schedule of rehearsals for *Oedipus Rex*, the cathedral, and the forthcoming new production of *The Rake's Progress* was confining. But at last, on the day after the *Symphony of Psalms* concert in the cathedral—Monday, 18 July, 1960—an open day arrived; and they were all able to go with me for a picnic to the cliff dwelling and pueblo ruins of El Rito de los Frijoles, in the Bandelier National Monument—a remnant of pre-Spanish history in New Mexico which never failed to move me with its evidences of early sedentary Indian life. These remained

so strong that yielding to the smallest impulse of imagination I could feel there like a revenant in an act of return after long absence—seven centuries, more or less—to a place which still spoke of daily life with its modest hungers and also of time-lost mystery. I tried to convey something of this to the picnickers—there would be only the four of us—and we set out with hampers of food and wine in my car at mid-morning.

We rose to the pink desert and crossed the Rio Grande, winding our way through the huge accidental elegances of the flesh-coloured sandstone erosions in all their formal variety which suggested sculpture and architecture. It was a fine high blue day, with far continents of horizon clouds (seeing these the modern pueblo elders would say to their children, 'See, your grandfathers are coming'). The sunlight in its brilliance looked to be somewhere between the colours of pale topaz and diamond.

Coming to the canyon we went idling along the trails leading to the excavated ruins of houses and *kiva* on the valley floor, where the thin little stream of El Rito de los Frijoles took its ancient way, and we paused frequently to gaze up at the dwelling combs hollowed out before the thirteenth century in the soft pale lime-stone. Craft climbed to the high levels and made his way in and out of several of the chambers empty in their millennial quiet. Nobody said much—the place completed our thoughts. There had been organised life there all that time ago, and it was gone, and the green of the valley floor simply proved once again the power of seeds, the detritus of the cliffs attested to the work of water and wind, and mounds covering still-buried chambers had through time taken on the inscrutable eloquence of natural earth forms. It was enough that it had lain in my power to make the gift of this place to the Stravinskys and Craft; and presently we went to a delicious little grove of tall cottonwoods which made a shifting mosaic of shade over some weathered tables and benches set out for picnickers. There in great content we opened our hampers and our bottles.

Madame and I faced Stravinsky and Craft across the table. We toasted everyone with our paper cups, out of which a chilled Portuguese rosé poured with some extra good flavour drawn from the air, the isolation—there was nobody anywhere near us—and the simplicity of the whole thing. It was a piercing event when for four or five minutes a sudden spare shower came down on us through the unclouded sunlight—tiny, ice-cold needles of rain

struck our warm faces and hands, there was just enough moisture to release an extra pungency from the thick sweetness of the cottonwood leaves, the day's heat was briefly suspended, and before there was any thought of going to the car for raincoats, the shower was over, and the picnic continued with carefreeness. Stravinsky seemed years younger. Madame was a source of peace. How restorative the country, and how blissful to be out of reach of affairs. I thought of picnics in Russian literature—Turgenev— and how simply the truly civilised took to the unspoiled natural.

—Stravinsky's face opposite me suddenly assumed a paralysed astonishment, and lifting his hand as little as possible for fear of inviting a wrong response pointed past me and Madame to something behind our backs. I could not tell whether he was in extremities of fear or of delight. He conveyed the necessity of absolute stillness as he stared fixedly into the near distance behind us. Good God, I thought, what of the several possibilities could he be staring at—a rattlesnake? a deer drawn by the scent of food? a bear? Madame said something to him in a low voice, in Russian. He did not answer. His pointing hand began to tremble, he dramatised a stupendous event. I began making wildly conjectural plans to deal with whatever crisis menaced us from behind. As slowly as I could in order not to excite whatever creature or condition he saw, I turned. In a small pool of dappled sunlight seated on his haunches, and inquiring of us with his nose what we might have to offer, was a red squirrel.

Returning to Santa Fe in the heated afternoon we felt drowsy with the virtue of a day in the open. Stravinsky was not talkative. I drove with extra caution, against my need of a nap. Content was upon us all, and I reflected on the fond habitude which marked the relations of Stravinsky, Madame, and Craft.

They were like any family. I had seen them humorously conspiratorial and private amid crowds, and occasionally irritable and out of sorts with each other in intimate moments of no importance, and I had pondered on the difficulties innate in Craft's position in that particular altitude of intellectual and artistic fame. Many persons older and longer intimate with the Stravinskys than himself made spiteful remarks about Craft, attributable to envy of the brilliant young man whose love and conviction concerning

Stravinsky had created the intimacy so resented by older, now outer, circles. Sometimes I had thought Craft almost indifferent to Stravinsky's comfort—small occasions when his help in the mechanics of an old man's getting through his non-artistic tasks might have meant much. In his energy of mind and person, Craft seemed at times unaware of the needs of the Maestro and Madame. I wondered if they were at moments hurt by him—he could be short with them in the presence of others. But the more I thought about it the more I saw what I was certain was a necessity—and that was, his preservation of his absolute independence lest he be overwhelmed by the position of a sort of highly special domestic. It was vital that he preserve his stance as the intellectual and musical complement to the Stravinsky ménage; and of his love they could in any case have no doubt. Moreover, I believe he thought it healthful for Stravinsky not to slide imperceptibly into undue dependence on him as upon a doer of errands and services through which by performing them himself Stravinsky would hold on longer to his timeless vitality. This, while it was not that of youth, was certainly not even becomingly close to the passive resignation which was expected of seventy-six-year-old men. No, Craft was obliged to remain himself, and let his unqualified devotion to the Stravinskys as persons and artists be taken for granted. They themselves took it so, I was sure. As for respect, he always addressed the Maestro as 'Mr Stravinsky' and Madame as 'Gnädige Frau'.

Driving back to Santa Fe I glanced into the rear-view mirror at one point. It gave full view of Madame and Craft. She was gazing out of the car window at the magnificent landscape with that concentration of an artist studying colour and form, her eyes half-closed the better to see her own vision as well as its actual object; and beside her, with his head on her shoulder, was Craft, asleep, filially reliant, and thoughtlessly accepted.

Working towards the new production of *The Rake's Progress* of 23 July, 1960, the company rehearsed by day in the various mock-up stages of the opera establishment, and by night on the main stage for scenery and lighting, and finally for the first full-ensemble rehearsal. It was a considerable part of Crosby's genius as administrator of the opera that he was able to provide more rehearsal

time than was available in any other opera house; and the schedules were as cunningly fitted as the parts of a Chinese puzzle box. Supreme professional, Stravinsky attended every full rehearsal for *The Rake's Progress*, which Craft conducted. No doubt they had conferred beforehand about details of performance, for I never saw Stravinsky halt him to give instructions. He was content to let the score unroll entirely under Craft's direction, while he himself sat at an end seat of a row down front with a music rack and his own score, under a patio parasol during the blazing days, and at night, with a music-stand light on his open pages. He conducted the rehearsal in a shadow performance of his own, vigorously, cueing every entrance, vocal or instrumental, and indicating dynamics by the degree of energy of his precise beat. Turning pages, he would lick his thumb and forefinger as usual, and from a few rows away one could hear his expressive inflection of breath to convey musical accent.

The cast was in general good, with notable characterisations, physical and vocal, by Loren Driscoll as Tom Rakewell and John Reardon as Nick Shadow. Again the orchestral writing, like Verdi's, was of the essence of theatre; projection of individual character in colour of instrumentation and style of melody. On first hearing Ann's exuberant soprano aria closing act one, 'I go, I go to him', I was as taken by it at the rehearsal as by a whirlwind, and I felt just as I had the first time I heard Leonora's *scena* '*Komm, O Hoffnung*' in *Fidelio*; and when the rehearsal reached the scene in Bedlam, the tender pathos of the flutes with their unearthly statement of lost folly, madness, and the sweetness of aberrant illusion made me marvel all over again at the breadth of Stravinsky's humanity, while competent musicians must have been marvelling at how he achieved effects both deeply emotive and technically severe.

At rehearsal one calm but chilly night, Stravinsky sat well-wrapped in scarf and topcoat, with a couple of his miniature Chivas Regal bottles at the ready against cold. His hand moving in his music light cast shadows on the far wing of the wooden stage frame. All was going beautifully, with hardly a pause by Craft to suggest a correction, when suddenly, sweeping across great distances, bringing dust, a powerful wind struck through the stage and the arena, and score pages began flipping. Here and there a violin bow was pressed down to the parts on the racks to hold the pages, and where a note or two was missed Craft sang out for it

and continued the rehearsal without pause. Stravinsky, beating away, giving cues, and establishing his own performance with one hand, held his score flat with the other. The wind was just passing through, but it lasted long enough to become a nuisance; and its final gust was so powerful that it called forth another tempest almost equally strong; for it ripped across Stravinsky's music stand at a moment when both his hands were in the air, and his pages were ruffled wildly back and forth. He lost his continuity. In his place at the end seat of the third row his own storm blew up —one natural force reacting in opposition to another. With the effect of a localised whirlwind, he stood up, shouted an execration in French or Russian, knocked his music stand over, the music light went out, he made shaking gestures and stamped his foot at the caprice of the wind, which having wrought its most perverse damage now subsided, as if in answer to his rage, but too late.

The rehearsal continued without break, for the players and singers looked only at Craft. Members of the theatre crew came running on their sneakers, set the Maestro's stand upright again, picked up his score, found the place for him, re-rigged his light connection, indicated that all was ready again, and were rewarded with a courteous bow. Once again he returned to his guardian performance of his work.

This opera now entered the history of the Santa Fe Opera as a repertory piece. Until Ingmar Bergman's production in Stockholm, the Santa Fe Opera remained the only house in the world where this masterwork of the twentieth-century lyric theatre was a regularly revived opera. It was interesting that Crosby's love for the work, which identified the company in its first season as an organisation as much committed to contemporary operatic works as to those of the past (many of them relatively unknown), began to bear fruit with the second production in terms of bringing audiences also to love the work. In the first season, the house for *The Rake's Progress* was perhaps sixty per cent sold. This second production would draw houses of perhaps eighty per cent. In its next presentation in 1962, the attendance was close to ninety per cent, and in the performances of 1966 and 1970, the work played to sold-out houses. Crosby's artistic vision and tenacity in honour of music he believed in contained a lesson on how to create the audience which great modern works deserved. I was told that Stravinsky was greatly moved by the Stockholm realisation of his opera; but before he saw Bergman's production, which I under-

stand was extraordinarily inspired, I heard him say that the later Santa Fe production of *The Rake's Progress* was the finest he knew.

For the opening performance of 23 July, Stravinsky, Madame, one or two others, and myself, sat together in the first row; and at the end of the opera, the house arose, Crosby came down the aisle and brought the Maestro to stand, a spotlight came on, and Stravinsky acknowledged the applause of cast, orchestra, and audience with his widest of smiles, in which he conveyed personal pleasure combined with a sense of high fellowship, which reached the individual member of the audience as if intended for him alone. It was an illustration of the power of his personality to transcend the impersonal. It was a revelation of the deep intuitive humanity ordinarily hidden within his formal and courtly manner.

Which is not to say that he was in private invariably amenable to even the most well-meant approaches.

For one day I had arranged a luncheon party, at the request of one of the schoolmistresses who acted in the name of social amenity. It seems that a member of the company who had a certain reputation as a considerable performer had complained that not yet, all season, had he met Stravinsky, and I was pressed to remedy what the lady of thoughtful manners regarded as a gross discourtesy. Innocently, I agreed, invited the neglected artist, and sent word to the Stravinskys asking if they would join me to meet another guest at lunch. When soon after receiving my message they were going with me to tea at Bynner's, Stravinsky, ascending Bynner's Chinese garden stairs with the aid of my arm, halted and said to me,

'What is this lunch party? Who is to be there?'

I had not named the guest whose feelings were to be soothed, and I now told who he was. Stravinsky with a tug at my arm resumed his ascent, always advancing only his right foot on each step, and said, with finality,

'I am not interested.'

No more social Samaritanism.

Stravinsky at meals was rarely interested in small-talk (*'ba-var-dage'*)

but rather in extended unravellings of ideas large enough to sustain thought, or else in epigrammatic opinions the more outrageous the better. Most of such came from him, and some of the best were jet-assisted by potions of Scotch whisky. At times the 'mood' was one of withdrawal.

I remember one very quiet Sunday evening supper when Madame and Craft and I sat alone with Stravinsky in the almost empty main dining room of La Fonda. Fred Harvey's most refined amber lanterns cast a depressing falsely Spanish dimness over all, and we were all in a quiet mood. I think it was the night following the first performance of the revival of *The Rake's Progress*. The conversation had no sequential line, there was an air of companionable fatigue about us, and I think we all felt a little nonsensical and perverse.

Early in the meal, which began with clandestine bolts of Scotch poured from miniature bottles—it being a New Mexico Sunday—Craft said without preliminary reference,

'Some day I simply have to conduct Wagner.' He grinned provocatively and his upper body, his hands, made an inadvertent nervous twitch such as often accompanied his talk. '*He's so awful!*' —this in a voice of exaggerated comic horror which did not entirely wash out the basic seriousness of his intention. Craft could produce a remarkable bronchial laugh, not merely an ordinary wheeze, but a faint chord of distinct notes which had an effect both harmonic and hilarious. I now heard it, and as always, it made me laugh also.

Stravinsky, whose views on Wagner were world-known, did not look at him; but his shoulders sagged, his head slumped between them, his chin almost reached his knuckles where his hands held his stick. His discouragement at the announcement was too great for anger. Craft continued in gleeful mischief somewhat in this vein:

'All that vaporising, and those aching tumescences prolonged as in *karezza*. Those literary references in the system of the *leitmotiv*, until we long for someone to arrive without his little name-card.'

Stravinsky seemed to sink physically lower and lower. He took refuge in more Scotch. I recalled, if he did not, the remark in the *Poetics: 'Le perpetuel devenir d'une musique qui n'avait aucun motif de commencer, comme elle n'a aucune raison de finir.'* Craft was mischievously absorbed in his profane project. Madame looked at me with a calmly patient smile, as if such a momentary tension between the two musicians were familiar, meaningless, and beyond her concern.

'I suppose every conductor,' said Craft, 'has now and then a glorious dream of unrestrained vulgarity in terms of sheer volume of noise. Wagner would be ideal for this. He's really so dreadful. I *must* conduct him.'

Craft's comic disclaimers—the modern chic of pretending to adore what is actually tasteless in the extreme, like the vogue for *kitsch* or camp or such objects as Tiffany lamps and beaded portières—did nothing to exculpate him in Stravinsky's increasingly depressed state and when the subject died away for lack of challenge, the rest of the supper consisted of desultory remarks by Stravinsky, many of which he did not mean but which ironically he uttered to irritate his own mood further.

His glasses kept sliding down his nose—this despite the rubber stoppers someone had told him to buy, and which he had found, I think, at Woolworth's. These were intended to fit on the side-bars of the spectacles behind each ear and prevent slippage. I remember how courteously grateful Stravinsky was when these were suggested to him by someone at the opera theatre. Now he wore them —but they were, contrary to instruction, affixed to his frames *in front* of the ears, so that their purpose was lost, and the glasses kept sliding, though he seemed content to slide them back, feeling that the problem had largely been solved by the mere addition of the rubber stops any which way.

Bending over his glass, he declared crossly in a husky sibilance, 'You want to say son of a bitch, *c'est à dire* son of Monteaux.'

Later, there was talk that Craft might conduct *Carmen* for the Santa Fe Opera.

'A most inferior work,' said Stravinsky, 'the summit of banality,' not looking at any of us.

The name of Benjamin Britten was mentioned.

'A ve-ry good accompanist.'

Madame mildly commented,

'Or you say something nice about someone so famous, Britten, Monteux, who is a friend, or you do not say anything.'

A silent, sardonic, forward inclination of the body, replied to this.

Soon,

'Now we must go,' said Madame. 'We must pack.' She sighed strenuously. 'We must pack for Europe, for here, for there, for New York, *c'est toujours ce va et vient.*'

For they were departing from Santa Fe the next day.

I saw them next when they returned to New York at eight in the morning on 7 December, on board the *S.S. Rotterdam*. At my suggestion they were coming to stay at the St Regis, where I was at the moment. They disembarked early, before all other passengers, with special escorts and waivers of the customs apparatus, and in a cavalcade of limousines, for there were many others to meet them at the pier, went rapidly across town to the hotel. The next engagement was in Washington in late December to prepare and conduct a production of *Le Rossignol*, which I planned to attend.

Meanwhile, in the same New York hotel, we met frequently, most often for quiet lunches together. A frequent resident of the hotel was, despite notoriety, now so familiar that the sight of him and his wife no longer caused heads to turn. This was Salvador Dali, whom the Stravinskys had known for years. One day as we found each other for lunch in the Oak Room, Stravinsky was thick-voiced in his greeting, given with a broad smile, which forecast something droll to come. As we were seated, he said,

'Vawnderful encounter just now upstairs with Dali,' and went on to say that the Dali apartment was in the same corridor as that of the Stravinskys. Evidently Dali was aware of this, for as they came along the corridor to descend for lunch, he was standing in ambush in his open door. As they approached, he stepped forth holding a little silver bell.

'It was the little bell carried before the priest when he goes through the street to bring the viaticum to a dying person,' said Stravinsky.

He paused and greeted Dali, who replied, '*Bonjour*, Igor, *bonjour*, Madame,' and then stood waiting.

'He was waiting for his moustaches to be noticed,' said Stravinsky—for it was in the period when Dali wore waxed spikes of moustache which reached to the corners of his eyes. 'But I said nothing, and Vera said nothing, we smiled *très doucement*, and started to go by.'

At that Dali rang his little silver bell.

'What is your little silver bell doing there?' asked Stravinsky.

'I carry it and I ring it,' replied Dali, and Stravinsky imitated him, 'so people will see my moustaches.'

The whole ridiculousness of conscious eccentricity was distilled into Stravinsky's report of the episode, and led to the reflection that Stravinsky had never, so far as I knew, in life or work, needed or desired to make an effect, or a 'scandal', for its own sake.

The Washington Opera company's *Rossignol* which Stravinsky conducted was despite a disagreeable auditorium a beautiful achievement. It was paired with *Oedipus Rex*, which had one unlucky aspect. This was that the Narrator was seated on a bar stool at the right of the stage, giving the effect of a night-club comedian in a dinner jacket, with his feet cocked informally on the rungs of the stool. Still, it seemed to me more or less what Cocteau, though not Stravinsky, deserved. It was a strenuous weekend—the works were given Friday and Saturday evenings and were recorded during the day Saturday and Sunday. I did not attend the recording session, but waited for the Stravinskys and Craft to return on Sunday to the quiet old hotel where they had been put up by the Washington Opera company.

They came late—the recording had run overtime. They were thirsty and hungry, looking forward to a satisfying lunch, with many restoratives, until their train for New York was to leave at three-thirty. But nobody had reckoned with the habits of Sunday in the national capital. The dining room was closed at two o'clock. The bar was not open on Sunday, liquor was never served on that day, room service was unavailable, and there was no time now to proceed to another restaurant even for food. As for drink, nobody had thought to provide any.

Stravinsky was exhausted and for the outburst of justified fury that followed he had once again to draw on the adrenalin which had served him through the recording. He was wrapped in his great fur coat, for he was sweating still from the exertions in the recording studio. No attaché of the opera or the recording unit was with him to see to his needs or comforts. His face, when he was told that he could have not even a bottle of Coca-Cola to assuage his thickened thirst, seemed positively enlarged with incredulous rage. He threw his hat away and shouted in the lobby of the hotel,

'*Ça m'emmerde!* It is not to be believed! What is this country! I am dyink from here'—he smote his belly—'and here'—he clutched his throat which still had a rehearsal towel wrapped around it—'and I can have nothink!'

Madame went upstairs to see that all the luggage was brought down. I had a car waiting. Stravinsky sat in the lobby in such a magnificent field of outrage that nothing could be said to him. There was an effect of people tiptoeing. Presently the car was loaded, we went to the station, and to the train, and into the

drawing room reserved for them. I went forward to the dining car to ask about food: drink I knew was out of the question. But the dining car was not yet ready, the train had time to wait before pulling out, and all I could do was bring a steward with a tray of ice and many bottles of ginger ale. Stravinsky greeted these as if they were to save his life, and actually I had been alarmed at his pallor, his rapid breathing, his parched lips and tongue.

'Oh my God,' he exclaimed, as he watched the Negro steward open and pour the foaming drink over ice, and called him 'my de-ar', and then pulled me to him and with his cold perspiration touching my face kissed me and thanked me before taking his first draught of the life-saving and soapy-tasting liquid.

So he entered 1961, for it was New Year's Day, which meant for him, for Madame, and Craft, only another day, and year, for work.

They arrived in Santa Fe on 2 July to prepare one of the opera's most superb events. This was a double bill consisting of a repetition of the *Oedipus Rex*, though with new costumes and set, and *Perséphone*, with costumes after designs by Madame and executed by Karinska, with whom she had worked as a designer in the Diaghilev company. The production of *Perséphone* was made particularly distinguished by the casting of Vera Zorina in the title role. She had previously recorded the work with Stravinsky, and in many performances with symphonic orchestras about the world had in a sense made the role her own. She was in residence in Santa Fe with her two young sons, and her reunion with the Stravinskys was that of a close friend.

Her engagement for the role of the goddess of the spring whose fate takes her to the world of shadows in Pluto's kingdom (the text of André Gide was given in the original French) was suggested by Stravinsky himself; and in later years she was to perform the work twice more with the company. Her exquisite beauty of person, her mastery of balletic movement, that magnetism of presence which reached an entire audience through her most simple glance, were supported by speech as lyrically lovely as any goddess need call forth. As with both Stravinskys, her artistic achievements rested on more than professional talent—it was a marvellously knowledgeable intelligence which gave inner light to her stage apparitions, which was, of course, an extremely rare

attribute among theatre artists, who mostly relied on acquired technique. It was this quality, for example, which Maurice Baring found so strong in Sarah Bernhardt, and which made that actress so fascinating a companion away from the theatre. As this held true for Zorina, she and the Stravinskys took particular joy in each other's company. When I met her through them, I also felt her spell, and when, from time to time, her husband Goddard Lieberson came to Santa Fe to join her and their sons, another dimension of brilliance, wit, and style was added to what seemed to me a charmed circle.

That summer Craft conducted *Oedipus Rex*, while Stravinsky reserved *Perséphone* for himself. I was again cast as the Narrator in the first work, which freed me to sit in the theatre after the intermission to see *Perséphone*. Two performances of the double bill were given—12 and 14 July. Everything worked to make them memorable, even the lightly playing air of the night, which floated the costumes of Perséphone and her maidens in folds and lifts which seemed to animate classical marble. Zorina created a formal suite of motion, not strictly dance, yet certainly aside from ordinary movement in walk or gesture, which was the essence of ideal antiquity as evoked by myth and sculpture. When she spoke the text in French as caressing as the entire gesture of her presence, we were taken to realms of spirit so true to the marvellous score that after the first performance, as I drove away from the theatre with him, Stravinsky said to me, using the personal name by which close friends knew Zorina, 'Brigitta is a great artist, but she does not "know" it!'

His inflection spoke volumes about the purity and penetration of her high sort of professionalism, about which there was nothing of prideful determination to make 'effects', but rather a combination of humility and penetration which seemed selfless. He also said in one of his interviews that he had never seen his ideal of Perséphone until her performance of the part.

Earlier in the year Crosby had conceived a plan which was appropriate and yet ambitious for a company so young as the Santa Fe Opera. This was to take representative productions of the current season to Europe on a tour to be sponsored by the State Department. During the winter he asked me to go to Washington with him to discuss the idea with the Assistant Secretary of State for cultural affairs. At a conference in Foggy Bottom, it was rapidly decided to take two evenings of opera in response to consultations

with the Embassy in Berlin—*The Ballad of Baby Doe*, by Douglas Moore, which the Ambassador thought would serve as an exhibit of United States subject matter, and the double bill of *Oedipus Rex* and *Perséphone*, provided Stravinsky would conduct *Perséphone* and Zorina would appear, while Craft would conduct the *Oedipus*. Crosby had already obtained the agreement of these members to tour with the five-year-old company. Dates were discussed and tentatively fixed. The Assistant Secretary was gratified at the lustre of the artists offered by the company, though he winced at the size of the casts and orchestra required, for his budget was as always under a strain. But he bore up well, and Crosby and I managed to contain our satisfaction at having the Santa Fe company presented abroad as the first opera company to be sponsored under the cultural exchange programme. We could have gone on with a few more luxuriating details of plans, but the Assistant Secretary, hand to forehead in Washington's symbolic gesture of sacrifice to incessant public service, said he must beg to be excused, his schedule was appalling, and he must now go to the lobby to see the Harlem Globetrotters off to Finland under his current programme of cultural exchange.

So it was that during the summer season the company was able to know the excitement of a forthcoming European tour to West Germany, and also Yugoslavia, which had been added to the original schedule. The casts of the works designated for the tour, which would follow immediately upon the close of the Santa Fe season, worked to perfect their performances. They were conscious of an honour bestowed. They enjoyed the breadth of idea in performing internationally. They were elated to belong to a troupe which included Stravinsky and Zorina. They asked each other how it felt to be going, and said it felt wonderful. I felt a mixture of the same elation and certain qualms about performing the Narrator abroad. But a fine undertone of adventure gave zest to the artists of the chosen works, and despite my dislike of flying—the company would go by chartered plane all together, except for the Stravinskys and Craft who had earlier commitments in Europe and would meet us in Berlin—I shared in the excitement.

My share soon turned to an objective one, however; for as the season advanced, everyone in the cast came to know, except myself, that I was not to be included in the tour. When I made reference to 'our' forthcoming adventure, colleagues changed the subject out of dismay that I had not been informed of the decision to cast

Stravinsky rehearsing the Santa Fe Opera orchestra in St Francis
Cathedral, Santa Fe, 1960 *Photos by Tony Perry*

Vera Zorina (*centre*) as Perséphone, Santa Fe Opera, 1961

a German actor for the Narrator in Berlin, and a Yugoslav for Belgrade. It was later made clear that the Department of State requested the general director, John Crosby, to utilise as the Narrator someone in the language of the country of performance; but I thought of other reasons for the change, and could not help but reflect that Germans and Yugoslavs, if they would not understand the Narrator in English, would no more understand the text of *Baby Doe* in English or of *Oedipus* in Latin. It was a disappointment of a minor sort, but I could honestly concede the justice of the decision, since the company must present its best talent in its first tour. Like much done in the name of good judgment, the decision had its ironic results, for the German actor was said to be unsatisfactory in performance, and a Yugoslav actor was unavailable, so that the Narrator was performed in Belgrade by the company's general director—in English.

During the hot Santa Fe summer days Madame would shop here and there while her husband and Craft were at work in the theatre or at other tasks—it was during that summer that Stravinsky was proceeding with the composition of *Noah and the Flood*. She would pause to rest in the shade of the great trees in the patio of Eleanor Bedell's shop on Palace Avenue, and there one day a friend of Miss Bedell's was introduced to her. He was in Santa Fe on vacation from his work with the Oxford University Press, and had come to town, where he had never been before, because of the presence of the Stravinskys. Like me, he had during his whole youth—he was still a young man—been devoted to Stravinsky and his work, collecting every recording of his, and works written about him in many languages. He wanted to see him as he conducted at the opera theatre.

'I am so tired,' said Madame, 'and I have so much shopping to do.'

Miss Bedell motioned towards the young man—his name was E. J. Allen—and asked why he might not take her car and drive Madame on her errands.

'That would be nice,' said Madame.

Allen, a quiet person, was hardly able to reply, but his agreement was evident, and the shopping expedition presently went on its way. It was the opening of a friendship of the most enduring

importance to him, to Madame, her husband, and Craft, and it was the last result Allen could have expected of a vacation trip to Santa Fe in 1961.

Meanwhile, the social aspects of that Santa Fe summer were like re-plays from other summers. We lunched and dined in the hotel patio, on rare occasions the Stravinskys went out to dine at the houses of opera patrons, and as always, Bynner's house was open to them whenever they felt like joining him and Hunt. One afternoon I took them there for tea. We sat as usual in the lower library of Bynner's house, it was cool, the ranks of books behind and above all the chairs and sofas made a rich backdrop, and Bynner was at his convivial best. While he and Hunt engaged Madame in conversation which if true to form combined bawdy wit with social comedy, Stravinsky, sitting by a small table where a silver pencil and a pad of memorandum paper were at hand for the vagrant thoughts which any writer likes to keep for their germinative value, suddenly took up the pad and pencil and said,

'Pol: I will compose a piece of music for you.'

I watched him carefully draw the five lines of the staff, and then saw him set down seven melodic notes, which he autographed and handed to me. It was this:

Considering that his entire day's output often amounted to no more than two or three bars of music to which he would listen again and again, in his mind, and on the muted piano, setting each note on paper with chirographic deliberateness, I was awed to be handed an original composition created for me in my presence. I was silenced by delight and gratitude at this conferral and he saw that I was.

Zorina was also present, and when it was time to go, she asked if she might drive Madame to the hotel, while I would bring the Maestro. As he came with me in my car, he was silent for a few moments, and then he mentioned that he had been told how, not long before, I had received a Papal honour by grace of Pius XII in a ceremony at the cathedral, 'for services to literature'. I confirmed this. A further silence, and then he said,

'It is ve-ry interesting. I have many times thought about it—why I have never become a Roman Catholic. You are born Roman Catholic?'

'Yes, Maestro.'

'Your writing is full of it—even your historical writing.'

'The Southwest was a Catholic country for hundreds of years.'

'Yes, but the *feeling*: I myself have a great feeling for Rome.'

'But so you do for Russia.'

'Yes, for Russia, of *course*. But the Latin, and the apostolic history of the papacy—many times I have thought of these things.'

I could not guess whether he was waiting for me to encourage him to undertake conversion, or whether—as one sometimes felt with him in his most cordial moments—he was saying more or less what he thought it would please his hearer to say; and passing by a missionary opportunity, such as I had never had inclination or talent for in any case, I thought to lighten the subject and leave it to him to continue it seriously if he chose, and I said,

'You know? I have always wondered why T. S. Eliot never actually swam the Tiber—he seems to me so altogether Roman Catholic despite his Anglicanism. I am told he prays the Rosary every day when he goes to the Anglican Mass.'

Religion disappeared when Stravinsky replied,

'We called on him in London at his flat. It was very strange. Very empty. Very comfortless. With his wife he is very happy.'

Still thinking of his propensity to say what would cost him little effort and give pleasure even if he set truth aside, I remembered an occasion I knew of through a man who escorted him to the table

at a dinner party in his Santa Fe residence. As they proceeded, the host—a bachelor of a certain temperament—said apologetically, deploring the absence of enough matched couples,

'Maestro, I am sorry not to have more ladies for you this evening,' to which Stravinsky replied with courteous mendacity,

'I prefer the other sex,' thus evidently intending to reassure his host on a number of counts.

In late August, the Stravinskys and Craft arrived in New York, where I had preceded them, and a few days later, I saw them off for Europe on the *Kungsholm* for Göteborg. Stravinsky was to go to Helsinki to conduct concerts and to receive the Sibelius Prize; then to Stockholm to see Bergman's production of *The Rake's Progress*; and presently he and the others would meet the opera company in Berlin for the performances there. I inspected the ship —it was the earlier one of that name—and found her to be as beautifully designed and fitted out as a great yacht, and I longed to sail with them all. (On a later crossing, a news camera crew accompanied them for a documentary about Stravinsky, who in several scenes gave every evidence of being in high spirits, and indeed at one moment, with the widest of smiles and the most rascally of voices said in reply to the question, Was he ever seasick? that on the contrary, 'I am never seasick, never! I am *sea-drunk!*')

But I could not sail, and on 20 September I went to the New York airport to take leave of the Santa Fe Opera artists, who were assembled there to fly to Berlin, and to wish them all triumph in their musical and diplomatic adventure. Lavish kisses and embraces. Childlike excitement under adult calm. Posed snapshots for publicity use. The delightful feeling of consequence, to be opera singers leaving for a foreign tour. A pang for the young, the beautiful, the confident, as at any setting out.

Madame wrote a postcard to me from Helsinki on 12 September 1961:

'Dearest Paul, here we are some 200 miles from Russia. The life is neat, calm and cosy—food is extremely good—we enjoy everything—only the rehearsals and concerts are enervating. With the change of time we are sleepy at unusual hours, the same with the meals. The Kungsholm was the best ship we ever had. She goes sometimes around the world—and I would like to do it . . . We

miss your company and we love you. Hope to have some news from you. Vera.'

A week later a card from Craft, sent from Stockholm, made a generous reference to my absence from the tour, and gave other news:

'. . . How sorry we all are that you won't be in Berlin . . . Your absence seems so unjust.

'I wish you could have seen Bergman's *Rake* . . . on the whole a tremendous and moving show. Very Swedish (not English) & very Gothick. The Tom was the best—a great singer, but we had a much better Shadow*—perhaps I am Miltonic but I think the Devil must be handsome. Bergman did the opera in 2 acts and we liked that, too. Costumes glorious—stage quite simple.

'The crossing was perhaps the most enjoyable so far & certainly the smoothest. The I.S.'s are well and join in sending love.'

Soon it was a fine satisfaction to read reports of the company's great success in both Berlin and Belgrade. When the tour was finished, Craft wrote from Zurich (10 October, 1961):

'Every tour must have its hero. Ours was John Crosby. Never losing his temper, hardly ever ruffled, sometimes working all night —John proved himself a real leader and won the admiration of everybody. In my opinion the company distinguished itself to the highest degree. A great, great deal of this was due to John alone —and John certainly had had less experience in Europe than any opera director in the world. He was also infinitely painstaking and gentle with the Stravinskys—and never did he ask them to do anything for his or the company's sake that might have tired or inconvenienced them. I only regret that he did not show his talents as a conductor. [All the performances were led by others] . . . I liked [Helen] Vanni as Jocasta—really satisfied with her, with [Donald] Gramm, with [Theodor] Uppman . . . Zorina was marvellous, and she is a wonderful person.

'The Stravinskys send love—they received your clippings [from the American press about the tour]. They enjoyed the boat, Bergman's *Rake*, Helsinki—but they were horrified by the wall in Berlin & Belgrade upset them, too; they have renounced all intentions ever to go to Russia.

'When will we ever see you? January? Mme S has a New York show the last week in January. But Santa Fe is a long time away. (I want to stay the whole summer this time . . .) We go to London

* John Reardon.

149

on the 15th—Savoy Hotel—until the 30th. We have a dinner with T.S.E. the 16th & one with E. M. Forster the 17th. I know you would love to be there with us.

'Please believe that [those who helped make the tour possible] could not have given to any better artistic cause (not just a "worthy" one) in the world.

Bob.'

The year 1962 held particular significance in the world of music, and the Santa Fe Opera was to make special observance of the fact. In that year Stravinsky reached his eightieth birthday; and Crosby, as general director of the opera, resolved to present all of the voice works composed by Stravinsky for the music theatre. In planning the season, it was more than once regretted that there was no Santa Fe opera ballet which could offer Stravinsky's dance pieces; but the idea of giving all the operas in honour of the composer's eightieth birthday year was in itself so large and original an undertaking that every time it was discussed in the planning stages, it seemed suitable for it to grow larger. The result, in a series of conversations between Crosby and myself, was a plan to give a Stravinsky Festival with many features added to the presentation of the operas. The general director would have his hands full enough with the season at the opera theatre, and therefore asked me as chairman of the board to carry on with planning and animating the other aspects of the Festival. As I was not yet committed to the full-time post of Director of the Center for Advanced Studies at Wesleyan University, to which I was summoned in the fall of that year, I had time to do the job, and more than enough eagerness to take part in our tribute to the Santa Fe Opera's greatest member and benefactor.

What we hoped to do was marshal all of Santa Fe's cultural resources, and a number from the world beyond the Southwest, to express the feeling of tribute and love which Santa Fe and its opera felt for Stravinsky on this milestone birthday. He would be given special homage around the world that year, but nowhere else, we believed, would so many elements be brought together to honour the anniversary.

As I sketched each phase of the Festival plans (aside from the preparation of the operas, which Crosby proceeded with) I kept

Stravinsky informed of what we planned. He agreed that it would be interesting to establish an Honorary Committee to sponsor the Festival. I asked him for names. His list was drawn from among his friends in the world's eye, and all agreed to serve:

W. H. Auden
Sir Isaiah Berlin
Witter Bynner
T. S. Eliot
Aldous Huxley
Pierre Monteux
St-John Perse
Artur Rubinstein

I spoke personally to those within reach—Auden, at a dinner of the National Institute of Arts and Letters, Bynner in Santa Fe. I wrote to the others, and had prompt replies from all but Perse and Rubinstein, whom I caught by long-distance telephone. They were all glad to be associated with Stravinsky in this way, though St-John Perse, who was at that time in Washington, had some difficulty in 'placing' the auspices of the Festival. In addition, we assembled an Executive Committee whose members were Crosby, Goddard Lieberson, Francis Robinson of the Metropolitan Opera, R. L. B. Tobin (my knowledgeable and generous fellow board-member) and myself.

We conceived the idea of inviting a small group of young American composers, to be nominated by some of the leading older contemporary masters of American music, to attend the opera season for the purpose of being present when Stravinsky was in rehearsal at the theatre or in the cathedral, and to share in the privilege of observing his working presence. They were also to hold seminars among themselves, conducted by members of the opera staff, in order to gain insights into the practical workings of an opera house. This plan was not uniformly successful, and in fact a certain young composer disgraced himself at one of the meetings by launching an abusive attack upon Stravinsky and his music in terms so intemperate and even obscene that the general director asked him to take his departure on the same day, with transportation provided by the Santa Fe Opera. Others took advantage of their opportunities in more serious ways. Unfortunately, several had brought themselves to expect intimate daily contact with Stravinsky, which under the pressure of schedules was not possible.

The third of the annual cathedral series was planned as a Festival event for 19 August, when Stravinsky would conduct his 1952 *Cantata*, and two days later, in the auditorium of the Museum of New Mexico, Craft would conduct the American concert première of Stravinsky's *The Flood*, with the participation of vocal and instrumental artists of the opera.

The Museum of New Mexico took part in the Festival by bringing to its galleries for three weeks of the summer a copious exhibition of designs, paintings, photographs, and sculpture under the title 'Stravinsky and the Dance: A Survey of Ballet Productions, 1910–1962', with a sumptuous catalogue prepared by the Dance Collection of the New York Public Library. The exhibition had been formed to honour Stravinsky's eightieth birthday by Wildenstein and Company, in conjunction with the New York Public Library, where it was first shown, and was further circulated by the Museum of Modern Art. It was a rich exposition of that aspect of Stravinsky's work which the Santa Fe Opera had not been able to represent—the ballet.

Further, the Festival undertook to present a series of five lectures on the general subject of 'Igor Stravinsky: His Contribution and Influence in the Arts of the 20th Century', to be given in the St Francis Auditorium of the Museum of New Mexico.

A statement by Sir Herbert Read in the catalogue of the exhibition might well have stood as the motto for the lecture series: 'It is given to some artists, whatever their craft, to be in virtue of their universality the representative artist of their age—a Dante, a Shakespeare, a Michelangelo, a Goethe. The most representative artist of our own twentieth century has been, not a poet or a painter, but a musician—Igor Stravinsky.'

And finally, at the opera theatre, along with works of the more standard repertoire in its regular season, the company was to present Stravinsky's complete operatic works—*Mavra, Renard, Le Rossignol, Perséphone, Oedipus Rex*, and *The Rake's Progress*. Opening on 1 August, and extending through the twenty-first, the Festival was the most comprehensive act of homage to Stravinsky given anywhere in that jubilee year. That it attracted less widespread attention than it deserved must have been the result of the opera's lack of a well-established and widely known apparatus of publicity—a lack traceable not to failure of foresight but to a sadly limited budget. No matter. The musical events were in themselves superb, the exhibition very fine, and some of the other features

highly distinguished. Those who were in Santa Fe for the whole Festival knew one of the richest rewards of their cultural lives.

The early part of the season was devoted to works in the regular repertoire, opening with Strauss's *Salomé*, which was soon followed by an extraordinary event on Wednesday, 25 July. This was a dramatised production of Arthur Honegger's *Jeanne d'Arc au Bûcher*, with Vera Zorina in the narrative role of the saint. She had given and continues to give the role in concert form with symphonic orchestras about the world. For this production she entered the physical as well as the spiritual raiment of Saint Joan and created a being of radiance, humility, suffering, and glory. The saint's monologues were supported by fine ceremonies of choreography devised and directed by John Butler, in which the dancer Vincent Warren made of a brief appearance a moment of remembered theatrical beauty and style.

The Stravinskys, long preceded by Craft, who was rehearsing the Festival operas, came to Santa Fe on Friday, 28 July, and four days later, on my birthday, 1 August, the Festival opened. I was as pleased as a child at the simultaneity of my personal date and the inauguration of an event so meaningful. Early in the day I was presented by Madame on behalf of herself, her husband, and Craft, with a pyramid of birthday presents, chief of which was a finely woven dark blue and green lap-robe which, as an addict of frequent catnaps every day, I take with me everywhere.

At three o'clock, the Stravinsky Festival was officially opened with this brief speech which I made to an audience assembled in the patio of the Museum of New Mexico:

Madame Stravinsky, honoured guests, fellow members of the Board, Ladies and Gentlemen:

This afternoon we initiate a series of events to do honour to the incomparable achievements of a voice of the human spirit which has uniquely spoken for the mind and heart of modern man for more than five decades.

Ladies and gentlemen, I introduce to you with these remarks the Santa Fe Opera Festival in honour of Igor Stravinsky, in the year of his eightieth anniversary. Our Festival will illustrate all aspects of his marvellously profuse creative life with the exception only of his directly symphonic literature, which however greatly we love it and

respond to it does lie outside the formal boundaries of our operatic institution and its resources.

In our Festival, we have the honour to offer a survey of Stravinsky's vital effect in the general history of twentieth century culture. To do anything like justice to our subject, a variety of occasions is required.

First, within the meaning of the word opera, where we claim our character, there is an enchanting and powerful aspect of Stravinsky's world to reveal. Accordingly, the Festival is presenting at the Opera Theatre all of Stravinsky's operatic works under his personal supervision. Opening with tonight's triple bill, the composer will conduct *Le Rossignol*.

In the orchestral resources of the company there are fine instrumentalists, and using their talents, and with the co-operation of the Santa Fe Chamber Music Society, two concerts of Stravinsky's compositions in the smaller forms are being given. A most significant part of Stravinsky's production has been devoted to sacred themes, and in any survey of his canon of work, these should be represented. Therefore, a concert of music by Stravinsky on sacred themes will be presented by the Festival in the Cathedral of Saint Francis under the patronage of His Excellency the Most Reverend Archbishop of Santa Fe, Dr Edwin Vincent Byrne, with the composer conducting part of the programme and his brilliant associate Robert Craft the rest of it.

Stravinsky's works for the opera and the ballet created a new idiom for the theatre. The Festival in collaboration with the Museum of New Mexico has arranged to show the exhibition *Stravinsky and the Dance* in the Museum's galleries, and there you may see original drawings and paintings inspired and required by his works for the stage, and encounter the strike of his own revelations of the playful, the tragic, and the profoundly contemplative attributes of life.

Such a Festival as this could perhaps as well be thought of as educational—and in our many revelations of Stravinsky's many aspects, we have included a frankly educational idea. Perhaps we have what could be called a Stravinsky Institute here, for the duration of the Festival; for the Festival Committee—with the benefit of notably stimulating suggestions by Mr Goddard Lieberson, for which I thank him most warmly—has tried to provide a means by which the living tradition of Stravinsky at work might be transmitted to a new generation of his fellow-composers in America. A carefully chosen representation of young American composers, selected by a committee of their seniors in their own art, are attending the Festival as guests of the company. It is their privilege to attend all rehearsals and preparatory sessions to observe Stravinsky in his working situations in theatre and concert. Further, seminars for the discussion of technical and aesthetic aspects of the works currently in production are to be

conducted for the young composers by members of the Opera's staff and by visiting experts.

Finally, the Opera has arranged a public series of Festival lectures on the general subject of *Igor Stravinsky: His Contribution and Influence in the Arts of the Twentieth Century*, including the fields of music, letters, and the visual arts. The first of these lectures will be delivered in the Museum auditorium this afternoon at four o'clock, by Mr Thomas Messer, director of the Guggenheim Museum of New York, after the conclusion of these ceremonies. Mr Messer will speak on the topic, *Igor Stravinsky and Twentieth Century Painting and Design*.

I believe I do this audience a service in announcing now the succeeding events in this series of Festival Lectures:

Next Wednesday, a week from today, at four o'clock in the Museum Auditorium, Dr Milton Babbitt of Princeton University will speak on *Recent Developments in the Music of Igor Stravinsky*.

On Friday, August 10, at four o'clock, Maestro Don Carlos Chavez, the eminent Mexican composer and conductor, will speak on *The Influence of Igor Stravinsky on the Music of the Americas*.

On Wednesday, August 15, at four o'clock, Professor Roger Shattuck, of the University of Texas, will speak on *Stravinsky and the Shape of Experience*.

And on Friday, August 17, at four o'clock, concluding the series, Mr Virgil Thomson, distinguished American composer and critic, will discuss *The Operatic Works of Igor Stravinsky*.

The history of Maestro Stravinsky's association with our company is a particularly appealing and intimate part of our annals. I want to ask now the Opera's General Director, Mr John O. Crosby, to give this audience a brief account of the association which more than any other has shed lustre upon our enterprise and has given us heart in our ambitions.

Crosby now took the podium and with grace and affection described the years of association earlier sketched in this book. He closed his statement by reading the following:

TELEGRAM RECEIVED FROM THE WHITE HOUSE, WASHINGTON, D.C.

July 30, 1962

John O. Crosby, General Director, The Santa Fe Opera,

Santa Fe, N.M.

THE SANTA FE OPERA DISTINGUISHES ITSELF AND HONOURS A VERY GREAT MAN IN PRESENTING THE FESTIVAL MARKING IGOR STRAVINSKY'S EIGHTIETH YEAR. THE SPIRIT OF THE MAN IS EVER YOUNG AND HIS MUSIC IS STILL REACHING OUT TO THOSE

BORDERLANDS WHERE GENUINE CREATION IN THE ARTS TAKES PLACE. THE MAESTRO HAS NOT ONLY BEEN A SOURCE OF GREAT ART HIMSELF, BUT HAS INSPIRED OTHERS IN MANY CREATIVE FIELDS. I SEND HIM AND MADAME STRAVINSKY MY WARM PERSONAL GREETINGS AND BEST WISHES TO ALL WHO MAKE THIS FESTIVAL POSSIBLE—

JOHN F. KENNEDY

I then resumed by saying,

We are immensely honoured by the expression of the President of the United States of those sentiments which our country and the world share with Santa Fe today.

Inseparable from the generous gift of his genius and his style to the Santa Fe Opera has been the opulent kindness which Maestro Stravinsky's wife has shown to the company in the five seasons of their presence with us.

Madame Stravinsky has herself known a beautiful career as an artist of the theatre, and aside from all her heart-warming gestures of friendliness to our artists, she has by her very presence given us a conviction of plausibility in our undertakings, whose virtues she has been quick to see, and whose faults she has allowed to pass by with the grace of an artist and a lady who knows that if growth is an uneven affair, it is yet a process of life which will not be denied.

With the most grateful respect, and as spokesman for the love which our associates all bear toward her and her illustrious husband and companion, I now have the honour to invite Madame Igor Stravinsky to perform that act which will declare officially open the Santa Fe Opera Festival in honour of her husband's eightieth anniversary.

Madame then cut the ribbon across the doorway leading from the patio to the museum galleries, while flashbulbs went off, and I ended by saying,

Ladies and gentlemen, in concluding these ceremonies, and inviting you to enter the Museum to see the exhibition *Stravinsky and the Dance*, and to reassemble for Mr Messer's lecture in the auditorium which will begin at four o'clock, I would ask you to let me say one more thing to you. It is this.

The stages of man's cultural history have often been designated by the name of that artist in each period whose lifetime's work seemed to make a coherent unit of style, purpose, and power of expression which spoke for his contemporaries in general. It is my belief that the

work of our beloved Maestro will require the central decades of the twentieth century to be known in cultural history as The Age of Stravinsky.

We now adjourn.

The Stravinskys attended all the lectures of the Festival series, which I introduced with the briefest possible remarks. The audiences were small—publicity had been too meagre to do much for the occasions, but it seemed to me sufficient that Stravinsky himself heard the tributes paid to him, though these were not uniformly attentive to the substance of music so that later he was unable to say that he had been continually 'interested'. He sat in the first or second row, wearing his beret, leaning a trifle forward—an attitude which reflected concentration. Thomas Messer, inaugurating the series, reached him intimately when he said of Stravinsky,

He has never shown any inclination to remove himself from the sharp edge of the most current contemporary issues and disputes.

And again, when he said,

. . . The surest and freest thought, that which goes directly to the core of the matter removing most decisively prevailing falseness, superficiality, and error—that thought in whatever kingdom of the arts it may originate—will take the lead and will inevitably impose itself upon the awareness of all fellow artists within and outside of its particular domain. It is such a thought also that often scares us for it confronts us with the annoying and uncomfortable necessity of having to rethink life and having to replace false, worn, if beloved premises, with a new, truer, but as yet harsh and dissonant reality. Eventually, to be sure, the manifestation of such a new reality again assumes nostalgic connotations and will be seen within a framework of beauty. But the time we require to absorb it temporarily separates us from those who first gave it form.

It is, then, the sharpness, the directness of thought given musical materiality that allows us today to pay homage to Igor Stravinsky at his eightieth birthday. In doing so we celebrate the achievements of a great musician, but beyond this, those of a thinker-shaper whose authority has extended beyond his own field into all the arts of the twentieth century. Through his music, directly, and through the effect of his musical thought upon all the arts of our time, he forces

us to rethink our lives and perhaps change them. All this simply because thought that no one had formulated for us before renders invalid, or at least places in a different light, universal concepts that we have held heretofore.

A week later, Babbitt, in a highly technical exposition of Stravinsky's musical fabric, held him spellbound, and I heard him declare later in thanking Babbitt that 'there is only one possible way to discuss music, and that is in technically musical terms'. Any other approach—association of ideas, images, analogies— bored him to extremity, even if delivered in the most loving jargon by non-musicians. Music critics he regarded at large as illiterate in their subject, even those with some instrumental experience or a minimal knack for reading scores.

With Carlos Chavez, Stravinsky was also delighted, for here was a man of music, as well as an old and sophisticated friend; and what was not spoken of by Don Carlos in his historical lecture was thoroughly examined in exchange at meals by the two. I recall one moment of that summer when, after lunching with them in the hotel patio, I left them at two o'clock, and passing by the same afternoon at about five o'clock saw them both still sitting at the same table, in expansive mind, energetically conversing in French.

One of the lecturers gave offence to Stravinsky by referring to him as 'old Papa sitting there, in his beret', and by a rather con- sistently condescending tone in appraising his work. Even in his compliments, the lecturer seemed to indulge his reservations; and it struck others that an occasion avowedly labelled as a celebration was not quite appropriate as the vehicle of acidulous comments, however objectively derived. But as a whole the lecture series was distinguished and I regretted it when a scheme to publish the papers in a book fell through.

On the opening night of the Festival, 1 August, when Stravinsky conducted *Le Rossignol*, there was a great reception of the com- poser; and throughout the span of the special events, he was acclaimed. When not conducting, he had seats in the first row, where a spotlight always sought him out for the audience. He would stand and bow, raising his arm in affectionate salute; and the Santa Fe audiences—augmented for the Festival by more than

the usual high percentage of visitors from far away—felt that he belonged to them in a special way.

On 8 August the double bill of *Perséphone* and *Oedipus Rex* was given—again a stylistically suitable pairing; and I always wished that an evening of Wagnerian dimensions (guilty words) consisting of these two works, with the addition of the ballets *Orpheus* and *Apollon Musagète*, could have been arranged. In this third production of *Oedipus* I asked to be excused from the role of the Narrator, and proposed instead that the distinguished and gifted poet, Winfield Townley Scott, who lived in Santa Fe, be cast in my place. Crosby agreed, furthering his idea that a man of letters should be used in the role rather than an actor; and Scott and I rejoiced that between us we enjoyed the privilege, even though it cost us both hours of terror. It was a newly designed and staged production, conducted for the first time by Crosby. Again it was an impressive evening, with Zorina once more lyrically creating her goddess. The rest of the operas gave an unexampled demonstration of Stravinsky's range in the vocal theatre, with *The Rake's Progress* as the company's major triumph in its repertoire of full-length works.

Yet again I brought Stravinsky to the cathedral—it was Sunday evening, 19 August, 1962—for a concert, this time for him to conduct his 1952 *Cantata*, that wonderful choral work calling upon early English poetry for its syllables. He used stanzas intermittently from the 'Lyke Wake Dirge' in the manner of a refrain, and placed other lines from the great anonymous early poetry of England, including 'O Westren winde', in a marvellous sequence reaching from earth and its longings to heaven and its hope— 'And Christ receive thy saule'. The spare instrumentation wove amidst the voices a texture thin as air and as life-giving. As in so many of his vocal works, Stravinsky here wedded his profound literary understanding with his music, without performing a mere 'setting' of text. As always, for musical reasons, he altered normal stresses of pronunciation where it suited him to do so, and instead of obscuring word meanings gave them new freshness by the startling prosodical effects required by his melodic conceptions.

Again the cathedral was filled, the audience rapt, the occasion lifted by the plain seriousness of the performance; and at the end, when I went with him to my car to drive him away, there were

people waiting in the courtyard behind the cathedral, among them the Archbishop and prelatic priests. Several cars were ranked there, with their headlamps shining; and I retain vividly a picture of the moment when the Archbishop came forward to Stravinsky. Darkness all about except for the headlamp beams, so that the light played in intermittent shafts. Suddenly a caprice of wind rose and tossed the red-violet mantle of the metropolitan prelate in strange wafts in and out of the lights. Stravinsky went to meet him. It was a curious effect of transposed senses—light became wind, and wind became darkness, and darkness movement. As they met, Byrne opened out his arms and received Stravinsky, and with both hands then slowly drew Stravinsky's head to his breast in a silent embrace which held peace in the midst of the tiny local storm of the elements in the courtyard. Once again two different but related powers exchanged their *mana*. The tableau held for a long instant. Then the scene broke, the wind whipped cassocks and colour, the Archbishop withdrew, never again to see Stravinsky at his cathedral, for within the year he died. It was also the last time I saw Archbishop Byrne, who gave the hospitality of his spirit, as it were, beyond vaults and transepts, to Stravinsky; as he had given something of the same to me in furthering my own projects.

Two evenings later, on Tuesday, as the final event of the 1962 Festival, the American concert première of *The Flood* was given in the museum auditorium in a performance much more interesting than the version with visual effects seen over a television network early in the year. Stravinsky and Madame were present, Craft conducted, and the work fulfilled its remarkable vision of man's primal earthly salvation entirely in the realm of sound, spoken, sung, played. Once again, references to the most primitive of experiences were brought into the most sophisticated consciousness by Stravinsky's unique intuitions of humanity's laminated historical memory—part of it conscious and formalised, the rest drifting in currents of the nether mind as if through a past drowned in the earth's waters.

We seemed in that Festival summer to be together more often than ever—Stravinsky, Madame, Craft, Zorina, Goddard Lieberson when he was free to leave his work in New York, Crosby when

Seeing the Stravinskys off on the westbound 'Super Chief' at Lamy, New Mexico, 1960: *below*, Mme Stravinsky, the author, the composer; *left* (from the left), Donald Berks, Mirandi Masocco Levy, Robert Craft

Photo by Le Gaun

18 August 1963, St Francis Cathedral, Santa Fe; Igor Stravinsky invested with the Papal knighthood of St Sylvester

pressures at the theatre allowed, myself. There was a gala feeling about our gatherings, great or small. Stravinsky was 'interested' when I proposed asking John and Faith Meem to come to lunch, along with Zorina; for Meem was the architect and scholar of U.S. Southwestern and north Mexican life who by his taste, vision, and gentle but persistent energy had throughout decades done most to save for Santa Fe its best historical likeness in arts and architecture.

Another day I brought to Stravinsky and Madame a copy of a book I had just read and found to be superb. It was *Patriotic Gore* by Edmund Wilson. Some days later Stravinsky said to me that the book was 'a masterpiece'. It gave me much pleasure at a later time to be able to repeat this to Wilson, who had written so early and often, and with such acuity, about Stravinsky. Wilson, to whom almost nothing in contemporary taste or achievement meant much, exclaimed, when I repeated Stravinsky's opinion of his book, 'Did he really! Did he really!'—with every evidence of gratification.

On another occasion, again at lunchtime, I witnessed a comedy of evasion and felt as sorry for the victim as much as I felt respect for him. This was an interesting composer, a master in his own field, who told a longish anecdote about the tyrannical airs and pretensions of Arnold Schönberg, the point of which was that Schönberg, irritably and Germanically jealous of his own grandeur, permitted no one, not any colleague, to address him by his first name, requiring even his wife to address him as 'Doktor Schönberg'. The narrator chuckled away at such nonsense; and without saying so, seemed to be working up to the privilege of addressing Stravinsky as 'Igor'. Stravinsky of course grasped the implication of the story. He responded to it, dashing the petitioner's hopes, by saying with extra charm,

'Yes, you see, my first name used in English does not fall gratefully upon my ears, unless it is in the voice of my vife.* In Russian, I am accustomed to the sound of my name in direct address as "Igor Fedorovich", which is a natural usage'—his charm grew more radiant with each phase of the crushing response—'but of course in English parlance this would not sound ve-ry natural. It is for this reason that I am not customarily addressed by my first name at all unless in the context of the Russian language or by a fellow countryman.'

* Madame pronounced his first name in English as if it were spelled 'Eager'.

The little bow in conclusion expressed three things—flat understanding of what the matter was all about, enjoyment of the evasive device for its own sake, and finality.

By this delicate negative demonstration, I am put in mind of another moment he told me about when he shattered protocol on the occasion of his 1962 trip to Russia. (The Stravinskys went after all to their homeland for a successful visit.) There was an audience with Khrushchev, said Stravinsky. They were seated close together, face to face, and the Soviet Chairman, in the custom of heads of state, took charge of the topic of conversation, beginning with remarks about music.

'It was ab-surd,' said Stravinsky to me. 'I interrupted him at once. Who could listen to his nonsense about music? I said, "We will not talk about music. *You* know nothing about music. We will talk about industry. *I* know something about industry." '

Evidently there was a pause to serve briefly as a gasp, and then Khrushchev, perhaps with relief, seeing the good sense of his visitor's point, threw apart his hands in a stout gesture of acceptance, and set forth on an enjoyable monologue about Soviet industrial achievements and plans. The audience became a success.

During the Festival summer there were eminent musical visitors, including Henri Sauguet, from France by way of Aspen, Virgil Thomson, Claudio Spiess, and others. One evening at El Nido, the restaurant near the opera to which Stravinsky enjoyed going for its excellent shrimp *rémoulade*, I gave a dinner party bringing together musical friends, including Henriette Wyeth (Mrs Peter Hurd), and her sons Peter and Michael, Sauguet, Thomson, Zorina, and others, to be with me and the Stravinskys and Craft. We were just lifting our first drinks when Stravinsky, next to me at table, suddenly gave an exaggerated gasp and pointing as if the squirrel of the Rito had returned in apparition, said hoarsely,

'No, Pol: this is dread-ful—we are thirteen at table!'

I counted, and he was right. It was time for rapid thought. Surveying the table, my eye lit upon Michael Hurd, who was fourteen years old.

'Ah! Maestro,' I said like someone quoting the law reassuringly, 'it is all right. Young Michael Hurd is not yet of legal age.'

Politely entering into my comedy, Stravinsky said with a judicial air,

'Ah, that is ve-ry good. We are safe.'

The party accelerated. Sauguet and Stravinsky conversed with animation in French.

At about this time, Miss Bedell gave a second exhibition of Madame's work in her Palace Avenue gallery. There were new paintings, drawings, and tapestries to be shown. At the private view, Stravinsky sat much of the time in the patio with Zorina and others greeting visitors on their way into the galleries. I sat with him at moments, and when she could leave her gallery crowd, Madame joined us. There was a convivial feeling—late sunlight rippling over us through the ancient trees within the walls, much gaiety in talk, and a series of quite uncounted Scotches which came along with the latening afternoon. Everyone was coming to dine with me later, but it was after seven when it was possible to break loose to go to El Nido. When it was time to go, Stravinsky rose genially to his feet, and leaning on his stick and smiling with an air of achievement, declared,

'I am dronk. Please, you will leave me at the hotel on your way to the dinner. Vera will go with you.'

Madame calmly accepted this, we took him to his rooms, and went on our way. Three hours later I brought Madame back to the hotel suite. She was working with her key to enter, and we had already said goodnight, when Stravinsky opened the door from within, making a small flourish. He was slightly flushed, but no longer with liquor. Bringing us in, he said,

'I came dronk, I slept one hour, I sent for some food, I have had supper, and then I have composed two bars!'

The statement was like a rascally declaration of a proper regimen for an artist's life. Madame said,

'Eager, you are all right?'

He made a great arc with an arm, indicating that not only he but the world was all right. Following his gesture, I saw the usual profusion of new books on one of the twin beds—we were in Madame's room—and on a table her painting materials; and through the open door into his room the window-side table where his paper and instruments of writing were laid, and next to it, the small muted piano which had been installed for him. Illustrious pilgrims, they had long ago mastered the technique of maintaining in temporary lodgings the essentials of their permanent life.

One morning that summer my telephone rang at eight o'clock and I heard Madame say in a voice so subdued and unhappy that I could hardly hear her,

'Pol: can you come?'

'Now?'

'Please. Here there is something wrong.'

'Of course. Immediately.'

'Thank you, yes, right away.'

In ten minutes I was knocking at her door of the suite and was admitted to join an atmosphere of deep dejection. Madame wore a flowing *robe de chambre*. Craft was in shirt, sweater, and slacks. In a corner, huddled it seemed almost into invisibility, was Stravinsky, staring at the floor and holding his cane with both hands. He wore his beret, a dark grey cardigan over a pale blue pyjama jacket, matching pyjama trousers, and slippers.

'What is it, dear Madame?' I asked in alarm.

'He is not good'—i.e. not well.

Stravinsky raised his head and looked at me tragically. He wrung my heart. He said,

'Pol: *je ne peux pas faire pipi.*'

It was laugh or cry, but I managed to do neither, for their concern was extreme, and I begged for explanations. It seemed, said Craft, that there had been some symptoms lately which required the opinion of a doctor. One was consulted, and late yesterday had made a tentative diagnosis which could not have been more upsetting, for it referred to the possibility of cancer of the urinary system; and all last evening, and through the night, and this morning, there had been total retention of urine. The worst possibilities seemed to be confirmed by the painful and unrelieved continence. My alarm at once became so great that I expressed it in rage.

'What a damned fool doctor,' I cried, while all the faces in the room regarded me sadly, 'how can he possibly make such a diagnosis so quickly! These things take elaborate tests. We must have a specialist, there must be another opinion, I certainly would not draw any dreadful conclusions from what has been done so far!'

'So, what can we do?' asked Madame, her lips white with nervous concern, her great eyes welling with tears. I kissed her hand.

'Has this ever happened before?' I asked.

Craft said,

'Not in so protracted a way.'

'I see.'

The three of us gradually grew into a committee formed to consider all aspects of the matter. Amazingly, we seemed to forget the patient, as we discussed possible hospitalisation, the summoning by air of a specialist from California, the necessary revision of all rehearsal schedules—Stravinsky was to be involved at the theatre for the evening of that very day—and Craft began to pace the small area near Madame's painting table, while she sat on the edge of the bed with the books, and I tried to pour confidence into her great rueful gaze. As each technical move was considered it seemed to bring a small start of hope in each of us, and none of us noticed that Stravinsky had left the room. Our first awareness of this was when he returned through the open inner door of the suite.

He was upright, smiling widely, his eyes lighted, and he came to us and said in his strong, authoritative rehearsal voice,

'Pol: *j'ai fait pipi!*'

Instantly all gloom was lifted. Madame sighed through a relieved laugh, and Craft put the collar of his shirt inside his sweater and took it out again.

'But how wonderful, Maestro!' I cried, and went to embrace him.

'You see?' he said, bending forward as to applause.

The world was again endurable. Madame asked if we would like coffee, room service was put to work, the light of Santa Fe was riding high into its morning, and that evening Stravinsky attended his scheduled rehearsal at the opera. So far as I know the difficulty never returned that summer.

On Wednesday, 22 August, with the Festival events all concluded, and the eightieth birthday fully solemnised by Santa Fe, the Stravinskys departed for California from the Albuquerque airport, to which I conveyed them. There was time for lunch in the airport, and a general tone of festivity suggested the suitability of champagne, which was brought. Aided by the altitude, the wine produced a feeling of gentle levitation. When the time came, I went out to the aeroplane with them all, and ascended the steps with Madame, following her husband and Craft, who had already installed themselves in two window seats, forward left, in the

165

cabin. She pointed at them and said to me with resignation, 'You see? They always have the window. I, never. Goodbye, dear-h.'

Earlier in that year, President and Mrs Kennedy had given a small dinner for the Stravinskys to honour the eightieth birthday. I was not present, but heard something of the event from Madame later. She said the President was entirely un-musical, but very clever, for sitting at his right, she was throughout dinner quizzed by him about details of her husband's career, his work, the character of his musical thought, so that when the time came for a toast to the guest of honour, the President was able to rise and acquit himself plausibly as one long familiar with Stravinsky's progress through the world.

One further detail of the event came to me long afterwards from Nicolas Nabokov, who had been a guest that evening. The drinks before dinner had been unusually large potions of Scotch; and wines had accompanied the food throughout. Stravinsky drank freely. As the dinner party rose, following the President from the room, a White House aide, himself obviously less used to high places than Stravinsky, asked with a patronising air,

'Well, Mr Stravinsky, how does it feel to be in the White House?'

Stravinsky replied,

'It feels very dronk.'

In the winter months of 1963 Thomas Messer was presenting at the Guggenheim Museum a life-span of the painting of Vassily Kandinsky—that painter whom I had revered through reproductions in my schooldays, and whose work I had lost touch with in the intervening years. One night at the Metropolitan Opera Club I asked Messer about the exhibition, and said the attending crowds had kept me away. He asked if I would like to see it after the opera.

'Tonight?'

'Yes. I can telephone now to have the guard let us in.'

It was a princely and generous proposal, and together with a couple of other friends, I went with Messer for a private view after midnight. He had hung the show chronologically, lighted it with subtlety, and my enthusiasm was high, particularly as Messer

himself was present to give an impromptu and learned lecture on the artist and the tangents of his thought and influence as we took our own time going down the museum's ammenoidal ramp.

During that winter the Stravinskys were at the Pierre Hotel, where I was asked to lunch or dine when I was in town from my post at Wesleyan. They were of course surrounded with the circumstances of the helplessly eminent—incessant messages by telephone and cable, vats of flowers, pyramids of books, sifted rosters of callers, reluctance to dine in public, the implausible security of a life elevated to an impersonal haven on a seventeenth floor. They bore it with comic stoicism, even when the elements were both tempting and defiant: on one winter day of violent beauty, with snow savaging its way down Fifth Avenue, Stravinsky must go out for a walk to feel the storm. Alone, he descended, wrapped in the fur coat, and with his stick took a few steps along the sidewalk against the blizzard. But it was too much for him. He made little headway, leaning over against the windy snow—was he transported to a St Petersburg winter in his heart? There came a gust of special fury—he was not only halted but like a castaway bare branch was blown bodily across the pavement and against the wall of the hotel. The doorman saw it happen, went to the rescue, and helped him indoors again. It was a reminder of the frailty one never thought of while listening to him.

On a visit in February, I told of my privileged midnight visit to the Kandinsky show.

'Ah!'—they had meant all season to go to see it, but like myself, had heard of the crowds so immense that hourly admission had had to be arranged so as not to overcrowd the viewers. A day or two later I had occasion to telephone Messer and incidentally mentioned the Stravinskys' disappointment at having to miss the show which would close on 7 April. Immediately Messer said,

'Try to arrange for a time when they could come an hour before the public opening. We would be honoured to show them the exhibition privately during that hour—and then please invite them to lunch with my wife and me afterwards.'

The Stravinskys were going out of town for concerts. Early in March the Maestro wrote me a note:

'To Paul Horgan my affectionate thoughts and thanks for his kind Febr 28th letter. That's OK for the Thomas Messer's invitation. We will be in NY after our March 21 concert and stay at the Pierre Hotel till the 8th April day of our sailing on "Bremen" to

Hamburg. For 2 or 3 days (when exactly I don't know) probably the beginning of April in Toronto for recordings.

'Looking forward to seeing you

'Devotedly
Yours
as ever
IStr'

Hollywood
March 3/63

The date finally arranged for turned out to be the last day of the Kandinsky exhibition—Sunday, 7 April. It was a success—but for one thing—Madame was recovering from influenza and could not attend.

The rest of us saw the show, again with the benefit of the director's guidance. He walked with Stravinsky, they took their time, and his love for the composer and his works found expression in being able to grant the privilege of the private hour in the museum, from eleven to twelve o'clock.

Afterwards we went with the Messers to a lunch party at the Stanhope Hotel. It was an event of high merriment, and once again Stravinsky, as in Houston with his pyramid of *merde*, showed his power to imagine an event and then demonstrate it visibly. He was describing an arrival at some destination or other by airliner. He joined his hands to create an aeroplane. He hunched his shoulders to suggest and focus forward energy. He spoke of the long descent—the approach as a speck in the sky, growing and growing —all the time flying the imaginary plane in infinitely small movement to suggest how a great speed at forty thousand feet looked almost stationary from the earth—and he brought the plane lower and nearer, and we felt the earth slowly rising to meet it, and suddenly we were in the earth's realm, and the plane was larger, it was coming in fast now, and—hunch and hands—it made those approaches of lift, lurch, recovery, glide, and a sense of the upswoop with qualm, and the down-settle again; and with sudden indrawn takes of breath he dramatised every felt loss of speed and height, and as we watched remembering the fall of the stomach in its own hollow as the condition of gravity took its changes, he landed the plane with an effect of headlong speed on the tablecloth, and made it turn a corner, and come to a stop, and we leaned back exhaling

168

as if we ourselves had made a safe descent and were glad of it. In other words, no experience, however common, was lost upon him, and no report of it was unworthy of a full re-creation, which meant that he never rationed his vitality in making a point, great or small.

Further—no situation was without its possibility of comedy for him, and it was not always possible to be certain when even with the aid of alcohol he was or was not intentional in saying something which would later find wide quotation. Example: the story told by Goddard Lieberson of how on arranging to leave Hamburg following a performance with the North German Radio, Stravinsky, after a luncheon heightened by drinking, went to the offices of the Lufthansa airline and with his most beguiling charm inquired, 'Please, you will tell me when the next Luftwaffe leaves for Paris . . .'

The Stravinskys' arrivals and departures were in themselves events of character, from the abstractions of anxiety to the critical curiosity accompanying any new condition or place. Once as I saw them off at the Grand Central Station on the 'Twentieth Century Limited' there was an animated chase like a passage in an old movie two-reeler. They had a suite of drawing rooms in the train. Madame was already resignedly encouched in one, with her books in reach, flowers in waxen green paper awaiting water, and when I came to say goodbye she embraced me and said 'Goodbye dear-h', and added that her husband was outside seeing to the luggage, if I wanted to take my leave of him.

I went to the inferno of damp cement and disheartening dim yellow light outside the train. There on two baggage trucks were thirty-eight pieces of luggage, which Stravinsky was counting with a forefinger. He was plainly not to be interrupted lest he lose count and have to start over. I waited at a small distance, where I found Samuel Dushkin. When the Maestro seemed to have completed his census, I started forward but not seeing me he darted into the far end of the Pullman and I therefore entered the near end hoping to meet him within and say goodbye. But he found what he wanted in the far vestibule of the car, went outside again, and with an item count in mind, began adding to it, by finger point, a completely fresh total of the cart baggage. This time he rounded the near cart towards me where I had emerged from my end of the Pullman,

and again without seeing me proceeded away from me, still counting. I then entered the car again at my end and walked its length
to meet him in the far vestibule. This time he entered by the doorway I had used and I thus found myself out on the platform while
he was within the car. The window shades of the suite were drawn
—I could not signal him within. I made one final try, walking
along the car to the end nearest the station, entered, and there in
the narrow entrance corridor we at last met; but it was a hurried
goodbye, as he was on his way outside to check one more detail
about the baggage, and there I left him.

Another time, awaiting the train at Lamy to go west, he heard
that a certain California orchestral conductor who had been in
Santa Fe to hear opera, was also to be on board.

'Oh, my God, he is so borink!' muttered the Maestro, and
glancing far up the brick platform of the tracks at Lamy he saw the
Californian and his wife waiting at the point where the 'Super
Chief's' last cars would halt. 'We will wait at this end,' added
Stravinsky, and led us to a green plot of grass with shade. Under a
tree we were almost invisible from the view far up the tracks, and
waiting became a pastoral pleasure in the cool shade, with the
many-blued mountains far off to our south and west. Mirandi and
Donald Berke had accompanied me in the leave-taking party.
Stravinsky was silent, giving the effect of depression. In his few
remarks of the moment, what seemed to come clear was that what
depressed him more than anything was an absence of talent on the
part of someone who sought to claim his attention. This was not
arrogance—it was rather a sort of ruefulness in which I thought
I felt another dimension of that self-dissatisfaction he revealed
after his public performances; the difference between an artist's
inner view of his perceptions and their outward and final expression, whether in work composed, written, painted, or performed.
'No talent,' he muttered, and we knew he was thinking of the un-
fortunate wretch at the other end of the platform who, it appeared,
had tried, but vainly, to see Stravinsky in Santa Fe. It was possible
to be polite to a nonentity who had no pretensions—but what did
one do with those who without the passport of talent, or better,
sought to enter his world? I think a kind of inverted rage at the
fact that so many who craved his acquaintance were ungifted was
what made him feel almost guilty on their behalf. Trivial persons
were pathetic at best, and intolerable at worst when they over-
reached themselves . . . The train at last: and entering at opposite

ends, the two musicians were spared all the way to California a confrontation which, though for different reasons, would have been uncomfortable for each.

In 1963 there was a significant arrival of the Stravinsky ménage at Albuquerque. I had received a telegram asking me to meet them and drive them to Santa Fe. They were coming from Chicago, having given several concerts at Ravinia Park with the Chicago Symphony Orchestra. Craft and Stravinsky had divided each programme—a comfortable arrangement which did not call too heavily on Stravinsky's energies. At eighty-one these were sometimes uncomfortably used up in a full-length programme.

The Albuquerque airport was thronged—several flights were coming and going at about the same time, and passengers were milling about at their concerns. I met my party at their gate, Madame and Craft went to see about luggage, and Stravinsky, looking fit, went with me to take a waiting-room bench. There was delay. He was still full of the recent concerts. He said the Chicago orchestra was the finest he had ever conducted, they were all virtuoso players, and what was better, marvellous sight readers. Their tone was marvellous. Each programme was *unglaublich.*

'And Bōp!' he cried enthusiastically, referring to Craft. 'You should have heard him conduct the *Tristan Vorspiel.*'

What! I said to myself, Wagner! Craft had gone and done it.

'A wonderful piece!' added Stravinsky, and my face fell empty at what seemed a conversion. His bland surprise was more fully revealed a few years later in a film interview. When he was asked about his famous views on Wagner, he calmly stated that he had revised them. 'It does not mean that I changed,' he said. 'I have added!' Further, he said, 'Everything who is creating does harm to something,' and I had a luxurious time working out applications of this: he had hated Wagner for doing harm originally? Or did he mean that he, Stravinsky, creating in his own mode, so antipodal to that of Wagner, had done harm to Wagner for their opposing principles? In any case, he stated, 'I have Wagner in my head. I have Wagner very much in my ears.' He could have added 'in my eyes', for on the wall behind him in the sequence filmed in his Hollywood house were two portraits of Wagner, one of them Renoir's portrait sketch. I smiled at this contrariness, but at his next utterance in the Albuquerque airport, I laughed out loud.

'*Ja,*' he said, 'Bōp was vawnderful—he was amazink in *Tristan.* My God! He drew out the first phrase, and held it, it was

impossible to play, yet he made them play it—' and in the bustling of the passenger crowd, he suddenly gave a vocal demonstration of how Craft had paced the celebrated opening theme for 'celli of the *Tristan* prelude:

'*Ta-re-e-e-e-e-e-e-e-e-ta-ra* . . .'

The sound he made, with its astounding hold and crescendo, was so loud that I had the impression of all movement in the airport coming to a halt, while a hundred and fifty people turned, startled, and stared to know what was happening. Stravinsky, oblivious, conducted his own sound as if giving instructions at rehearsal, and with more gaiety enunciated the answering theme in the oboe:

'*Ta-ra-ra-re-e* . . .'

Then again the second statement of the main theme, again in a voice growing so loud it echoed off the ceiling. The Chicago orchestra sat invisibly about him and he gave full expression to their imaginary playing. The energy he sent forth from his bench was commanding. It held almost everyone there motionless until, quite unaware of anyone about, he was finished with his demonstration, and then as he returned to conversational speech, the dazed public were freed from strangeness to go on about their business. He said,

'There was not enough bow for them to play it, but Bōp made them, and it was *épatant!*'

The power of his voice, the intense musical intention he conveyed through it, is, now, still 'very much in my ears'.

Presently, when the other affairs were arranged, we set out for Santa Fe, where, instead of going to the hotel, they had accepted arrangements to stay in an apartment complex with a small kitchen where Madame could prepare little meals if she felt like it. There was also room service if they needed it, and a place to park their car, which had been driven from California for them by E. J. Allen, and there was hope of a comfortable domesticity, such as others found there.

Alas, this was not to be.

It turned out to be a strange, a disheartening, summer season in

many ways. The physical circumstances were not all they had hoped for—the rooms were dark, cars came and went and parked too closely nearby (all the apartments were ground-floor bungalows), room service was willing but slow, as often was the case in the Southwest there were occasional insect visitors such as centipedes or large spiders, there was no hint of the comforting elegance which was taken for granted in such lodgments as the Bauer-Grünwald, the Paris Ritz, the Hassler, the Boston Ritz-Carlton, even the Pierre with its sterile amplitudes. The unlovely sounds of tourist America carried from apartment to apartment.

All such might have been borne with ironic stoicism if the spiritual climate had been rewarding; but this summer it was not so. To the amazement of those who habitually saw the Stravinskys and worked to make their residence in Santa Fe as comfortable as possible—Crosby on their arrival sent an impressive vessel of Chivas Regal—there was in that season a tone of emotional and even artistic inhospitality which was disconcerting. There was an attitude of inattention to the Stravinskys on the part of certain members of the opera staff who at first were excused on the grounds of production pressure and the rest; but as the summer wore on without all the customary courtesies the Stravinskys were puzzled and finally hurt; and when one day it came to the ears of Madame that a small youthful faction of the musicians were heard mocking her husband's work at rehearsal—he was preparing his *Mass* for a concert at the cathedral to be given on 18 August—she was on his behalf deeply outraged. She worked to keep knowledge of such disrespect from him, but to me and to Zorina she spoke bitterly.

'They are saying that my husband is no longer competent with the musicians. They are laughing at him if he makes a mistake with the score. Why do they act this way? Who are they to be *méprisants*? When they have done something in the world perhaps they will have a right to criticise. Of *course* he is an old man. Of *course* he may forget now and then. But he is an artist and he is serious. He has given them the best he can give for 'ears [years] and now *on se moque de lui*. This is not good. I am unhappy.'

I could hardly believe that all this could be so, but I presently heard from others reports of the same behaviour. I was disheartened but not amazed when Madame said,

'We shall never return to Santa Fe.'

I knew she meant it, for her power of conviction was as strong as

173

her character, and where her husband was thoughtlessly ill-treated was no place to which she would allow him to be exposed again. Stravinsky was too intuitive not to feel it all, and though to mention it would have been below his dignity, he showed 'certain mood' which it was tactful to ascribe to the effects of the altitude of Santa Fe. There was nothing I could do to help remedy the shabby cause for the Stravinskys' personal displeasure; but I was indignant on their behalf, and I felt sorry for those few members of the then musical staff too young for humility, and too egotistic to defer to achieved position. Their limitation of knowledge and deficiency of good manners made it impossible for them to feel a great artist's strong love for even his humblest materials—the love which could induce Stravinsky to write, 'What incomparable instrumental writing is Bach's. You can smell the resin in his violin parts, taste the reeds in the oboes.' There spoke the complete master of the actual as well as the ideal who deserved better. He spoke as such again on being asked, 'What is technique?' when he replied, 'The whole man. We learn how to use it but we cannot acquire it in the first place; or perhaps I should say that we are born with the ability to acquire it,' thus conveying his own presence in a totality too subtle for the callow to grasp. I could not help applying a phrase of his to any young people to whom the far past had no significance, not to mention the past which survived all fresh into their very lifetimes, for in identifying the particular character of the saxophone, he once remarked with witty precision its 'juvenile-delinquent personality'.

My sense of regret may have reached so deeply into my feelings as to produce a curious dream which came to me one night during their last days in Santa Fe. In my dream, in placeless surroundings, I saw Stravinsky. With solemnity he regarded me, and slowly made the sign of the cross over me. I was transfixed for a moment, gazing at him; and then in the dream I hastily responded by making the sign of the cross over myself in concert with his grave gestures. When I awoke I wrote down the essence of the scene, which had both elated and troubled me.

Meanwhile Stravinsky and Craft worked through rehearsals to bring the works for the cathedral concert to readiness for performance on 18 August:

Claudio Monteverdi   Excerpts from *Vespro della*
                                       Beata Vergine (1610)
              Deus, in adiutorium meum
              Sonata sopra Sancta Maria
              Magnificat anima mea Dominum
              Et misericordia
              Esurientes
              Sicut locutus est
              Sicut erat
              Amen
                        Conducted by
                        ROBERT CRAFT

Igor Stravinsky   *Mass* (1948)
        Kyrie   Credo
        Gloria   Sanctus
                        Agnus Dei
                      Conducted by
                      IGOR STRAVINSKY

(Pope John XXIII asked Maestro Igor Stravinsky to conduct
a performance of this Mass at the Vatican during the coming
year. The Holy Father's death intervening, Maestro Stravinsky now dedicates tonight's performance to his memory.)

CHORUS AND ORCHESTRA
of
THE SANTA FE OPERA

JOHN CROSBY, *General Director*
JOHN MORIARTY, *Chorus Master*

A greater throng than ever made its way into the cathedral on
that Sunday evening; for not only was the musical fabric of the
evening of special interest—and it proved to be the most movingly
performed of any of the four sacred concerts—but an event was
immediately to follow the concert which had stirred up added
interest. It was known that in the previous autumn Pope John
XXIII had signed the patent creating Stravinsky a knight commander with star of the Papal Order of St Sylvester; and Archbishop Byrne had planned to invest the Maestro with the insignia
of the order on this occasion. Unhappily, the Archbishop's death
during the winter deprived the event of his stately offices, and,

since a new Archbishop had not yet been designated, the Vicar General of the Archdiocese, Monsignor George V. Rieffer, assisted by the Chancellor, Monsignor M. J. Rodríguez, would act instead. The late Pope and the deceased Archbishop were in many thoughts that evening—not least in mine, for it was at the hands of the latter that I had some years before received the Papal knighthood of St Gregory of which Stravinsky knew; and it was in this character that I was asked to sponsor and accompany Stravinsky for his own accolade. In my role of the evening I was required to appear in the uniform of the order of St Gregory. As I did not own the uniform itself I borrowed one from Chief Justice David Chavez of the New Mexico Supreme Court. It fitted me well. With it I wore the sword of the order, which was needed later.

At the conclusion of the *Mass*, with its plea for peace in the Lamb of God, as simple and elemental as a stillness of water, the voices without flourish, the closing chorale for brasses and woodwinds as personal as hardly uttered thought, the sanctuary was cleared of musicians and their racks. Then, following the two celebrants, Stravinsky and I came from the sacristy to the high altar. He held my arm with one hand and his stick with the other. I brought him to the kneel on the altar's lowest step and retired to the side while the Papal patent was read aloud in Latin. He bowed his head over his hands clasped on his stick. I never saw his bearing more serious. He was coming under the blessing of Rome and he knew that the Order of St Sylvester was almost invariably reserved for Roman Catholics.

It was in itself somewhat anomalous that Stravinsky was accepting the decoration, even though it came from the august friend whom he had loved well; for he once told me that it was his inflexible principle to refuse all honours—degrees, decorations, citations, and the rest. When I happened to mention this to Craft, he said that Stravinsky's position in respect of official recognitions of any sort arose from the fact that he had once been persuaded to put himself up for election to the Institut de France during his period as a French citizen—but without success. The process of personal campaigning for the chair vacated by the death of Paul Dukas must in any case have been repugnant to him, with its calls of ingratiation upon the most powerful of the members, the mustering of votes, the supplicatory posture which no candidate was spared, but he complied—only to be passed over in favour

of the composer Florent Schmitt, whose gifts were of another order than Stravinsky's. Since then, Stravinsky scorned electioneering, and refused even unsought honours—but only up to a point; for in recent years he had received without protest various distinctions, such as a chair in the American Academy of Arts and Letters, certain decorations during a Latin-American tour, the Medal of Freedom from President Kennedy, the Sibelius Prize, and such. St Sylvester was most acceptable of all.

At a signal from the Vicar General, I drew my sword, gave the salute with it, remembering how from my days with the cavalry sabre as a cadet, and handed it hilt-first to the celebrant, who then, speaking the text of the accolade, touched Stravinsky on each shoulder with the blade, returned it to me, and then leaned down to place the collar of the order around his neck. This done, in a moment of suspended hush, Monsignor Rodríguez in recognition of the desires of everyone in the cathedral began to applaud; and in a second the great crowd responded with an explosion of its own applause.

Stravinsky knew what to do with applause, even at a sacred ceremony. He rose, stood away from the step, turned, took my arm, and began to march us to the chancel rail, while the ovation seemed to double and redouble. We reached the rail and stood, while he bowed and bowed, it seemed to me, for between five and ten minutes, holding on to me, while I stood at attention, for fear of seeming to accept any of the applause for myself. At last he indicated that he would turn and go. The tumult followed us out of sight. I could feel his arm trembling in mine. The applause was not so much for the great artist, the recent concert, the new knight commander, it seemed to me, but for the small, exhausted, powerful man who again made himself seem to belong to each individual in the crowd even as he received its collective tribute. I was elated for him; but I was also heavied in my feeling, for the certainty of the farewell that was coming.

He was so tired after the concert that once at his lodgings he retreated to his bed, while in all the other rooms the last gestures of packing went on; for Madame was determined that as soon as her husband's and Craft's professional promises were fulfilled, they should none of them endure any further the discomforts,

physical and emotional, of that summer in Santa Fe. Against all sensible persuasion, they were leaving by motor before midnight, going west to their California place. Loyalist friends were there to say goodbye. Zorina helped Madame. The car was loaded by Craft and Allen. All was being done with a haste which saddened me as much as the fact of their going. How they must long to leave a place where they had not been happy! I thought.

I went softly to the bedroom. The door was open. Stravinsky was lying down. He saw me, beckoned to me, took my hand. The bed was low, it was awkward to bend over it to speak to him, I hesitated to sit beside him upon it. It seemed a sensible solution to kneel on the floor beside him. I felt a closeness to his spirit. He caught this. He was not surprised, nor was I, when I said, now not dreaming,

'Maestro, give me your blessing.'

Seriously with a light patriarchal grace, he put his hand on my head and said a few words in Russian and then signed the cross over me. I felt blessed, as he felt the power to bless. We said goodbye. I went to find Madame, we embraced. There was a feeling of tears, if not their actual flow. I did not wait to see them all leave. They departed, all exhausted, close to midnight.

We heard that they drove all night, and early in the morning in the deserts deep in Arizona, Madame, at the wheel, going seventy miles an hour, almost fell asleep. Craft, who was beside her, felt the car sailing in a fast curve to leave the road. Just in time he swung the wheel around, the car recovered, and Madame was shocked awake again. In their habit of survival, they were all saved.

Though Craft returned in later seasons to conduct at the opera, the Stravinskys never came back to Santa Fe.

Craft wrote in 1969, 'Stravinsky has always known when he and his work require a change of scene, a fact that helps to explain his sudden, restless junketings about the globe.'

For the five years following the end of the Santa Fe experience, the Stravinskys seemed to be on tour more often than not. When their passages brought them through New York, they would usually put up at the Pierre, and there I would come to see them. I find record in my pocket diaries of many lunch and dinner

engagements between the times of their travels. On 4 January, 1963, Stravinsky wrote me a note in red ink, 'Happy New Year dearest Paul (Horgan) How to thank you for this new mark of affection (and taste!)'—a little silver ruler I'd sent. 'Tomorrow morning going with Bob to Philadelphia for concerts (Vera staying here at Pierre)—Will be there one week afterwards one week here, one day in Washington DC to repeat the concert and back to hotel Pierre till the end of January. Will we see you? Say "YES" Love IStr.' It was a complicated schedule, but he seemed to thrive on it. I came to see them after that fortnight, and heard how for the Philadelphia concerts—a pair—he had been driven from New York, after all, instead of staying in Philadelphia; and had encountered furious blizzards on the road, had persisted, and had arrived safe and ready to conduct, returning to New York immediately after the performances.

It was a time of intermittent contact with them all, for my work at Wesleyan was ever more demanding, requiring travel on my part—to Europe, to the West Coast where unluckily when I was in California the Stravinskys were away, so that I never saw them in their Hollywood house. But by now I had a fair notion of what it would interest them to read, and one author I always tried to reach Stravinsky with was Alan Moorehead, whom he declared to be his favourite modern writer (presumably of non-fictional works). It was not always possible to anticipate his acquisitions, for on 6 December, 1963, he wrote me, 'Dearest Paul Horgan, just reading "Cooper's Creek" (this new masterpiece of Moorehead) when I received your copy. How very nice of you. When are you coming to NY? Love IStr.'

It may have been that year at Christmas when I joined the Stravinskys at the Liebersons' New York house, after the Christmas dinner they had all just celebrated. There was a late-afternoon atmosphere of companionable surfeit—fine food, fine drink, ingenious gifts in profusion, great drifts of festive wrapping paper and ribbons on floor and furniture.

Often we dined upstairs at the Pierre, and if there was a programme on television of interest to Stravinsky, he watched it in silence with intense attention. I remember one documentary film having to do with an intimate study of the social habits of African apes, and the careful beguilements of the white expeditioners as they sought to win the intimacy of the wild primates. I watched Stravinsky more than I did the screen, for in silence he at moments

enacted the behaviour of the animals, mimicking them *in advance* of their own reactions with intuition which was comic yet wonderful in its accuracy and serious respect for the creature life in the film. How light, and again, how deep was his empathetic mastery of the unity discernible in all life.

In May 1966, I arrived at the Pierre for an evening. He was asleep in his bedroom. Madame had some new paintings of hers to show me. She was always reaching for further dimensions of her technique in handling her materials, and we were occupied for quite some time in talking about her work, and then the painting of others. No less than her husband's, her whole inner life was governed by the aesthetic; but it was difficult for her to give enough time to her painting because of the constant movement of their days—and, now, increasingly, the needs attendant upon Stravinsky's state of health. She would describe how she must often drive to and from the doctors in various cities, and of how many an errand was needed to fill prescriptions, and the rest. This was not given in complaint—there was no question of her dedication to her first duty, which was her husband's welfare. But she was, for all her attunement to the visionary nature of her art, an uncompromising realist; and she saw no reason to soften or ignore the unpalatable circumstance when it came along. Something of this must have accounted for her remarkable psychological health. As her own years advanced she retained her beauty, her capacity for impulsive gaiety which always seemed youthful, and her clear strength for the ordeals of age which if not yet entirely consuming were impossible not to expect in anyone's ninth decade.

Presently word came that Stravinsky had awakened and on being told I was present, he sent for me. He was lying on his bed, and he explained that he was resting because that day he had been given one of the frequently scheduled transfusions he must undergo because his blood was 'too thick'. We embraced, and he said,

'You are very good looking.'

Fatuous satisfaction at this must have appeared in my expression. It was enough to recall to his inner ear what he had really meant to say, and he now promptly said it:

'You are looking very good.'

I could not help laughing. He pursed his mouth and breathed audibly, nodding seriously at the advantage of good health itself.

A few weeks later I had a tiresome operation which required me to take an apartment in New York for the summer in order to be near the doctors for post-surgical examination and observation. It was nothing serious, but it had dull aftermaths, and I had a slow and irritable convalescence. My natural hypochondria was exacerbated by a sense of indignation at feeling protractedly less than my adequate best. My friend Donald Berke generously gave up his summer to look after routine requirements of my small household on the East River, and by the good sense mingled in his sympathy he kept my self-indulgent qualms at a minimum. When a day or two after my release from the hospital I declared my disappointment at not being able to hear Stravinsky conduct *The Symphony of Psalms* in Philharmonic Hall as the concluding event of the festival of his works being given that summer by the Philharmonic Symphony Orchestra, Berke said,

'Then we will go.'

'Shouldn't I ask the doctor?'

'Of course not,' he said. 'You can go if you feel like it. We'll go just for the last half. That won't be too tiring.'

The programme was to consist of the *Symphony in Three Movements*, and *The Flood*, conducted by Craft, followed by the intermission, and then by Stravinsky with *The Symphony of Psalms*. Calculated to a nicety, our arrival brought us to Lincoln Center just at the end of the intermission. We had obtained seats on the centre aisle halfway down the hall. It was Saturday evening, 23 July, 1966. We were seated just in time to see the entrance of Stravinsky.

The house rose.

He walked with new difficulty, using his stick. I was once again moved by his continuing, under physical limitations, now on the increase, I was afraid, the public duties attendant upon his commitments. He came to the podium and with expressionless face, set aside the stick, turned to the house and gave the Mariinsky bow. The applause did not subside when he turned around to face the orchestra and chorus with his hands clasped in front of him. It seemed like many minutes before he was permitted to give the chorus its signal to rise, lift his furled hands over the orchestra, and activate the staccato chord for percussion and woodwinds which declares the work.

I was perhaps more than ordinarily susceptible in my weakened state; but it remains my conviction that that performance of *The*

181

Symphony of Psalms, led by the composer in his eighty-sixth year, remains the summit of all musical performance which I have ever heard. His extraordinary vigour, his orchestral and auditory conception more acute than I had ever found it, and the glory of the writing itself—all brought me such exaltation as I had never known before in the concert room. This was not merely the gratification of the sensuous pleasure one has in splendours of sound, or of the satisfaction for the intellectual faculty of detecting to the extent of one's ability the structure of such an abstraction as a masterpiece of music. It was rather to a communion of spirit wholly achieved by means of tonal art that one was lifted. It was not that I was able to forget Stravinsky, there, as the work unfolded, or cease to marvel at his mastery of the imperfect instrument of his body, with its paralytic numbness in its entire right side; I was indeed very conscious of his every act, and this realisation of the sublime through the fallibly human was as much part of my emotional and spiritual lofting as any of the rest of it. 'One hopes,' he said once, 'to worship God with a little art if one has any, and if one hasn't, and cannot recognise it in others, then one can at least burn a little incense.' The dry grain of his productive intellect was as much present as the well-springs of his lyric power. What he was saying with his music as well as with his gradually diminishing body was his praise of being. When he brought the work to its protracted close, '*Alleluia*' and '*Laudate Dominum*', I held my hand across my eyes, in tears. I did not then know it, but it was the last time I was to hear him conduct.

I returned to my apartment and lay awake the whole night in a state of translated feeling and a certainty of having been healed. The night sounds of the river—tugboats throwing a wash as they churned by, and the deep shaking diapason of great freighters as they signalled their rounding the river curve of Hellgate, the audible slide of the current when no shipping passed—became part of an enchantment. Exhausted and at peace I gave thanks.

Pursued by their demonic timetables, the Stravinskys were to depart from New York two days following the concert; and at midday on Sunday I went to take my leave. Compliments, responses, scoldings of critics who had written routinely of the concert, sounded dilute and dreary as I uttered them, but Stravinsky—he

was alone for Madame was out paying a call, and Craft had already flown to Texas for a concert—received my feeling instead, and said to me of the critics, 'All they think about is *L'Oiseau de feu.*' His disgust was however not in the least petty—it had about it a deep organic detachment—as of a higher order of life noting the behaviour of a lower. 'They like my music for never the right reasons,' he had said earlier, and he once quoted a letter from Verdi which said, 'For the artist it is a joy to be hated by the critics.'

In his eighties he was asked by a performer, 'You are working very hard?' and he replied, 'All my life.'

The terms were consistent, and his own. At various times he had articulated the motive attitudes behind his work. 'I was guided by no system whatever in the writing of *Le Sacre du printemps*,' he said in an interview. 'I had only my ear to help me. I heard and I wrote what I heard. I was the vessel through which the score passed.' He told a seminar at the University of Texas, 'I think very little about problems . . . In my brain are two elements—intervals and rhythm.' He said to the same gathering of students, 'Something comes into my ear and I write it down,' thus giving the simplest real description of the creative process I have ever heard.

Craft wrote, 'He rarely employs and never thinks of the vocabulary of musical theory . . . he recently remarked of [the final chord in *Le Sacre du printemps*] that he could not explain or justify it at the time but that his "ear accepted it with joy".' It was the perfect illustration of the artist's *non-theoretic* possession and conviction as he works. Systems are based on him, not he on them. 'Music,' as he wrote on one of the sketch pages for *Le Sacre du printemps*, 'exists if there is rhythm, as life exists if there is a pulse.' This led to his orchestral innovations, first of all in *Le Sacre du printemps*, and Craft wrote of these, 'One imagines the glee with which he must have added the knowledge to his growing arsenal of academically affronting effects.'

It has always seemed to me clear that the rhetorical respiration of his music reflected directly his own breathing and the metre of his speech. A small illustration comes to mind in remembering the frequent stress he placed on the upbeat in his compositions— like a quick intake of breath—and the gestures with which he

accompanied his remarks. The physical connection of himself to the abstract stuff of composition was suggested when in a film documentary he said, 'I like to feel the vibrations' of the tones, and illustrated this by recalling that in his deafness Beethoven, when composing at the piano, would place a pencil between his teeth and touch the end of it to the instrument; and in the film Stravinsky did the same to show us how. Possibly he sometimes allowed the piano to act the role of *planchette*—even as some writers do with the typewriter—but for a directly musical reason, hearing, changing, refining what tones emerged as he struck the keys in search of his precise intention.

His professionalism had in it a lofty freedom from preconception which paradoxically reminds us of Lord Byron's inspired and at times snobbish amateurism: Gerald Heard asked Stravinsky about the nature of his creative process, and received this reply: 'I don't know if there is a creative process as such. Only the pleasure. I like to compose music much more than the music itself . . .' In the same conversation he said later, 'Listening to your [own] work always gives you surprises—and always bad surprises.'

They were, as in every 'maker's' life, dry periods. He said to Dushkin, 'You must have faith', and these remarks I take to myself as a writer, as I am sure other workers in the arts would do. 'You must have faith. When I was younger, and ideas didn't come, I felt desperate and I thought everything was finished. But now I have faith, and I know ideas will come. The waiting in anguish is the price one must pay.' Years later, smiling widely, while touching on the same idea, he said, 'I can wait as an insect can wait. I am somebody who is waiting all his life.' And when the idea would come, he said, 'First ideas are very important; they come from God. And if after working and working and working, I return to these ideas, then I know they're good.' I could not help but be reminded of my own habit of keeping all of my countless notes, for one never knows which one may suddenly show signs of organic life, putting forth new tangents, which in turn extend themselves, until a whole structure can be seen in its very act of formation.

Someone once asked Stravinsky how he felt when starting a new work—the sort of question familiar to anyone whose work reaches a public. He answered, 'Are you happy to be awakened?'—for him to compose was to be awake. Despite lively disclaimers, he could

not be entirely detached from the consequences of his work. Dushkin once attempted to reassure him during one of his diatribes against critics, saying, 'No one can please everyone,' adding, 'Even God does not please everyone.' Stravinsky jumped up and shouted, 'Especially God!'

For at eighty, he made this statement:

'I regard my talent as God-given and I pray to Him daily for the strength to use it. When I discovered that I had been made custodian of this gift, in my earliest childhood, I pledged myself to God to be worthy of it, but I have received uncovenanted mercies all my life.' And he added, with a humility felt but not frequently revealed, 'The custodian has too often kept faith on his all-too-worldly terms.'

Book 3

TO THE END

AFTER 1966 Stravinsky's conducting engagements became less frequent, and I heard reports of increasing difficulties with health. There were intermittent, painful, and frightening periods of hospitalisation in Los Angeles, and in 1969 the household moved to New York to seek more varied medical care. They took an apartment in a hotel on Central Park South. There I would call, or dine, and I find one notation for an evening which I marked as 'radiant'.

Stravinsky was now really frail. He seemed almost to ration his utterances; but when they came, they were, even concerning commonplaces, touched with his particular acerbity which combined a droll assumption of agreement by his listeners with a view they might never have come to for themselves. His hold on life was a marvel. Time and again he alarmed everyone by a spell of critically extreme illness—a crisis of the blood, or the circulation, or respiration—but in a few days, inquiring by long-distance telephone, I would hear that he was much improved and again at work.

But presently he must go to a New York hospital for surgery, and his discouragement was so great, it was mingled with so much angry disdain for illness and all its dreadful apparatus, that he took to muteness, and according to a tale told by Zorina, he refused to speak to his nurses, only giving directions in his sickroom by imperious flicks of a finger, indicating what he wanted as though conducting.

It was all the more wonderful, then, that Allen was able to send me a note in June 1969, saying, 'I know that you will be happy to hear that I.S. is much improved, eating now, the morale a little improved, and even working: completing the 4th fugue of four from *The Well-Tempered Clavier* (instrumentations).' Fifty-eight years earlier, from Ustilug, his Russian home, he had written to Roerich concerning their joint inspiration for *Le Sacre du printemps*, 'I expect to start composing in the fall, and health permitting, I hope to finish in the spring.' Health permitting! Now in 1969, possibly already mortally ill, he was, at a weight of eighty-seven pounds in his eighty-seventh year, orchestrating Bach for a little while each day. Working? 'All my life.' . . .

189

Allen, who had moved east from California to take a post at the Wesleyan University Library, was by now a friend so intimate and essential to the Stravinskys that in the increasing worries and needs of the Maestro's illness he had asked for and had been granted leave by Wyman Parker, the University Librarian, to stay in New York to do what he could—and it was much—for the afflicted family. The strain had been great on Madame, and Allen added in his note, 'Vera, however, is suffering from a bad heart and has to remain in bed . . . Meanwhile, V. wanted you to have this—' an amusing book about the Ritz Hotel in Paris.

When she was again well enough, I was invited to call—it was 4 December, 1969. I saw Madame alone for a while, and then Allen brought Stravinsky to us in his small, somehow clever-looking wheelchair. The Maestro's face was pink, he made the ride in the wheelchair resemble a child's animated excursion, and I exclaimed,

'How marvellous you look!'

'What else?' he replied with gaiety. I bent to kiss his hand, and with strength which astonished me he pulled my hand to his lips. We settled down to a conversation.

Madame said they were looking for a permanent place of their own—an apartment they could buy. She had been all over town to see various possibilities, but found them so expensive that they had decided on nothing. They liked best the idea of a place overlooking the East River.

'Eager so much liked the view from the hospital, to see the boats, and the lights of the bridges. We would like to have a place over there.'

'Oh, yes,' I exclaimed. 'I remember the same thing from the summer when I was here in the hospital, and later in my sublet flat. It is where I would like to live if I had to live in town.'

'But you have no idea,' said Madame, 'what they ask. We could never afford it.'

'I know,' I said. 'I don't know how it could ever be managed.'

'Pol,' said Stravinsky, like one settling a problem with final practicality, 'you should buy the river.'

The farcical amplitude of this delighted us all. The Maestro, at our laughter, gave his effect of taking a bow. We went rambling along. He spoke of 'the fragments of life', making the point that the essential matter in both living and in 'making' was to 'put them together'. He was, of course, voicing his belief in form and

design. He spoke of powers, and their use, and also said with an air of wisdom that there were other powers which could not be *used*—this in a religious reference. I said, in a kinship with both my childhood and his wholly simple faith beyond sophistication,

'Every time I pass the cathedral here, I go in, and light a candle, and say a prayer for your well-being.'

He thanked me silently.

All through this meeting, I was moved by the extraordinary sensitiveness which Allen showed in his care for Stravinsky. He saw signals which no one else did. He never took his eyes off Stravinsky's face. How he knew it, I could not say, but at one moment, he understood that Stravinsky wanted to be moved from the wheelchair to the sofa; went to him took him up in his arms —Allen was tall and strongly made—and resettled him on the sofa. In a few minutes, this proved not so comfortable as Stravinsky wanted it to be, and again, without the exchange of a word, or even a preliminary gesture visible to me, Allen moved him to the wheelchair again. There was tenderness as well as efficiency in Allen's intuitive alertness, and it was easy to see why he had been so fondly taken into the household. His affinity with Russian life was great—he was studying the language, Madame said he was making excellent progress, he had grown a Russian beard, dark and handsomely trimmed, and, in his case as in mine, a devotion conceived in a youthhood far removed from Stravinsky was now fulfilled in close friendship with him, his wife, and Craft.

With nurses both night and day, it was now not possible for Stravinsky to go out to dine as we used to do; but it was important for Madame to have an occasional brief respite from her voluntary confinement to the apartment, and I invited her and Craft to dine out with me on 19 January, 1970.

I came a little early to fetch them, for Craft had agreed to show me some of the Stravinsky manuscripts—a comprehensive collection—which were then undergoing appraisal. By now Madame had made the hotel apartment a livable place, with some of her own paintings on the walls, and more by Léger, Tchelitchev, Bakst, and others. There were, as always, books in profusion, many in large folio size containing reproductions of works of art.

'How is he?' I asked.

The report was better again, but there had been a serious set-back the previous week—'worse than at any time in the past eight months', said Craft—a thrombosis in the left ankle. But Stravinsky was now already recovering from this.

'We'll see him in a moment,' said Craft, and then produced some of the manuscripts, showing them to me on a low long table before a sofa. They were in themselves works of art. The chirography was extraordinary in its precision, purity, life, order upon the page, utter clarity. Each page looked as if it were designed by a master designer of typography. Their beauty as objects was allied to that of the graphic arts. They were finished scores. Their precision could not possibly be misinterpreted by later generations. I could not imagine another musical archive by such a master brought to such completeness and beauty of visual style. I turned a few pages. It was a direct encounter.

Presently Craft took me to Stravinsky, who was in his own room.

It was a small, rather narrow room, but in its formal neatness it seemed larger than it was. The light was low everywhere but in one place—that was where Stravinsky was disposed, upright, in his small wheelchair, his back to the wall, and the lamp glowing over his shoulder upon the pages of a book which rested on a cushion, on a carefully folded throw, on his lap. He wore one of his cardigans. In his left hand he held a little dictionary. To his left was an ordered desk; to his right, a neat upright piano. He was in effect in a niche between the two pieces of furniture. He looked small—smaller than I had ever seen him; but his smile of welcome was full of that joke of surprise which he could always counterfeit to give a common event some extra dimension. He looked so frail that I was fearful of greeting him physically, but Craft said,

'Go ahead—kiss him. He wants you to.'

I leaned down and touched his cheek with my lips. He responded with a small nod. I saw that the book he was reading was Henri Troyat's biography, *Pouchkine*. Merely to make sounds, I asked,

'Is it a good book?'

Stravinsky replied, so softly that Craft leaned down to him and repeated the words to me:

'A biography of Pushkin is no ordinary affair,' and bowed in the old way of confirmation of his own statement. The dictionary he held was in French. Even in his high literacy in that language, he enjoyed meditating on even familiar words with the aid of a lexicon

Igor and Vera Stravinsky setting out for a drive in Central Park, New York, 1969

—a lifelong habit. This meant that he was reading slowly. Time itself was still his to command. His profile was now heroic, craggy, when seen in the scale of the diminishment of all else about him. He volunteered no remarks, but his awareness was so keen that as Craft and I talked commonplaces, he followed our words from one to the other as if watching a tennis match. He was participating in our society in silence, which rather reminded me of how autistic children enter their surroundings in full awareness while seeming not to do so. Presently Craft, preparing Stravinsky for our absence for the remainder of the evening, said in a gentle subterfuge,

'We are going downstairs a little while to have a drink.'

Stravinsky caught a breath in his playful manner and said with longing in his almost vanished voice, so that Craft again had to repeat for him,

'I will come with you.'

The pathetic impossibility of this resulted in Craft's instant decision not to leave at all. He was right: Stravinsky so plainly longed not to be abandoned. Craft said, with a fond air of daring to hope for an unexpected privilege,

'If *you* will have a drink with *us*, we will stay here and have it with you.'

'*Merci*,' Stravinsky indicated through a gesture.

Room service then responded to our altered plans. We ordered drinks and dinner. The waiter came, wheeled a rickety table in place, Stravinsky came in his rolling chair to the table, Craft next to him, Madame and myself facing them. A glass of watered-down Scotch was provided for Stravinsky. He made a social matter of pantomiming a toast.

What developed then was a miniature contest for life itself—for Craft, keeping up a running exhortation, like a coach putting 'spirit' into his player, urged food upon Stravinsky, who responded like an earnest team member, so that the game took on a seriousness which stood for much more than the mere moment of its playing. It was as stark and poignant, as sweet and desperate, as the Schubert song about *Death and the Maiden*, or one of those Dürer engravings counterposing flesh and skeleton. In loving urgency, like one who is sure he can save what may soon be lost, Craft, throughout the dinner, devoted himself wholly to the nourishment of Stravinsky. A contest in a nursery style developed —though in deadly earnest—as Craft kept saying, '*Mangez-les*', pointing to lima beans, and assuring the Maestro that there was

much protein to be had in them; and the rare, delicately cut-up beef—'*Mangez-le*', it gives strength. Stravinsky took mouthful upon mouthful, in determined effort to win, no matter what the odds. 'He is eating better than for weeks,' said Craft softly in an aside to Madame and me. And then, 'Drink a little Scotch', he would say in his role of coach, and the striving tiny athlete did what he was cheered on to do. In French, Craft, watching every successful bite, said that with his strength recovered (it was coming fast now, all this excellent protein), in the spring, they would go to Paris, and stay at the Ritz, where, as Stravinsky must remember, the food was so good, the garden so charming, the wine so marvellous, remember the Richebourg '61, and Souvchinsky would come to call, and Boulez, and there would be those lovely long drives late in the afternoon when Paris was most beautiful . . . He took a lima bean on his own fork and posed it to Stravinsky and said, '*Mangez-la, c'est la proteine*'—both of them hungry for the same great life, and so was I.

Madame meanwhile said to me,

'Bob is so sweet to him, so kind, so attentive,' and then in her uncompromising realism, she added, 'So unexpected, too'—for she had known for years Craft's cult of refusing to show his feeling directly to Stravinsky, or to give him any intimate attention such as he now gave with a sense of the marvel of Stravinsky's whole life, work, and presence.

'Splendid,' said Craft, watching Stravinsky's unceasing movement of fork from plate to lips, 'you are doing splendidly, and later we will hear some music . . .'

So it was that after dinner Stravinsky was established on a sofa, his shoeless feet in neat plain black socks resting on a cushion on the floor, while Madame and I sat together at another side of the room. Craft, after bringing scores, set the phonograph going. He came to sit beside Stravinsky to read score with him, turning the pages, pointing out significant details in them, half conducting, indicating by finger on the page important entrances of instruments or various thematic matters.

They played the first three movements of Beethoven's string quartet op. 125, and the last movement of the piano sonata op. 111. When I say 'played', I mean that they participated; that music was

never more powerfully conveyed to me than by their active musical intelligences; that Stravinsky's concentration was so complete and consuming that I felt in the presence of an act of creation. His lower lip was stuck forward, as if to inhale the music in an extra sense. His head was bent over the score, causing the few strands of hair at the base of his small powerful skull to stick out more than ever, and his breathing was shallow, rapid, regular, and expelled in gusts with, I thought, wastefully terrible force. It was another urgent—almost desperate—act of nourishment: Craft working to retain life itself in the noble musical mind with that sustenance which it still craved; that which—who knew how soon?—it would soon no longer be able to receive. I was moved almost past enduring. Madame, listening with me, knew what I felt; and though brave and real to the fullest, habitually ready to admit any truth, she now said proudly to me in defiance of truth, in her most dovelike tone, at the presence of so much realisation in life, '*That is not a dying man!*'

Stravinsky and Craft were unaware of us. Madame then said,

'If you want to go now, go'—this towards the end of op. 111. 'They will be at it for a long time.'

'Shall I say goodnight?'

'No, just go.'

I went to get my coat. She came with me. They did not notice us as we moved to the foyer. On the way I made a gesture of admiration for Bakst's drawing of her done when she was in her twenties. It showed her at her most ripe young beauty. She told me to wait a moment, went to her bedroom, and returned with a framed reproduction of the drawing, and gave it to me with a kiss.

I left in stealth and great disarray of thought and feeling; for it was the actually tremendous intensity of how Stravinsky listened to the master whom he had come to love above all others late in life, it was what came into the room through the vital concentration of Stravinsky's reception of the music which made me hear it *through him*; and since I was familiar with that music of Beethoven and ordinarily would be ready to agree with anyone about its power, it was, on this night, the longing power of Stravinsky as he listened which had exhausted me so that I could endure it no longer. It had been a contest between the certainty of death and the survival of art, neither of which could avert the particular victory of the other.

On a Sunday evening—17 May, 1970—I came again for dinner. Allen was there with Madame and Craft. The table was laid, and there was a curious air of optimism which must have been called forth by the finally accepted limits of strength; for since my last visit there had been several more trying episodes with crises and periods of hospitalisation 'for tests'.

I had been given news from time to time, and one day in Middletown Allen brought me a copy of *Retrospectives and Conclusions*, the final volume of the five in which dialogues between Stravinsky and Craft, together with diaries by Craft, had appeared. Stravinsky and Craft had both inscribed it to me. It may be one of the last, perhaps even the very last, autograph Stravinsky ever gave. In wavering print he had written, 'To Paul, with lowe, I.S.—1.30.70', and the use of the German 'w' sound for the English 'v' reflected his increasing tendency in those days to retreat from English and speak in German or French to everyone but Madame, to whom he now habitually spoke in Russian—'Russian, the exiled language of my heart', as he had put it earlier. Craft added his own initials.

Another late autograph was inscribed on his photograph by Stravinsky for young Peter Lieberson, who loved Stravinsky as greatly as his parents did, and who understood Stravinsky's last music so well that his discussion of it was welcome to Stravinsky, who had said to him,

'What will you do?'—meaning in life.

Peter replied,

'I want to become a composer.'

Stravinsky, not dismissively, but with respect for the young man's hopes, yet was obliged to say,

'It is not enough to want.'

When on that Sunday evening Stravinsky was brought to the table by a nurse, I had a shiver of recognition of how he had grown even smaller since I had seen him. His face seemed to have receded about his eyes, so that they had a newly prominent look. He was stooped as he sat. His great hands were like exposed roots in winter, all gnarl and frosty fibre. About his throat was a scarf, with its ends tucked into his cardigan. He was placed at the head of the table, still the patriarch at his own board. I was seated to his left, Madame to his right, Allen next to her, Craft next to me. A current of good feeling went from each to the other of us. It was, despite everything, a joyful condition that we were all together with Stravinsky. In one of those small silent marvels of communica-

tion of which he had always been capable, but which was now particularly extraordinary, he made us feel his own pleasure.

When drinks were before us, I saw that his was the palest ration of his favourite, for I had seen the nurse mix it, when perhaps a teaspoon of the liquor had been put in a tumbler half full of water. The doctors had forbidden liquor for him, and tonight's potion was simply a signal of festivity, like the 'cambric tea' of nursery imitations of grown-up tea parties.

Stravinsky looked deliberately around the table at each of us. It was in no sense a bestowal of a lingering farewell, though I for one, and possibly others, could not but think of the notion. On the contrary, his gaze was an expression of the keenest social pleasure and fondness, and when his survey ended with me at his left, he lifted his glass—weakly at an angle so that its contents were almost tipped out—and with beautiful formal manners, he said,

'Pol, *hier haben wir eine sehr gemütliche Gesellschaft.*'

With that he touched my glass with his, and bowed in a silent toast to us all, and took a sip. We drank with him. Food came. He ate two or three mouthfuls. Our talk rattled on in general, none of it directed with pointed consideration towards him, and he joined in none of it. His simple presence was enough to satisfy him, and—alas—us. We were in high spirits, our give-and-take while not ignoring him did not pause from time to time to discern and attend to any needs he may have had. It was therefore to our surprise that he suddenly halted all talk by saying in a strong voice, low in pitch, while crumpling into himself as if the better to plumb his condition to its fullest,

'I am dronk.'

One or two sips of water scarcely flavoured with Scotch? It told us much. Allen rose at once and went to the wheelchair and turned it from the table. The nurse heard something of our reaction, came from the bedroom, and relieving Allen at the steering knobs of the chair, wheeled Stravinsky from sight to see him into bed. I watched until his door was closed. Ah, ah—under my breath. I never saw him again.

At the table, his disappearance was granted the dignity of not being commented upon. The others were by now used to such sudden lapses of vitality. What could be done for him was being done, there, behind the closed door. Meanwhile, there he was, living, by the simple fact reassuring, and cherished in the life which continued about him.

197

The party resumed its conviviality. We talked of Russian writers —Madame remembered Mandelstam and the poems he had written to her long ago. Someone brought up Turgenev, which led to a discussion of the general inadequacy of translations of Russian literature. I was reading for the first time the Aylmer Maude versions of *Anna Karenina* and *War and Peace*, having previously known only the Constance Garnett translations, and I quoted the illuminating and original remark of Edmund Wilson to me: 'The trouble with Constance Garnett's translations is that

TO PAUL

with LOWE

75. *& R.C.*

1.30.70

The last autograph (in a copy of *Retrospectives and Conclusions*)

she makes all the Russian writers sound alike.' Madame remembered a passage from a Russian writer—a word had been translated as 'assiduous', and declared that this was not the proper shade of meaning. She searched her thought for a better word, and then said, 'I will find the dictionary', went and returned with one in Russian, saying, 'We still have about fifty dictionaries even here', turned a few pages, and then exclaimed with satisfaction, 'The proper word is "diligent".'

The *Gesellschaft* lingered for almost three hours, while we sat at table in the Old World fashion, drinking coffee and liqueurs in companionable comfort. It was good to see Madame so much at peace, so relieved of tension, looking so handsome and taking so much pleasure in animated conversation which relieved

her for even a little while of the concern which heavied her usual days and nights. Just below our idle, spoken, convivial thoughts at the table, silently there was another—for me, for everyone there, I felt sure—of the life in the next room.

In that summer—1970—I was astonished when they told me that they were taking Stravinsky abroad, to Evian, away from the hot months in New York. I could not imagine how he could endure such a commotion and effort as a flight to and from Europe. Nevertheless, they went, and evidently he stood the journey well.

I was in London in August, and saw a notable production of *Les Noces*, handsomely choreographed after Nijinska. Once again I had the sense of being beaten into awareness by the powerful rhythmic drive of the work, and every sort of atavism came to mind, hearing and seeing the ritual enacted in the peasant wedding, and I felt Stravinsky's humaneness of intuition as his ballet proclaimed its programme of the mystery celebrating the coming together of two human beings in formalised love as it was consummated by marriage. How subject, I thought, mankind remains to the pathos and the power of ancient ways.

Mirandi was living in London, where her husband was producing films. I had a lively reunion with her, and our shared interest in everything concerning the Stravinskys gave us much to talk about. We fell into the habit of lunching together every Sunday. On one of these days she joined me with a fine promising rattle of her heavy gold bangles, her eyes lighted with laughter and information. She had made a point of telephoning to Madame at Evian just before lunch so she could bring me the latest news.

'Marvellous,' she said in the husky, humorous voice she kept for her best stories. 'Vera sounded wonderful, she sent her love.'

'How is the Maestro?'

'He is not very strong, but he seems comfortable. They take drives in the country, he enjoys seeing everything, and the hotel is marvellous. But they are leaving tomorrow—no, day after tomorrow.'

'Where?'

'Back to New York. Vera was glad I called. She wanted me to do something for them.'

'Oh? What was it?'

'Wonderful. She said it was about the photographer.'

'What photographer?'

'Please,' asked Madame, 'there is that photographer to come to photograph my husband. But we cannot. He is to come tomorrow. We are so busy. I am packing, packing. The airplane is to take us the next day. My husband is too tired. He should not be bothered. Why should there be photographers? Please tell him not to come.'

'But who is he?' asked Mirandi.

'The name I do not think of at the moment. He has an appointment for a long time. He must not come.'

'Do you want me to find him and cancel the appointment?'

'Yes, please.'

'Then tell me how to look for him.'

'He is married to a princess in England.'

'Do you mean Lord Snowdon?'

Madame, as if it were her own triumph, cried,

'That is who! Please tell him we are so busy, I do not want my husband to be bothered.'

Thinking of Kensington Palace, Mirandi said,

'Is he at home, now, in London?'

'No, he is in Sardinia.'

'Sardinia! But where in Sardinia?'

'He is with the Aga Khan,' said Madame—surely a sufficient address for anyone.

Mirandi's head was now in a whirl, but she had a clear thought.

'He is a very fine photographer,' she said, 'an artist; and he is very sympathetic and moving in his pictures of old people. He would make some beautiful pictures of the Maestro.'

'So, he should come?' asked Madame doubtfully.

'I would certainly let him come. After all, he needn't take all day.'

A silent moment for thought, and then Madame said,

'Very well. He may come. Do not do anything.'

'I won't,' promised Mirandi.

'So he is after all to take the pictures?' I said.

'Tomorrow.'

'I went to visit them, you know,' said Mirandi, 'earlier this summer.—He is so changed. I hardly dared touch him.' She spoke with love, and then, in her own sense of the historical, which so often embraced the comic as well as the formidable, she said,

'Did I ever tell you about the terrible morning in Hollywood when I called him "Pussycat"?'

'No. But you have always called him Pussycat.'

'I know.'

'He loved it.'

'I know. But wait.'

One morning in the usual routine Mirandi went next door in Hollywood to see her neighbours, who were soon to move to New York. Stravinsky was not yet at work. He seemed somewhat preoccupied, if not dejected. She went to his chair, leaned over him, kissed him on his head, and said,

'Good morning, darling Pussycat.'

What occurred then appalled her.

Stravinsky threw away something—his stick, or a book, or whatever—and shouted,

'I think I have lived lonk enough and worked hard enough, not without some recognised achievement, to have earned the privilege of not beink addressed as "Pussycat"!'

Mirandi said she felt herself go pale—she had seen his gusts of anger before, but never had felt one directed at herself. Shaken, she apologised. He frowned staring ahead into his mood. He was the last one whom she ever meant to offend.

'Good heavens,' I said. 'What did you do then?'

'Nothing much more then, but I *tell* you, I was trembling. After that, I always called him Maestro, like everybody else.'

In New York again at the end of summer, Stravinsky endured further vagaries of health. I was in touch by telephone, and saw Madame and Craft now and then, but my duties that winter were so particularly heavy, and Madame's preoccupations and worries were so woeful, that it was not until an evening in January—Wednesday, the twentieth, 1971—that there was occasion for an evening together, though of course I could not see Stravinsky, as only the household now had access to him.

But on that evening Madame invited me to accompany her to the opening of a new production of *A Midsummer Night's Dream*, to be followed by supper. Craft and Rita Christensen, the Danish nurse who with skill was principally taking care of Stravinsky, were also with us. Weary beyond amenity, Madame nodded and slept

during most of the play, despite its glaring, harsh, and stuntish production. Craft and I endured it awake, and at the end, he said to me with one of his smiles of intellectual mischief, after we had shrugged over the production's style, 'It is not even a very good *play*.' I agreed with him, despite passages of magic poetry in the text.

We went from the theatre to Madame's supper party at the Pavillon, where we were joined by the Liebersons and Dominique Nabokov (her husband, Nicolas, was unwell).

Here it was most easing to see Madame rise to the atmosphere of her supper party with her fullest charm. She seated me to her right, and to my right was Zorina. My situation could not have been improved. Stravinsky was much in all our minds, immobilised as he was across town; and in a real sense the measure of our gaiety that evening was the measure of how our thought of him, and the memory of previous times when he was present, knitted us together in his name. We toasted him. Then Madame turned to me and said for my ear alone,

'He is not good'—meaning that he was extremely unwell. It was very much like her that even as we were gathered to enjoy a party, she could recognise and speak of what was so full of unremitting ache for her. The toast reminded Lieberson and Craft of amusing anecdotes about him, and spirits rose, and presently Madame turned to me with a lustrous smile and asked,

'Did I ever tell you how I first met Stravinsky?'—I always liked her pronunciation of his name: 'Stra-veen-sky.'

'No, never.'

'So, I will tell you.' Her smile began to fill with loving recollection. She made her familiar little labial movement as if tasting her words in advance. She looked beautiful if weary that evening, but now behind the face of a lady of eighty ('I used to deny my age,' she had said not long before to Zorina, 'but now I am proud of it') I saw the timeless glow of a young woman's love, and she said,

'It was this way. It started this way.' It was in 1921. The Diaghilev company was in the midst of ballet preparations—rehearsals, costumes, *maquettes* for scenery, endless talks about changes in script and score. 'This was in Paris. One evening D'aghilev'—they always pronounced the name this way—'D'aghilev came and said we would go to dine in Montmartre. He said, I have Stra-*veen*-sky downstairs in a cab. Come. He is in very bad mood. *Be kind to him.*' Madame turned full upon me and I felt a

lovely and explicit reflection of joy as she said, with a ghost of wonderfully feminine gallantry, 'And I was.'

Shortly before that evening, which I think of as filled with rose-coloured light and warmth, Madame had at last found an apartment which was suitable in every way, and Stravinsky had bought it for her. He looked forward to having his own home again, where paintings, books, instruments, could once again be assembled about him. There was much to do. They had hoped to move before Christmas, but there were the usual delays of redecorating and equipping the place, and the weeks went by without seeing the rooms ready. But possessions and furniture were gradually being transferred from the old hotel suite to the new apartment; and Madame was at moments happy in these new preoccupations. As for her husband, he was, at eighty-nine, still putting a few notes on paper every day, according to Allen, when it suddenly became necessary for him to be taken once again to the hospital. The shock to him was great. It would be hard to think of anyone who would more fastidiously loathe the public business of stretchers, ambulances, and passages through elevators and lobbies than he. But there was again—though a diminished one—another of those extraordinary resurges of recuperative power which he had shown so often in the past many years; and when he was brought back from the hospital it was to his new home.

Five days later while listening to early-morning news on television I heard that he was dead. I then realised that for weeks—even months—I had turned on the TV with a denied sense of dread of this very news. Now, here it was. I changed all my arrangements for the week. The day was 6 April, 1971. I drove at once to New York and on arrival, speaking to Lillian Libman, the secretary-manager of the household, placed myself at the disposal of Madame and Craft. There was, evidently, nothing for me to do, but I wanted to be in town in case I might be of use. That evening there was to be a private Russian Orthodox prayer service and Miss Libman said that Madame asked for me to be present.

I entered a feeling of vigil. I felt absent from myself all day long.

The Age of Stravinsky ended at dawn on that day. Of his nine decades of life, five had had, for me, a nourishing union, at first far, then nearer; and in my heavied thought on that day there was yet a living edge of gratitude that my life had been touched by my encounters with his work and his presence.

I thought of Mirandi in London and telephoned to her. She had heard the news, but knew of no plans; and when I offered to have flowers sent to the bier in her name, she was thankful. She would telephone to Madame. We could say little more to each other.

That evening when I came to the service being held for him I was nervous. If this was the death of a man, it was also the death of an epoch; and personal feelings were mixed in turmoil with a sense of the time now bereft of its strongest aesthetic spirit.

I came into a large square room containing perhaps thirty persons. My eye was immediately drawn to a figure sitting alone on a modest straight chair, facing a mounded hillock of flowers over a coffin. It was Madame. A black lace veil was clouded about her head. She was wanly beautiful. About her was a wide space which now and then someone crossed to speak to her. Her great eyes seemed larger than ever. Her manner was spacious and gentle. She held murmured conversations with the particular friends whom she had summoned that evening. I recognised George Balanchine, Lincoln Kirstein, Elliott Carter, among others, and of course Craft and Allen, and Miss Libman. There was a sustained hush. I saw faces marked by mystery and sorrow. Contemplating the hill of flowers, thinking of what lay beneath it, I mentally made various offices of prayer. Presently Allen came to me and asked me to cross the terrible open space separating Madame from the world.

When I came to her, she raised her cheek for me to kiss and I kissed also her hand. Her noble composure remained unbroken as she held on to my hand and spoke to me, while awaiting the entry of the bishop, his thurifers, and the chanters who would sing the service.

She said they knew all day yesterday that the end must come very soon. She said they wept all day, helpless to relieve him of his suffering. She said he had been home only five days in their new apartment, but he had been very happy, asking to be taken in his wheelchair through the rooms again and again, and he would say over and over, 'It is ours, it is ours.' He loved, however briefly, the

look of Central Park from the windows, and as a surprise for him she had bought a bird, a canary, and wherever Stravinsky was taken in the apartment, he could hear the bird singing. It was a wonderful singer, joyous and strong in its jubilee of sound, and he listened ecstatically as long as he could. When suddenly his last crisis came, he lay in his room, his breathing was horrifying to hear —Madame as I stood holding her hand imitated how the breathing sounded and my heart beat hard for hearing it.

How can she be so strong? I kept asking myself. I feared that I must be tiring her, for so long as I would be by her side, she would for my sake continue to speak to me. I heard the echoes of that breathing, and I imagined the abstract tiny glory and sweetness of the singing bird.

After what seemed to me a shamelessly long time for me to be by her side, someone else approached, and I bent to her, and we kissed, cheek and cheek, in Russian style, and I left her as the other visitors came to whisper their words for her, and for him.

Not long afterwards the small procession of religious, followed by the bishop, in his tall cylindrical head-dress from which black veils fell over the back of his black robes, entered from a side room. The prayer service began. Incense from a swinging thurible billowed about the mounded flowers. The prayers began in Slavonic, now intoned, now spoken. Madame crossed herself each time the bishop did according to the liturgy. There was a group of male singers, all young, who sang the responses in magnificent tone and simplicity, with the bass voices predominating. It was a long liturgy, Byzantium audible and visible. At one moment Madame made as if to kneel but her strength for once failed her and she briefly stood instead. Craft was beside her. He was white as paper and impassive. At moments I could only half-believe what was happening and why; at others I was pierced by the finality of it. At the end, when the small procession took its way out of the funeral chapel, the bishop paused to speak to Madame. When he left her, I went away myself.

The next morning at ten o'clock at the side altar of Saint Theresa of Jesus at Saint Patrick's Cathedral a Requiem Mass, at my request, was said for Stravinsky. Father Moher, the celebrant, agreed to say it in Latin. What had Stravinsky written so long

ago? 'I have always considered that a special language, and not that of current converse, was required for subjects touching on the sublime . . .,' a view consonant with my own for that, and any, sacred occasion. It was a private Mass to which I had invited those who had special relations and feelings concerning Stravinsky. There were several whom I could not reach, but among those attending with me were John Crosby, Anne Fremantle, Robert Giroux, Charles Henderson, Thomas and Remi Messer, Charles Reilly, and Francis and Shirley (Hazzard) Steegmuller.

I remained in New York all week, until Stravinsky's public memorial service at three o'clock Friday afternoon. The actual funeral and burial would occur in Venice during the following week. On Friday, not knowing that a place had been reserved for me within the undertaker's chapel, I joined a queue of people, three abreast, which reached from Madison Avenue to Fifth Avenue. It advanced with infinite slowness. It was made up largely of young people—many of them very young, in the beards, beads, jeans, of their generation. They must truly have heard Stravinsky.

When the line turned the corner, and I reached the door, an usher was obliged to refuse admittance to me or any more other people: the rooms were crowded to the street. I went to Saint Patrick's Cathedral and spent an hour in the name of the dead.

In Venice, on 15 April, 1971, he was buried from the ancient church of SS Giovanni e Paolo. There Craft—summoning in his grief what strength I could not imagine—conducted Stravinsky's *Requiem Canticles*. At the same hour, in Middletown, I listened to Stravinsky's recording of the same work, and also his own performance of *The Symphony of Psalms*. '*Libera me*', I echoed, and '*Alleluia*', and '*Laudate Dominum*'.

In May, Madame and Craft returned from abroad, where, after the Venetian burial, they had sought rest first in North Africa and then in Paris. Late one afternoon shortly afterwards I came to see them to ask if they would approve my writing this book. They agreed with interest and generosity. I did not stay long, but invited them to dine with me on the evening before I was to leave to go west for the summer.

It was the first time I had seen the new apartment. It was spacious and handsome. On a low bookshelf stood one of Snowdon's

photographs of Stravinsky from the summer of 1970 at Evian—
one of that last group ever taken of him. It shocked me. With his
beret topping his costume, Stravinsky faced the camera with eyes
made enormous by the further shrinkage of the flesh of his face.
He held a fixed, powerful stare. The texture of his flesh was
shrunken and withered like bark, or skin long submerged in water.
Seeing me look at it, Madame described the session when the
photographs were made.

She found Snowdon charming and considerate, but like all
professionals he was thinking first of his purpose, and he had many
requests and instructions for his sitter. Stravinsky sat quietly
facing the camera, not answering anything Snowdon said to him.
Madame told me:

'I had to stand by the camera and translate everything to my
husband in Russian, and I made remarks, and gestures, to amuse
him, and to bring *légèreté* into his expression. He would answer me
in Russian, and Snowdon took pictures during such moments.
Finally my husband was bored, or tired, and that was all. Snowdon
had dinner with us, and said to me, "What a pity he does not know
English." '

Suddenly I heard ruffles and trills coming from a remote corridor of the New York apartment, notes which carried piercingly,
rising to clear heights. It was the canary. Its tiny, detached rapture
seemed to contain allusions too poignant for immediate remark.

I was leaving for the West on 10 June to be gone all summer.
Madame and Craft came to dine with me on the ninth in New
York. Waiting for them, I was troubled to know what, or what not,
to speak of concerning Stravinsky.

But I need not have worried. They arrived, sat down with me,
and almost at once began to tell of events which we had not previously talked of. I felt an almost exhausting strength in their love
for Stravinsky as they spoke of him, even coming to some of the
most intimate and difficult details of his death and afterwards.

They were still filled with the splendour and solemnity of the
service in Venice which moved from SS Giovanni e Paolo to the
burial at the island cemetery of San Michele. Venice, said Craft,
was chosen long ago for this event by Stravinsky himself, 'because
it was the Pope's parish'—Roncalli's. The world had come to pay

its tribute—though, said Craft, no official notice or message of any kind was sent by the United States.

'The Mayor of Venice,' he added with understated irony, 'paid for the music at the funeral.'

All the anonymous people of Venice hung over the bridges, filled the walks, crossed themselves as the cortège of gondolas went along the canals. The thought of John XXIII led Craft to relate how, on his last birthday, 18 June, 1970, Stravinsky dressed and wore the full insignia of his Papal knighthood.

Madame said that the day before the end, her husband kept trying to make the sign of the cross, over and over, but could only touch his brow, 'Father', and his breast, 'Son', but was too weak to reach his shoulders for 'Holy' and 'Ghost'. Over and over. He looked at them, and what hurt them most was his awareness that he saw how they knew he was dying.

I remembered something Stravinsky said in his *Conversations*: 'Ravel died gradually. That is the worst.'

They described to me the astonishing strength of his handclasp as he reached for them. His fingers were curved into hooks to take his wife's and Craft's hands.

'He did not want to let go,' said Madame.

Craft said to her now,

'When he put your hand to his face he knew he was dying.'

A death mask was taken. Craft said it was done without including the ears, as Beethoven's was—'That instrument of all great composers. Still, there is something noble about the mask, though the mouth is distorted.'

Passing Stravinsky's room in the apartment after the return from Venice, Craft for many days could not enter it, as the death mask was there. Finally, 'It had to be done,' he said, and he went in to confront it.

'Have you seen it?' I asked Madame.

'No.'

Craft said,

'You must—you will find something true even so.'

Later that evening, during our dinner after a shift of talk, and a little pause, Madame said to me,

208

Portrait of Vera de Bosset (Stravinsky) by Léon Bakst, 1922. Collection of Vera Stravinsky

'There is something I think about. I want to ask you.—What is the difference between belief and faith?'

It was a question large enough to take up the working hours of someone like Thomas Aquinas and it stirred me for the suggestion it made of the direction her thought was taking in that time in her life. But I must reply, and I said,

'I will take a risk in answering. I will say that belief is engendered by an intellectual faculty, while faith comes from a higher faculty—something of the whole being beyond intellectual formulation. Is this nonsense?'

Craft said,

'That is a profound statement.'

I thought, whatever the merit of the distinction I posed, that Madame seemed to take comfort from it.

I left the following day for the West. We exchanged a few letters during the summer. They had again gone abroad. Craft wrote to me on 27 July from the Hôtel du Palais in Biarritz, which Mirandi, visiting them there later, characterised as 'truly the original Steinberg drawing of the Hôtel Splendide'. He was kind enough to thank me for 'helping to keep Madame's spirits up. I'm afraid,' he wrote, 'they fell rather far in Venice, which is why we are here. *Everything* reminded her, and she began to go out to the grave all alone, without telling me, and it is quite a walk as well as a long ride on the *vaporetto*. She seemed quite calm in Rome after seeing the RAI film of the funeral—which I could not take, and simply left.' They had gone to Rome to see Zorina in a performance of *Perséphone* at the Santa Cecilia with Prêtre conducting, and also to consult Giacomo Manzù about making the design and cutting it for Stravinsky's gravestone. 'Then,' Craft continued, 'two hours later, with Manzù *chez lui*, she wanted to show her appreciation and kissed him, whereupon Manzù started to cry and told her that Stravinsky was the greatest inspiration in his life, and that he must have the gold cross of a great king. (Incidentally, the Vatican is giving the white marble.) At this point, Mme startled me by saying, "But you know, I keep expecting him to come back." Another indication of the terrible loneliness she feels came on the road here. Suddenly, in a restaurant, south of Aix, she began to sob, but never said a word.'

I think often of Stravinsky's last earthly delight—the bird Madame had waiting for him on his final return home, the bird whose song had so startled me on my first visit to that home. For him, she said, it sang and sang and gave him much joy. His own words, given in 1939, come to mind from the chapter under the heading 'The Phenomenon of Music', in the *Poetics*. He spoke of 'the most banal example . . . including the song of a bird. All this pleases us, diverts us, delights us. We may even say, "What lovely music!" But all such are of course merely promises of music; it takes a human being to keep them . . .'

The last scene of *Le Rossignol* might speak for anyone coming to the end of Stravinsky's life, though not of his music.

> *Death stands in the Emperor's bedchamber . . .*
> *Torn by his aching conscience, the dying ruler calls*
> *in vain for his musicians to make him forget. But*
> *the nightingale returns and so charms Death with*
> *its song that he agrees to allow the Emperor his*
> *life. The Emperor revives and offers his saviour a*
> *place at court, but the bird refuses and returns to*
> *its woodland haunts with the promise that it will*
> *sing each evening. Now the courtiers enter, pre-*
> *pared to find the Emperor dead. They are*
> *astounded when he sits up in bed and bids them*
> *'Good morning!'*

The nightingale, death, and the Emperor bring before us music in nature, and the mortal change of all things, and man's insistence on immortality—themes which belong within Stravinsky's vision, even as the magician's wit of the Emperor's last words. Every artist is committed in his own degree to that which never dies.

Appendices & Index

Appendix A
The Memorials

By grace of the various institutions involved, the following commemorations concerning Igor Stravinsky's activities in Santa Fe, New Mexico, have been cast in bronze and installed as indicated.

In the theatre of the Santa Fe Opera:

> THIS TABLET WAS ERECTED IN GRATEFUL AND DEVOTED MEMORY OF
> IGOR STRAVINSKY
> 1882–1971
> BY THE BOARD OF DIRECTORS OF THE OPERA ASSOCIATION OF NEW MEXICO TO RECALL THE INCOMPARABLE DISTINCTION AND THE BRILLIANT ARTISTIC ASSISTANCE HE CONFERRED UPON THE SANTA FE OPERA BY HIS PARTICIPATION HERE IN THE COMPANY'S PRODUCTIONS OF HIS WORKS FOR THE MUSIC THEATRE—THE RAKE'S PROGRESS, MAVRA, OEDIPUS REX, PERSÉPHONE, LE ROSSIGNOL, RENARD— DURING THE YEARS 1957–1963, WITH JOHN O. CROSBY AS GENERAL DIRECTOR.

In the St Francis Auditorium of the Museum of New Mexico:

> IN THIS AUDITORIUM ON AUGUST 21, 1962, THE AMERICAN CONCERT PREMIÈRE OF THE FLOOD BY
> IGOR STRAVINSKY
> WAS PERFORMED IN THE COMPOSER'S PRESENCE BY ROBERT CRAFT, CONDUCTOR, WITH VOCAL AND INSTRUMENTAL ARTISTS OF THE SANTA FE OPERA, JOHN O. CROSBY, GENERAL DIRECTOR.

In the Cathedral of St Francis at Santa Fe:

IN THIS CATHEDRAL UNDER THE INITIAL PATRONAGE OF THE MOST
REVEREND DOCTOR EDWIN VINCENT BYRNE,
ARCHBISHOP OF SANTA FE,

IGOR STRAVINSKY

CONDUCTED

THRENI, JULY 12, 1959
SYMPHONY OF PSALMS, JULY 17, 1960
CANTATA (1952), AUGUST 19, 1962
MASS, AUGUST 18, 1963.

THESE PERFORMANCES WERE OFFERED FREE TO THE PEOPLE OF SANTA
FE WITH THE PARTICIPATION OF VOCAL AND INSTRUMENTAL ARTISTS
OF THE SANTE FE OPERA, JOHN O. CROSBY, GENERAL DIRECTOR.

IN 1962, POPE JOHN XXIII OF BLESSED MEMORY ASKED MAESTRO
STRAVINSKY TO CONDUCT A PERFORMANCE OF THE MASS AT THE
VATICAN DURING THE FOLLOWING YEAR. THE HOLY FATHER'S DEATH
INTERVENING, THE COMPOSER DEDICATED THE 1963 CATHEDRAL OF
SAINT FRANCIS PERFORMANCE OF THE MASS TO THE MEMORY OF HIS
AUGUST FRIEND.

UPON THE CONCLUSION OF THE PERFORMANCE HERE, MAESTRO
STRAVINSKY WAS INVESTED BY THE VICAR GENERAL OF SANTA FE
WITH THE PAPAL KNIGHTHOOD OF SAINT SYLVESTER IN THE DEGREE
OF COMMANDER WITH STAR, WHICH HAD BEEN CONFERRED UPON HIM
BY POPE JOHN SHORTLY BEFORE DEATH ENDED THE PONTIFF'S REIGN.
THIS OCCASION MARKED THE LAST APPEARANCE OF IGOR STRAVINSKY
IN SANTA FE.

Appendix B
Acknowledgments

FOR assistance in various forms contributing to the realisation of this book I gratefully acknowledge my indebtedness to the following persons: Madame Igor Stravinsky, Miss Virginia Rice, Mrs Tania Senff, Mrs Peter Hurd, Miss Vera Zorina, Mrs Ralph Levy; Messrs Robert Giroux, Robert Craft, Donald Berke, Goddard Lieberson, Thomas Messer, E. J. Allen, Peter Hurd, Professor Edward Williamson, Edmund Fuller, and John O. Crosby and Edward Purrington of the Santa Fe Opera; and to Joseph Slater, Director of the Aspen Institute of Humanistic Studies where as Scholar in Residence in 1971 I wrote much of my text; and to the following books which in one respect or another sustained me with information:

Armitage, Merle, ed. *Igor Stravinsky (articles and critiques)*. New York, 1936.

Craft, Robert. *Commentary to The Rite of Spring Sketches, 1911–1913*. London, 1969.

Goossens, Sir Eugene. *Overture and Beginners, A Musical Autobiography*. London, 1951.

Rosenfeld, Paul. *By Way of Art*. New York, 1928.

——. *Discoveries of a Music Critic*. New York, 1936.

——. *Musical Chronicle, 1917–1923*. New York, 1923.

——. *Musical Portraits*. New York, 1920.

Stravinsky, Igor. *An Autobiography*. New York, 1936.

——. *Poetics of Music in the Form of Six Lessons*. Cambridge, 1947. (Bi-lingual edition, French and English, Cambridge, 1970.)

Stravinsky, Igor, and Robert Craft. *Conversations with Igor Stravinsky*. Garden City, 1959.

——. *Dialogues and a Diary*. Garden City, 1963.

——. *Expositions and Developments*. Garden City, 1962.

——. *Memories and Commentaries*. Garden City, 1960.

——. *Retrospectives and Conclusions*. New York, 1969.

——. *Themes and Episodes*. New York, 1966.

Van Vechten, Carl. *Interpreters*. New York, 1920.

——. *Music After the Great War*. New York, 1915.

———. *Music and Bad Manners*. New York, 1916.

Wilson, Edmund. *The American Earthquake*. Garden City, 1958.

White, Eric Walter. *Stravinsky. The Composer and His Works*. Berkeley and Los Angeles, 1966.

For two particular usages I have drawn upon the wits of others. The first, on pp. 17–18, 'to make a career of the landscape' I heard years ago in New Mexico from Francis Fergusson. The sense of the other, on pp. 55–7, on 'making remarks', I owe to Sir Max Beerbohm's essay, 'First Meetings with W. B. Yeats', the *Listener*, 6 January, 1955.

The Dial, 1921–1929, was a useful aid to memory.

The synopsis of the last scene of *Le Rossignol* quoted on page 210 is taken from Carl Van Vechten's *Music After the Great War*.

Documentary film footage about Stravinsky has proved useful in a few passages of this work, and I wish particularly to cite with gratitude glimpses of Stravinsky in the films produced by the National Film Board of Canada, and by Rolf Liebermann and Richard Leacock for NDR. I viewed reruns of these films through the kindness of National Educational Television, in New York.

I am grateful to Madame Igor Stravinsky for permission to quote brief extracts from correspondence which I received from her husband and herself; and to Robert Craft and E. J. Allen for permission to quote briefly from their communications to me.

Index